PAINTERS, PAINTINGS AND BOOKS

An Essay on Indo-Persian Technical Literature, 12-19th Centuries

PAINTERS, PAINTINGS AND BOOKS

An Essay on Indo-Persian Technical Literature, 12-19th Centuries

YVES PORTER
(transl. by Mrs. S. Butani)

MANOHAR
Centre for Human Sciences, New Delhi
2026

Peinture et arts du livre
Paris-Téhéran, 1992
Bibliothèque Iranienne no. 35

First edition (English) 1994
Reprinted 2026

ISBN 978-81-7304-750-3

Published by
Ajay Kumar Jain for
Manohar Publishers & Distributors
4753/23, Ansari Road, Daryaganj,
New Delhi-110002

Printed at
Replika Press Pvt. Ltd.

To the artists, craftsmen and *ahl-e ma'ni.*
To my parents.

TRANSLITERATION

The transliteration of the Persian and Urdu words is given here in a simplified system :

a	ا	s	ص
b	ب	z	ض
p	پ	t	ط
t	ت	z	ظ
s	ث	‘	ع
j	ج	gh	غ
c	چ	f	ف
h	ح	q	ق
kh	خ	k	ك
d	د	g	گ
z	ذ	l	ل
r	ر	m	م
z	ز	n	ن
zh	ژ	v/u	و
s	س	h/e	ه
sh	ش	y/i	ی
		’(*hamza*)	ء

The vernacular Indian words are followed by a *.
Accents and long vowels are only noted in the Bibliography, Glossary and Index.
Bibliographical references are abridged in the notes; the complete references will be found in the Bibliography.

CONTENTS

PREFACE

This book is the revised and translated version of a Ph. D. thesis in Iranian Studies submitted at the University of Paris III – Sorbonne Nouvelle, under the direction of Prof. Charles-Henri de Fouchécour. It was defended in 1988.

First of all, I am indebted to Dr Bernard Hourcade, Director of the Institut Francais de Recherche en Iran, for giving me an opportunity of spending three years in India. During this period, I had the chance to stay at the Indo-French Archaeological Mission (MAFI), thanks to its director, Dr H.-P. Francfort, and I was affiliated to the Centre for Historical Studies, School of Social Sciences, Jawaharlal Nehru University, thanks to the support of Prof.Harbans Mukhia and Prof. Muzaffar Alam. Prof. M. Alam also took an interest in the process of the production of the book. I am particularly grateful to Dr Olivier Guillaume, Director of the Centre for Human Sciences of the French Embassy in India for funding the translation of this book and facilitating its publication in India.

During my stay in India, I visited many libraries. I would like to thank some of the persons I met in these libraries, especially Mrs Zaibunia, Madras University Library, Dr A. R. Bedar, Khuda Bakhsh Library, Patna; Mr Rahmat Ali Khan, Salar Jung Library, Hyderabad and Mr Shaukat Ali Khan, Tonk Library.

I shall also never forget the valuable aid and support I received at Jaipur, at the house of Kanwar Sangram Singh of Nawalgarh, where one of the last traditional artists' studios survives, mainly thanks to the efforts of Mrs Brigitte Singh. She welcomed me from the very beginning and made it possible for me to observe the artists at work in Nawalgarh House's studio.

I should also like to express my thanks, for different reasons to Sholeh Sadr, Paola Manfredi, Valmik Thapar, Jagdish Mittal, Saleem Kidwai, Meraj Khan, Nalini Thakur, the Sabha Mahila Sangh–without forgetting Poonam and Om Prakash–and to the French team, Christine, Valentine, Claire. They all contributed towards making my stay in India unforgettable.

TABLE OF PLATES

British Library, Add. 16 561, fol. 36 b. (colour 3)

6. Marbled flowers in the technique of Necmeddin. Marbled pigments on paper, Turkey, 20th century. 44 x 33,5 cm. Private collection (see page 49). (colour 4)

7. Three men in landscape with animals. Page from a dispersed manuscript showing an unfinished painting. Pink, gold and black ink on paper. Shiraz, end of 16th century. Page, 31,8 x 21,2 cm. Private collection (see page 94). (b.&w. 3)

8.Pounced drawing, showing a man riding a horse. Ink and charcoal on paper. The whole outline of the drawing is pierced by pin holes. Jodhpur, early 19th century. 33,5 x 24 cm. Private collection (see page 65). (b.&w. 4)

9. *Dibace*. Fronstispiece from a manuscript of the *Makhzan al-asrar* of Nezami copied in 1538 by Mir 'Ali Mashhadi and illuminated by Mahmud Mozahheb on *khanbaliq* gold flecked paper for the Shaybanid sultan Abu al-Ghazi 'Abd al-'Aziz. This page contains the beginning of the text. (See page 113). B.N. Suppl. Persan 985, fol. 2 b; 39,5 x 19 cm. (b.&w. 5)

10. Writing and painting tools: a bronze pen-case, a reed pen, pen-case scissors, polisher, two *jadval-kesh* (see page 59), an ink spoon, a compas, two brush tips. Iran and India, 19th century. Private collection. (b.&w.6)

11. The calligrapher 'Abd al-Rahim and the painter Dowlat in the atelier. Painted by Dowlat ca. 1610 at the colophon of a *Khamse* of Nezami ordered by Akbar. The painter is drawing in front of the calligrapher 'Abd al-Rahim 'Anbarin-qalam, author of this manuscript, in a corner of the palace (see page 151). One can see on the floor some of the tools of the workshop. British Library, Or 12 208, fol. 325 b; 30 x 19,5 cm. (colour 5)

12. Scene from a bazar. Illustration from a *Majales al-'oshshaq* probably copied at Shiraz by the end of the 16th century. One can see among the shops, some dyers at work, and paper sellers. B.N., Suppl. Persan 775, fol. 152 a. 28 x 16 cm. (colour 6)

13. Bookbinder. Page from the *Album of the Crafts of Kashmir*, (see pl. 4) showing a bookbinder and his tools. India, ca. 1850-1860. India Office Library, Add Or 1 700. (b.&w. 7)

INTRODUCTION

The excellence and repute of Persian painting are neither unknown nor need they be proved. Several thousands of these paintings have been preserved in various collections all over the world and many have been identified and listed in catalogues. Numerous art lovers and historians have focused their attention on this form of Persian art. What is the point then in returning to a subject already so well known? The difference, however, between this study on painting and previous ones lies in the fact that here the paintings themselves will only be referred to incidentally.

My initial idea was as follows: what should a 20th century artist who is a stranger to the Iranian world do if he wants to paint Persian miniatures? The answer that comes immediately to mind is obviously to copy from a model. The artist should pick up his brushes, open his book of Persian painting at the page of his choice and get ready to start his copy. But where should he start? What type of paper will he require? What colours should he use? And how should he apply them on the paper? Thinned into water-colour or in thick gouache? How, in truth, does one reproduce these glossy flat tints, these extraordinarily delicate features, these intangible beards and curls? We could imagine then that like the description by Cennino Cennini of how to illustrate drapery and how to produce ultramarine for the Virgin's cloak[1] there exists in Persian also some text in which we might find an answer to our questions.

That is how I started my research. However, once I had progressively familiarised myself with some texts, it did not take me long to note that they would not be able to answer my questions fully. On the other hand, the study of these texts proved to be productive in other ways. First of all, these texts had to be located. Indeed, as R. Ettinghausen has said, the Muslim world, in comparison with China or Europe, does not have well-developed technical literature on the arts.[2] This author also notes that the few technical texts which have come down to us are often found inserted within works of a more extensive nature, such as compilations or encyclopaedias. It should moreover be noted that the proportion of technical texts in Persian that have been published or translated, is very small. It was therefore necessary, first of all, to make an inventory of these texts. Once the corpus had been gathered, the direction that the study would take had to be defined, and the material collected had to be organised. The relative lack of precision of the texts, and the difficulty in identifying all technical terms and expressions led to the creation of a lexicon which served as the basis for further work. It then became possible from the study of various texts, and some experiments conducted personally, or observed as done by others, to trace the different stages in the production of the illuminated book, not only its material aspect (ground, pigments, instruments) but also with regard to those who take part in its execution. The diversity of the sometimes very fragmentary information necessarily imposed some limits on the subject. At what point should the study start? The title chosen specifies that the study relates to *Persian texts*; that is where the limit has been fixed. As it happens, the oldest Persian texts concerning painting date from the end of the 12th century. That then is yet another limit within whose bounds we will keep. And the most recent text studied brings us up to the middle of the nineteenth century!

We have noted that Persian painting is well known. However, the history of painting in the Iranian world has yet to be written. Indeed, no existing work encompassing *the totality* of Iranian history, considers painting in the Iranian world from the overall viewpoint of pictorial representations on various types of grounds. Now one could also wonder whether there exists some kind of unity in time and in the various supports on which Persian painting is executed. It is in fact rare that studies on Persian painting treat at the same time mural painting and ceramics together with miniatures, not to mention other plastic arts. Now, does the miniature, or rather manuscript painting,[3] possess some specific character which it does not share with other forms of painting? To study this idea we would need to consider a very extensive cultural area, and examine a period ranging from protohistory to the present day. The objective of our study is not to write this history but to contribute to its writing by bringing to light some essentially technical elements of analysis.

Why is the 12th century the starting point of our study? This chronological landmark is not an arbitrary one; it remains, for the time being, the crucial period before which practically no manuscript painting is known to us, nor any technical text about these paintings. The oldest Persian texts giving technical information about painting and the arts of the book are undoubtedly the *Farrokh-name* by Jamali Yazdi (580/1185) and the *Bayan al-sana'at* by Teflisi (d. 600/1206). This chronological starting point certainly does not constitute a historical or technological barrier, separating the period before and after the 12th century; it could well be pushed further back if new sources were to be discovered.

Art historians, nevertheless, often consider the history of Persian painting as starting in the middle of the 14th century. Thus, a study by B.W. Robinson, "A Survey of Persian Painting (1350-1896)"[4] starts with the following words: "Any survey of classical Persian painting must begin with Dust Mohammad's account".[5]

A passage from this text may have induced the author to adopt this bias; it reads as follows: "The art of painting flourished both in Cathay and in the territory of the Franks till the sultanate of Abu Sa'id (1317-1334). It was then that Ustad Ahmad Musa, who learnt the art of painting from his father, unveiled the face of painting, and invented the kind of painting which is current at the present time".[6]

It is quite clear, according to Dust Mohammad, that painting existed before Ahmad Musa, but in a different "genre". And beginning the history of "classical" Persian painting with this painter is truly nothing but a bias on the part of Robinson; the translation of the title of his article in the French résumé is, moreover, clearer: "Peinture *classique* iranienne", as it confines the field of study to a conventional period known as "classical".

It is this absence of a break that we are going to retrace here, by trying to show that there is a continuity and a unity in the history of Persian painting and that these did not make an *ex nihilo* appearance in the 13th or the 14th century. It is certain that to reconstruct this continuity, we are obliged to survey a very vast geographical area and also pictorial remains that are very diverse in nature. On the basis of scanty remains of mural paintings, painted ceramics and fragments of manuscripts, we hope to prove that the Persian pictorial tradition existed before the 12th century; some literary references will support or confirm the existence of this tradition.

The successful differentiation of colour manufacturing processes or certainty about their specificity of period or region could become a criterion for identifying some paintings. To do this, it is necessary to establish the degree of technicality that Iranian artists had achieved just before the period in which documents become available for study, that is to say the end of the 12th century.

However, while it can be noted that the styles do evolve and vary during the course of history, the techniques, on the other hand, in mural painting for example, do not appear to change much between the last phase of Pendzhikent and the Safavid frescoes. An in-depth study of the pigments and techniques used in the mural paintings of the Iranian world show how little the materials and techniques evolved during the course of time. Besides, although we cannot draw the same conclusions as regards the arts of the book due to lack of material for study, we can at least assume that at the dawn of the 13th century, the Iranian artist possessed more or less the same technical means as the 9th century painter of Manichaean manuscripts.

The appearance of paper at the end of the 8th century marks undoubtedly an important revolution in the arts of the book. Other innovations, in the preparation of pigments for example, are largely due to alchemists who, by their experiments, produced, if not new materials, at least a better understanding of those already existing. Indeed, if we compare on the one hand the pigments detected in the analyses of the frescoes in Central Asia and those mentioned in ancient sources (Pliny, Vitruvius, *Silpa-Sastra*) on the other, the pigments mentioned in the Persian texts and those still used today in certain "traditional" schools, we would be astonished to note that the materials used are, to a considerable extent, the same.[7] This comparison shows for example the great use made of "earths" in pre-Islamic painting, ranging from clay white to green. This is a notable fact because, as we shall see subsequently, the later texts make practically no mention of any earth.

However, while this comparison also shows that numerous pigments were already present before the 12th century, one factor which it is difficult to estimate from such a distance is the degree of elaborateness achieved in the making of the pigments, and consequently the exact nuance of the colours; indeed, the analyses made to this day of the pigments of mural paintings in the Iranian world (pre-Islamic as well as Muslim period) do not enable us to make a judgement about the refinement of the processes used nor of the nuance obtained. Only some analyses of microtraces could give an idea of the process used. It is obvious, moreover, that the exact colour desired cannot be inferred simply from formulas contained in texts. Consequently, the mere presence or absence of a colour can hardly be an adequate criterion for dating. To achieve this, it would be necessary to draw up a colour chart capable of supplying the palette of a region at a given period, keeping in mind the factors which lead to the ageing of pigments. This would have to be done on the basis of actual examples, remains of paintings, and experiments. This aspect widely oversteps the bounds of our study; it would, however, undoubtedly be a good means of obtaining some sufficiently precise criteria which could serve to identify not only the nature of the pigments but also the method and the extent of their preparation. Stylistic analyses and the archaeological context can, moreover, supply, in many cases, a more rapid and more precise dating. This analysis of pigments has a role to play not so much in the dating of the paintings as in the variations of technical quality.

It therefore seems that at the period when our study begins the essential materials used are already known, and that the evolution that is to follow is mostly in the form of the perfecting and refining of the techniques. We will probably have to await the period of direct and sustained contacts with other worlds before some techniques, totally unknown to the Iranian world, make their appearance.

The oldest references to the techniques of painting in the Iranian world have undoubtedly to be sought for in scientific and encyclopaedic texts. Indeed, like Pliny's *Natural History,* these deal with the characteristics of the elements and their use, and they sometimes supply information about painting.

The oldest Muslim-Arab scientific texts (Jabir, Razi) already contain some descriptions about the production of certain materials, such as cinnabar or minium, used in painting. The treatises on mineralogy by Biruni or by Tifashi also describe numerous elements which can be used in painting.

In fact, the oldest available technical text devoted entirely to the Muslim arts of the book which has been preserved, is undoubtedly the *'Umdat.al-kuttab*, dated 1025 and attributed to Ebn Badis, or perhaps, as M.T. Danesh-Pazhuh suggests,[8] the work of the calligrapher Ebn Bawwab. In the Iranian world, the oldest technical text which discusses matters relating to painting and to the arts of the book is perhaps the *Farrokh-name* by Jamali-ye Yazdi (580/1185). In this encyclopaedia, one chapter is devoted to the solutions of metals and elements that can be used in painting, although painting itself is not explicitly mentioned (chap. 12); another chapter concerns "the skills of the arts of the book and calligraphy" (chap. 13). The *Nozhat name-ye 'ala'i* of Shahmardan b. Abi'l-Kheyr al-Razi similarly contains a chapter about the use of metals in the manufacture of objects of art (I, 6) and another on the various sciences and techniques, includes colouring (II, 6).[9]

This kind of literature concerning the characteristics of the elements (*khavvas*) is also found in the *Bayan al-sana'at* by Teflisi (d. 600/1206). In this work, one chapter is devoted to colours used in painting (chap. 9); two others describe the inks, invisible inks and the way to remove marks (chapters 10 and 11).[10]

In texts apparently much later, the *Majmu 'at al-sanaye'* dated 1624[11] at the latest, we again find some features common with these old texts; we find formulas for dissolving metals and some "tricks" for the arts of the book, but at a much more elaborate stage.

Lastly, it seems logical to imagine treatises written by painters and meant for their colleagues or students. The void in Persian literature on this matter can be considered to be surprising. While there are numerous calligraphers who, in addition to their artistic works, have left behind some literary, poetic or technical works, I know of just one treatise on painting written by a painter: it is the *Qanun al-sovar* by Sadeq Beyg Afshar "Sadeqi".[12]

Some *Tazkere* or collections of biographies, containing particularly the biographies of artists, are also of capital importance. Of notable mention among these texts are the passage from the *Tarikh-e Rashidi* of Mirza Haydar Dughlat, the *Preface* of Dust Mohammad, the *tazkere* of Sam Mirza and of Qazi Ahmad and the *History* of Eskandar Beyg.[13] In fact these biographical texts are often incomprehensible if they are not accompanied by a technical study.

The study of this material has enabled us to retrace progressively the different stages in the production of an illuminated manuscript, from the making of the support right up to the finishing stages of the binding.

The texts examined, all of them in Persian, originate from Iran and from India. However, for obvious and most unfortunate reasons, it has not been possible to study all the material preserved in Iran. Only a few published texts and some observations made during a journey to Iran, in 1982, could be used. On the other hand, a whole universe opened itself up to us in India where numerous, practically unexplored sources furnished an important part of the material for study; the area provided also good scope for the observation of traditional practices.

Lastly, some manuscripts preserved in European libraries were also consulted.

The study of techniques, particularly in the East, has till now, been confined essentially to crafts and to industry; it constituted a minor subject in ethnology and more recently in archaeology. Painting and Iranian arts of the book in general have very rarely been the subject of technical analyses. C. Huart has perhaps been a pioneer in this field; in his *Calligraphes et miniaturistes de l'Orient musulman* (1908), he gave some information about pigments, types of paper and some tools of the arts of the book. In the framework of the monumental *Survey of Persian Art* by A. Pope, A.P. Laurie has supplied some data about the colours used in the "Perso-Mesopotamian" school of the 13th century.[14] It is however just a brief, general view of the question and most of the information is formulated as hypotheses, with the author noting that "no information based on the study of actual pigments was available". No reference is made to Persian texts. In this same work, T. Behzad supplies earlier formulas apparently of his own invention (he mentions no sources); they are probably the last links in an oral tradition. We should also point out the few pages on techniques, which are found in Norah Titley's *Persian Miniature Painting*;[15] it gives, though too briefly, some interesting details about the various operations, the production of the paper, the colours and the paintings. Some authors have already made use of Persian texts, particularly with relation to the biographical aspects of the history of painting. Mention should be made, among others, of T. Arnold who, in his remarkable work *Painting in Islam*, while freely making use of Arabic and Persian texts, sketches a most unconventional history of painting. We should also mention the work carried out by Ivan Stchoukine who has remained undaunted in his study of Persian sources for his numerous analyses of Persian paintings.[16]

However, there has long been a certain tendency in the literature of art history to surround the making of miniatures with a halo of mystery. The result is that we find, in works on Persian painting, phrases such as the following: "The basic substances used for the preparation of these colours are known to us even if the thousand and one professional tricks of the trade that went into their patient making have undoubtedly been lost forever".[17] Similarly, S.C. Welch asserts[18] that the mediums or binding material were made, and continue to be made, according to secret formulae. A cursory glance through the texts shows that there is nothing secretive about these formulae. It is quite common to hear amateurs say that "miniatures" are painted with brushes having a single hair! Similarly, the magnifying glass, which is supposed to be an indispensable tool for the execution of details, has certainly never been used by "miniature" painters.

It was therefore necessary to sweep away this "halo of mystery" from Persian painting and its techniques, by considering it from a more objective angle. While it is difficult to recreate paintings on the basis of texts, it is possible, on the other hand, to reconstruct the various stages in the production of a book.

This study is devoted to following the different stages in the making of a painted manuscript. The production of the manuscript is considered first of all with regard to the materials and the techniques used. The various manufacturing stages are described, starting from the preparation of the ground (essentially paper) and some observations concerning the rules of composition and layout, going on through the creation of the colours right up to the various subjects of the paintings and types of binding. A short chapter gives an overall summary of the history of mural painting and ceramics, running parallel to the history of manuscript paintings.

A second part aims at illustrating the material and human means which make the production of manuscript paintings possible. The painter, man and artist, his origin, his training and his status are analysed first of all. We know from some texts, and marginal notes in some manuscripts, that these painters worked in workshops, the most well known under royal patronage. We will therefore attempt to show how these workshops functioned, how they were organised and how tasks were distributed. The production of large sumptuous painted manuscripts involves, in many cases, a considerable investment in materials and in men. It cannot therefore be considered without the structure which makes it possible, that is to say the workshop and the entire body of professionals working in it.

It seems moreover that manuscript painting and the rest of the work constitute a whole and follow certain standards of composition which take into account not just the painting itself but also the calligraphy which surrounds it, the illuminations and even the binding. It is within the workshop that such a cohesion of work can be obtained.

NOTES

1. Cennino Cennini, *Il libro dell'Arte.*
2. "*Abri* paintings", p. 345.
3. The meaning of the word "miniature" has departed so much today from its original meaning of "illuminated design" to take on the modern significance of "tiny model", that we will try, as much as possible, not to use it.
4. *Art et Société,* ed. C. Adle, pp. 13-82.
5. His text is dated 951 or 953/1543-1546; it should be noted that in his article, Robinson confuses two people of the same name, Dust Mohammad Gushvani, a calligrapher who is the author of this text, and Dust Mosavver; see article by Y. Zoka on this subject, "*Dust Mohammad*".
6. Transl. *B.W.G.*, p. 184; ed. p. 197 and after.
7. See tables in Annexe 1.
8. *Rang-sazi,* p. 30.
9. Z.Vesel, pp. 27-31.
10. Ed. I. Afshar, pp. 345-357; to correct, p. 355, *bab-e dahom* (chap. 10) into *bab-e yazdahom* (chap. 11).
11. Ethe, vol. 1 no. 2781
12. See Bibliography for editions of the text.
13. See Bibliography for the references to the editions.
14. A. Pope, pp. 1918-1920.
15. pp. 216-250.
16. See Bibliography.
17. A.M. Kevorkian and J.P. Sicre, p. 72.
18. *Persian Paintings*, p. 11.

PART I

TECHNIQUES OF PAINTING AND ARTS OF THE BOOK

Most of the texts of the pre-Islamic period have only come down to us by way of later copies or translations. Yet, the book existed, probably in the form of codex or scrolls. There are many examples of titles of books from the Sasanid period, such as the Pehlevi translation of the *Pancatantra,* the *Vis va Ramin* or the *Shahbuhragan* which Mani gave as a gift to Shapur. Sasanid libraries are also known, particularly Khosrow I's library in Gondishapur.[1] However, practically no Sasanid manuscript has come down to us. *A fortiori* no illuminated manuscript of this period is materially known to us. Yet, Arab sources do mention in several places the existence of pre-Islamic illuminated manuscripts. Undoubtedly the most well-known of the Sasanid illuminated manuscripts is the *Khoday-name.*[2] Other titles of books are mentioned in Arab sources.[3] Finally, A. Tafazzoli mentions, in his list of Sasanid professions, the *nibegan-negar*, the painter of manuscripts.[4]

We can therefore deduce from these few scraps of information, that the pre-Islamic Iranian world had a good knowledge of books and that these were considered precious, since they were kept in royal libraries and were probably illuminated.

Perhaps the oldest illuminated manuscripts of the Iranian world that have come down to us are the Manichaean fragments discovered in the region of Turfan by A. von Le Coq.[5] Some of these fragments date back to the 6th or the 7th centuries; most of them however date from the 8th and 9th centuries. Although produced by Uighur Turks, these fragments are considered to be the ancestors of the Iranian illuminated manuscripts. These fragments however give a poor idea of what the Manichaean manuscripts must have looked like; several sources describe their extraordinary exuberance.[6] As we shall see further on, Iranian literature abounds in quotations in which Mani is described as a marvellous painter. This idea is already mentioned in the *Kephalaia.*[7] The *Arzhang*, a book written by Mani, is described as a preciously illuminated manuscript, and Mahmud of Ghazni had a copy of it in his library.[8]

As is the case for the pre-Islamic manuscripts, there was until recently practically no knowledge of the first Muslim manuscripts. Indeed, three centuries separate the birth of Islam from the first known Arab illustrated work, the *Sovar al-kavakeb* of 'Abd al-Rahman al-Sufi (1009). Some oriental libraries take pride in possessing Korans written by the hand of 'Ali himself or documents dating to early Islamic times. These manuscripts date back more to the 9th than to the 7th century; they do not have any decoration either (some of these manuscripts, written on parchment, have been mounted, at later periods, on decorated margins). On the other hand, the recent reappearance of the painted fragment of a manuscript, dating from the 9th century[9] enables us to question, or even put back to earlier period the commonly accepted date of 1009 (date of the *Sovar al-kavakeb*).

Before the end of the 12th century, some sources indicated the existence of illuminated manuscripts.[10] That is how we know that the original copy of the *Alfie va shalfie*, a work by Hakim Azraqi Heravi (who died before 465/1072) dedicated to Toghan Shah of Herat, had 72 illustrations.[11]

Similarly, Ravandi[12] says that in 570/1175 Toghrul b. Arslan ordered a collection of poems, which was calligraphed by the uncle of Ravandi and illustrated by Jamal Naqqash-e Esfahani.[13] Other references to the production of illuminated books are also found in the *Rahat al-sodur*:

> "Toghrul Arslan started to write a Koran in thirty parts, and he brought all that he wrote to the painters and the illuminators so that they could overlay it with gold solution; and each of the thirty volumes cost a hundred dinars. Some (volumes) of this Koran have remained with the king, others with Bak Tamr Padshah, others with the painters".[14]

Further on, this author adds:

> "I saw that the Korans and the books, when they were taken out of the *madrasa* and the libraries, were sent to the painters in Hamadan, who erased the mentions of *vaqf* and traced there (instead) the names and nicknames of these barbarians, then made gifts of them".[15]

These few quotations do indeed testify to a tradition of manuscript paintings of probably pre-Islamic origin. It is however certain that the major part of the Persian painted manuscripts that we know were made after the 13th century. Let us now examine the techniques.

1

THE GROUND

Among the grounds used before the appearance of paper, parchment occupies an important place. It is indeed known that the *Avesta* was written on 12000 skins.[16] Similarly, Jahshiyari says that the Iranians wrote on skins.[17] Some documents from Mount Mugh in Sogdiana, in the early 8th century, as well as some Saka fragments from the 7th to the 10th centuries are also written on leather.[18] The bark of some trees and wood were also used; at Kyzil, some fragments of texts with Brahmi characters from the 5th century written on the bark of the birch tree, have been found.[19] Ebn Nadim also mentions several Iranian books found in Isfahan during the 10th century, which were written on bark. The 140 documents of Toprak Kala in old Khwarazmian are on wood and leather.[20] Most of the Kharoshti documents from Niya, brought to light by A. Stein, are in the form of wooden slabs.[21] Some Pehlevi papyruses, dating from the occupation of Egypt in 619, have been the subject of several publications.[22]

1. Paper

- *The origin of paper in the Iranian world*

As J.P. Drege[23] says, "For a long time it was believed (...) that paper had been invented by a certain Cai Lun in 105 A.D. till some excavations in Xinjiang in 1933, then more recently in Shaanxi and in Gansu, brought to light some fragments of paper which archaeologists evaluate as dating to the 1st century B.C."

The oldest fragments of Chinese paper are not written on; they are made of hemp and china grass. In fact, if we credit Cai Lun with having discovered paper, it is probably because he introduced the manufacture of paper from bark and developed its production to the detriment of silk. Subsequently, we find paper made from *Broussonetia* fibres, mulberry, cane, and after the 10th century bamboo.[24]

Paper was made first of all with the help of a fixed mould, a wooden framework on which were stretched out threads of silk or braided horse hair. Towards the 2nd century, at the end of the Han dynasty, it was replaced by a mobile mould, quite similar to the one later known in the West.

After the 5th century, paper was sized with starch. From the time of the Hans, some paper was dyed. Under the Tangs, an animal gum, and then a vegetable gum replaced starch. Watermarks appeared at the end of the 10th century. It was only from the 12th or the 13th century that hydraulic power was used.

In Xinjiang as in Tibet where paper appeared in the 7th century, the making of paper was adapted to local conditions and resources.

The scroll, made of a series of sheets stuck one onto the other, was the oldest form of the book in China. The pleated, and then the quire form, succeeded the scroll. Calligraphy was done preferably on paper made from hemp, up to the Song period, then on paper from bark. Painting, on the other hand, continued to be done for a long time on silk.[25]

The sands of Taklamakan have preserved fragments, at times of considerable size, of manuscripts on paper. Written in various languages and at periods varying from the 2nd to the 9th centuries, these fragments are, in a way, the precursors of the Persian book. Among these, some fragments originating from Qotco and Toyoq are painted and date back to the 8th and 9th centuries.[26]

The Judeo-Persian fragment of Dandan-Uiluq discovered by A. Stein[27] and published by D.S. Margoliouth is probably the oldest Persian text preserved on paper, known to date. Indeed, the oldest Persian manuscript, apart from this document, is supposed to be the treatise of Movaffaq b. 'Ali Herati, composed between 961 and 976, the copy of which, dated 1055, is preserved in Vienna. The research conducted by D.S. Margoliouth on this Judeo-Persian fragment led him to suggest the date of 718.

We know moreover, that at this date the Sogdians knew how to make paper, having learnt it perhaps during the establishment of colonies in Buddhist sites as far away as Tuen Huang, where Sogdian manuscripts have been found as also in Turfan.[28] The Persian word *kaghaz* comes moreover from the Sogdian *k'Gdyh*; it has passed into

Uighur in the form of the word *kaghda* and into Turkish in the form *kagit*.[29] Under the Sasanids, Chinese paper was known but was restricted to official use.[30]

- *The first Muslim paper*

The history of the beginnings of paper in Samarkand, under Ziyad b. Saleh (d. 752) is related by Sa'alebi.[31] We know that following the battle of Talas, in 751 some Chinese prisoners taught the invaders how to make paper. However, it would seem that these prisoners had not themselves been workers specialised in the manufacture of paper, and that they merely repeated what they had seen being done in their country. This would perhaps explain how, contrary to the Chinese manner, the first "Arab" paper made in Samarkand included old rags mixed with the pulp of plants. It is likely that the paper makers of Samarkand first of all mixed some woven fibres, particularly flax, with other raw plant fibres, and progressively increased the quantity of the former. The *Hodud al-'alam*[32] mentions that "there is in Samarkand a monastery of Manichaeans called *noqushak* where paper is made which is sent all over the world". Samarkand paper remains, till the 18th century, the model for the best paper in the East.

In the Arab world, the oldest fragment of paper preserved, found in Egypt, dates from 796-815.[33] According to Yaqut, a paper mill had been installed in Bagdad by al-Fazl Barmaki, brother of the vizir Ja'far Barmak who had been the governor of Khorasan in 794-795. It was situated in the Dar al-ghazz area.[34] This fact is mentioned also by Ebn Khaldun.[35]

The paper of the first centuries of Islam is known to us mainly through Ebn Nadim.[36] According to the list of the names of papers he supplied, and thanks to the identification proposed by C. Huart,[37] it is possible to suggest some hypotheses. The list is as follows:

1. *fara'uni* : this name, apparently, designates a variety of paper meant to compete with the papyrus of Egypt.
2. *soleymani* : named after Soleyman b. Rashid, Director of the finances of Khorasan under Harun al-Rashid.
3. *ja'fari* : from the name of the vizir Ja'far Barmak.
4. *talhi* : named after Talha b. Taher of the Taheride dynasty (822-828)
5. *tâheri* : from Tâher II (844-862) of this same dynasty.
6. *nuhi* : from Nuh I b. Nasr, of the Samanid dynasty (942-954).

It appears, according to the identifications made by C. Huart, that most of the paper mentioned comes from the east of the Caliphate and particularly from Khorasan. It should be noted that no doubt from the Taheride dynasty onwards, Iran produced paper, the manufacture of which was undertaken by the Samanids, and that this paper was known in Bagdad where it was probably exported. It is strange on the other hand, that Ebn Nadim does not mention the evolution of paper in the West, particularly that of Syria, known some centuries later for its good paper. But perhaps in the 10th century, the Muslim West still preferred papyrus? Indeed, paper only reached Sicily, a big centre for the production of papyrus, in the 10th century.

At that time, Biruni, in his *Kitab al-Hind*,[38] recalls a not so distant past when paper was not yet known. He writes:

> "Muslims, too, used in the early times of Islam to write on hides (...) The copies of the Koran were written on the hides of gazelles, as are still nowadays the copies of the Thora. (...) The *kirtas* is made in Egypt, being cut out of the papyrus stalk. Written on this material, the orders of the Khalifs went out into all the world until shortly before our time. Papyrus has this advantage over vellum, that you can neither rub out nor change anything on it, because thereby it would be destroyed. It was in China that paper was first manufactured. Chinese prisoners introduced the fabrication of paper into Samarkand, and thereupon it was made in various places, so as to meet the existing want."

Paper making in Iran and in India

The Iranian world

Apart from the list of names of paper left by Ebn Nadim, we know practically nothing about pre-Timurid Iranian paper. Jamali-ye Yazdi and Teflisi (12th century) mention paper as a commonly used material; Rashid al-din, while discussing the distribution of water in his domain (*Shahrestan-e Rashidi*), mentions some paper mills. Elsewhere, he points out that beautiful paper should be used for the books produced in the workshops that he has set up and he even mentions their formats.[39] The comments by Ravandi that we quoted earlier, unfortunately give no detail about the type and the origin of the paper used. Some information about the *varraq* or paper seller[40] indicate that the paper trade was extensive enough to keep a group of professionals fully occupied. The Arab historian Abu Hamid al-Gharnati says: "Paper from Samarkand has supplanted paper from Egypt, just as this had replaced the *maghrebi*. Paper made in Balkh compares favourably with the paper made in Irak, in Khorasan and in India".[41]

Hojviri (5th/11th centuries) relates how the sheets of the manuscripts of Abu Nuwas and of Jahez ended up as the lining of hats or as book bindings.[42] This fact would indicate that the price of new paper must have been high enough to prevent its being used for such petty things. We will see later that paper was likewise reprocessed in India.

In the 15th century, Simi mentions paper coming from Baghdad, Damascus, Amol, Samarkand, and Bengal.[43] Soltan 'Ali (920/1514) makes no mention of any strictly Iranian paper. He simply refers to *khata'i* paper and paper from Samarkand.[44]

Although this is not mentioned in the treatises, Herat also must have produced some paper during the Timurid period since Babur saw some paper mills there.[45]

At the end of the 16th century, the Turk 'Ali Efendi mentions paper from various sources, six at least being definitely of Indian origin.[46]

The types of non-Indian paper that he mentions are from Turkestan, *habashi* from Abyssinia, *demashqi* from Damascus, *samarqandi* from Samarkand, and *guni-ye Tabrizi*, which is coloured paper from Tabriz.

According to the remarks made by Chardin and Du Mans (see below), it would appear that the quality of Persian paper of the mid-17th century, had deteriorated a lot.[47] The production of Iranian paper seems to have further declined in the 18th century and become practically non-existent in the 19th century.[48] It appears, on the other hand, that in the 17th and 18th centuries, Indian paper was used in Iran and in the Ottoman empire, as is testified not only by the above-mentioned treatises, but also in a remark made in the *Dastur al-moluk*, a Safavid work on administration (around 1137/1725) in which it is specified that the *majles-nevis*, Secretary to the Chancery, receives 30 reams of paper from Dowlatabad.[49]

India

Paper arrived in India much later than in the Iranian world. Indeed, as Biruni mentions, the Indians in the 10th century wrote mainly on palmyra leaves or on bark. Perhaps the oldest references to paper dates from the reign of Balban (1266-1286). The historian Barni tells us how this king had a firman washed, perhaps with the intention of reusing the paper, or simply to annul the decree that it contained.[50] In the *khateme* of his *Qeran al-sa'deyn* (682/1284), Amir Khosrow composed a poem in praise of *Shami* paper, a term which some authors understand as meaning "paper from Syria"; they have concluded from this that "Syrian" paper was manufactured in Delhi during this period.[51] In fact, the text is unfortunately much less explicit:[52]

- "Syrian" paper springs from the colour of dawn/
  Its dawn-like finery (its whiteness) comes from the evening (of Syria).[53]
- It is a spotless silk, but its substance, formerly/
  was made from flax and from raw silk.
- The silk thread came in the skein/
  it is a marvellous silk that can be torn into pieces.
- The elements (of the paper) are brought together by water/
  but its destruction also is brought about by water.
- It has been so flattened by beating/
  that its back folds over at a single stroke.
- May there be a passage across the handle of the blade/
  may it (the paper) present its head from the blade to the scissors(?)
- May the eye of the needle pull the *mastar* (ruling)/
  may it draw the curve of the quire's thread.
- In short, may the aim of the arrow be, at all times/
  inspired solely by the love of the pen.
- May it (the paper) act on the princely face/
  so that destiny may discover a last meaning.

This difficult passage plays on the double meanings of words (*sham* means "evening" as well as "Syria"). Nevertheless, at no place is it specifically mentioned that this *shami* paper was made in Delhi.

Some contemporary Indian historians point out that paper was imported from Khorasan or from Isfahan.[54] However, eyen if this is probably true, particularly in the case of paper from Sarmarkand, I have found no trace of it in texts yet.

We noted earlier that some sheets of precious manuscripts had been turned into linings for hats or into bindings for books. Hamid Qalandar, in his work *Kheyr al-majales* (around 754/1354) also mentions some sheets of manuscripts being used for wrapping sweets.[55] As we already noted earlier, the price of new paper must have been too high for it to be used as a packaging material.

In short, we know little about the manufacture of paper in India before the 15th century. I. Habib notes that the caste system probably played an important role in hampering the development of new techniques in India. Thus, it is very probable that a new technique such as paper making, must, for a long time, have remained in the hands of immigrant craftsmen or those who had converted to Islam.[56] It is interesting to note that even today the manual manufacture of paper still remains restricted mostly to Muslims.

In the 15th century, Simi is the only one who mentions paper coming from Bengal. In Kashmir, the making of paper was probably introduced by Zeyn al-'Abedin (1417-1467), king of Kashmir, who learnt it in Samarkand where he was detained for several years. Thereafter, paper from Kashmir earned an excellent reputation.[57]

Paper from Deccan

By the end of the 16th century, paper from Dowlatabad was known and had spread not only over India but also in Persia and in the Ottoman Empire. The *Manaqeb-e honarvaran* by 'Ali Efendi, (995/1586) is probably the oldest source to mention it. In the 18th century once again, Dowlatabad paper is mentioned in Persia, as we have seen, in the *Dastur al-moluk*, a manual on administration.[58] Considering that the place-name Dowlatabad, is very common in Iran, Afghanistan and India, there may well be no particular reason to believe that this relates to the Dowlatabad of the Deccan. Indeed, as the latter is very far from Isfahan, one may wonder why the *majles-nevis* of the Saffavid court would procure reams of paper from so distant a source.

However, the Deccan seems to have produced a fairly large variety of paper the importance of which has not yet been properly estimated. Paper from Dowlatabad is mentioned numerous times in Indian sources. During the reign of Akbar, this paper is mentioned in the *Haft eqlim*[59] (1002/1593) and in the *Resale-ye Khoshnevisi*;[60] a century later, it is mentioned, once again, in the *Bayaz-e khoshbu'i* (1109-1698).[61] In the 18th century, it seems to have been replaced by paper from Ahmadabad.[62] It may be noted that, five kilometres from Dowlatabad, on the road to Khuldabad, there is a little market-town by the name of Kaghazpuri. It was no doubt at this place where there were several reservoirs, and not at the foot of the impregnable fortress, that this renowned paper was produced.

Apart from Dowlatabad paper, 'Ali Efendi mentions five other varieties of paper of Indian origin:

- *'adel-shahi*, from the name of the dynasty which ruled in Bijapur (Deccan) 1486-1696, also mentioned in the *Resale-ye-Khosh-nevisi*,[63]
- *hendi*, Indian,
- *nezam-shahi*, dynasty 1490-1636, Ahmadnagar (Deccan),
- *qasem-beygi*,
- *hariri-ye hendi*, Indian silk paper.

In addition to 'Ali Efendi, at least two other texts mention *qasem-beygi* paper; the *Bayaz-e khoshbu'i*, dated to 1109/1698[64] and the *Kholasat al-mojarrabat* (before 1766).[65] There are several personalities with the name Qasem Beyg in Indian history during the 15th and 16th centuries. Three of them are of Iranian origin. One of them served 'Ala' al-din Bahmani in his foreign regiments, became the governor of Dowlatabad in 1471 and continued to occupy this position until at least 1485.[66] Another Qasem Beyg, a doctor, served in the court of Burhan Nezamshah (1510-1554), then in that of Hosein Nezamshah (1554-64).[67] A third Qasem Beyg, of Tabriz, was a scholar in the court of Akbar; he translated the *Mo'jam al-boldan* of Yaqut into Persian, served the prince Murad in Malwa, during the 36th year of the reign of Akbar and died in 1007/1599.[68] On account of the date of the writing of the *Manaqeb* (1586), the most likely one would seem to be the first Qasem Beyg, the governor of Dowlatabad.

Under Akbar, then under Jahangir, Sialkot in Upper Panjab, also developed the manufacture of paper. We find in the *Kholasat al-tavarikh* of Sujan Ray (1107/1695) the following:[69]

> "In this city beautiful paper is made, particularly the paper of Man Singh (Akbar's general governor of Panjab) and also paper from silk, and the "special paper" of Jahangir, equally beautiful and of fine material, of lasting whiteness and purity; they are distributed in the neighbouring regions."

Paper from Sialkot is also mentioned in the *Bayaz-e khoshbu'i*.[70] The *Mer'at-e Ahmadi* of 'Ali Mohammad Khan (1175/1764),[71] considers the Ahmadabad paper as superior to all the others:

"Although the Dowlatabad and the Kashmir paper are of good

> quality, yet neither can compete in whiteness and lustre with the paper of Ahmadabad."

Lucknow produced hemp paper, as W. Hoey has observed (see below). Abu al-Fazl mentions paper from Bihar,[72] and the *Bahar-e 'ajam* mentions that of Moradabad, in Uttar Pradesh.[73] Although it would seem that Jaunpur also had been a city which produced paper, I have not yet found any reference to this in any Persian text. The "treatise on the manufacture of paper of Delhi" which we are going to see later, implies that paper was manufactured in this city, but this is not otherwise acknowledged.

Techniques for manufacturing paper

Probably the oldest description of the manufacture of paper that we have in the Muslim world is the one given in the *'Umdat al-kuttab.*[74]

The raw material used is flax (*qunnab*). After its leaves have been removed, the flax is soaked and then combed till it softens. Then it is soaked in quicklime overnight, hand-rubbed and put out to dry in the sun; the operation is repeated several times. After this, the flax is soaked in pure water for seven days, the water being changed daily. When all the lime has been washed away the flax is finely crushed in a mortar and once again soaked and dissolved till it attains a silky viscosity. The pulp is then put into moulds of the desired shape. These are made from a screen of strands of stretched straw, placed on a frame with sliding edges the base of which is constructed from widely spaced slats. The pulp is flattened by hand on the frame, in such a way as to spread the thickness evenly over the entire surface. Once flattened and drained, the sheet takes shape. It is then placed flat on a board subsequently on a wall where it remains until it dries and falls.[75]

The technique described in this text is fairly rudimentary and the paper obtained must have been quite basic. As we shall see, improvements are, in fact, introduced during the centuries, which enabled the speeding up and the perfecting of the production.

Very little information is available on paper-making from the 13th to the 18th century. Some remarks by Chardin and by Raphael du Mans tell us something about 17th century Iranian paper.

"Paper making is a very rudimentary process in Persia; this arises from the fact that they only use cotton cloth, most of which is dyed and painted; moreover their paper is greyish, dirty, thick and lacks consistency. They use a lot of paper from Europe, after having sized it".[76]

"They make paper everywhere in their country; it is composed, like ours, of scraps of cotton and of silk; but as their canvases are mostly oil painted, and cotton is neither strong nor resistant, their paper is not as white as ours and it tears when it is folded".[77]

Of the three treatises on the manufacture of paper mentioned by Storey,[78] none is dated; there is however reason to believe that they are quite recent (Storey dates them as 19th century) and are of Indian origin.

The treatise of the Decourdemanche collection[79] is not so much a technical work as, in fact, a mythical history of paper, supposedly invented by Abraham who was inspired by the Archangel Gabriel (fol. 3a): it then goes on to tell us more about the duties of the apprentice to the master paper maker and about his profession than about the manufacture of paper itself.

The "treatise on the manufacture of Delhi paper",[80] undoubtedly Indian, gives some details about the making of the pulp. The basic material here is the rag (*tat pati**). The rags are soaked in a vat made of stone and plaster. They are beaten with a device which is unfortunately only succinctly described (*tarkibesh mota'laq be molaheze*, its shape is according to need), but it seems apparently to be moved manually. It must be a kind of pounding device which pounds the rags in the vat (*anra bekuband va carkh dehand*, they pound them and operate the wheel). The pounding continues for several days after which the pulp is squeezed and left to dry, then washed with a mixture of tin oxide and soda. The operation is repeated several times till the rags form a smooth white paste. The process of preparing the paste lasts a whole month during hot, dry weather and almost fifty days in humid or cold weather.

The description of the manufacture of sheets of paper from the paste prepared in this manner is given in a very summarized fashion in this text: once the paste has been obtained, a mould (*qaleb-e tayyari*) is plunged into the vat; (when a film of paste deposits itself on the screen of the mould, the latter is raised up and) it is placed on a board to drain; (the sheet is then raised and) is left to dry; then it is polished and is ready for use.

A plate from a mid-19th century album, illustrating the crafts of Kashmir,[81] gives us a few more precisions. Here the pounding of the rags (*karbas*) is done by a hydraulic mill. The paste is then washed in a cloth sheet held stretched out between two people and poured into a vat. To lift up the sheets, a mould[82] is used, composed of a screen made from orange tree twigs (*narang*) and of a wooden frame on which the screen is placed. The worker plunges the mould into the vat and raises it up gently; the frame is left to drain out, then the sheet is lifted from the frame and put under a press. When it has dried, the sheet is trimmed at the edges with a knife, then polished.

W. Hoey observed, in 1880, the way paper was manufactured in Lucknow.[83] He describes, among other things, the way in which *arwali** paper, or paper made from hemp rags "in the traditional manner" is manufactured; he says that this kind of paper, which is particularly suited to manuscripts, is not much in demand at the time of writing:

> "*Arwali* paper is made of old *tat** (hemp rags) which are sold for one rupee a *maund*.[84] Four maunds of these are soaked in a tank (*hauz*), with twenty *sir* of soda (*sajji**) and 15 *sir* of lime (*chuna**). The pulp is pounded with a sledge-hammer (*dhekali**), then washed. This process is repeated about thirty times within four months; once the paste is ready, the sheets are raised with a mould."

It is interesting to note that in general paper making has evolved little, practically, up to the present day; indeed, it is still possible today to observe its being produced in certain areas in the same manner as several centuries ago. Mechanization is minimal. I have had the opportunity of seeing paper being produced at Sanganer (Rajasthan) where it continues to be made manually.

The pulp is prepared essentially from old paper; the best quality paper is made from a mixture of old paper and rags. The pulp is washed in the traditional manner: two men attach a large piece of cloth around their loins and place the pulp inside. Standing in a tank, they beat this cloth sack in the water (exactly as is shown in the plate from the *Album of the Crafts of Kashmir*). After several washings, the paste is left to drain, then it is put into the vat where the worker stirs it in such a way as to keep it floating in the water. The frame is in the form of a rectangle of wood on which spaced out slats are stretched; the screen, made of woven twigs, is placed on this frame. The frame is plunged into the vat at an angle and progressively brought to the horizontal position. A slight to and fro movement enables the pulp to spread out evenly; then the frame is raised and held at a slight angle by a wooden rod so as to drain out the surplus water. The screen is then separated from the frame, taking with it the sheet of paper; this is detached from the screen and is placed on gauze. When one ream is complete (25 to 50 sheets, depending on the thickness, all separated by gauzes) it is pressed between two boards with a screw press to extract most of the water. The gauzes are then removed and the paper put out to dry.

W Hoey makes similar observations about *wasli* paper, produced from old paper and used to make cardboard, and about *zard-kaghaz*, also made from recycled paper, but of a finer grain.[85]

Technical improvements :

1) Mobile form : The adoption of a mobile form in which the frame and the screen are separate, represents a considerable improvement in the manufacture of paper. As we saw earlier, the Chinese used a mobile form as early as the 2nd century. The form described in the *'Umdat* appears to be only partially mobile: the bars of the frame are mobile but apparently the screen itself cannot be separated from the frame. The forms described in the *Album of the Crafts of Kashmir* resemble those that are still used today.

2) The press is only mentioned in the *'Umdat* in the chapter concerning tools used for book binding.[86] In this work, two types of presses (*mi'sar*) are described: the one with a rope, used in Egypt, Irak and Khorasan, and the one with a screw, also called Solomon's press.

In the manufacture of paper the press has the advantage of tightening the grain of the still humid paper and of getting rid of most of the water. In the plate from the *Album of the Crafts of Kashmir*, the press consists of just two boards with stones on top. It is not mentioned in the "Delhi treatise".

3) The hydraulic mill: In China, hydraulic power seems to have been used only after the 12th or 13th centuries.[87] Practically no texts are known to us describing the application of hydraulic power to paper-making. Rashid al-din mentions a *kaghaz-khane* installed on the waters of the *Shahrestan-e Rashidi*; were these perhaps mills?[88] Babur notices some paper mills (*juvaz-e kaghazlir*) at Herat and in Samarkand.[89] In Europe, some hydraulic devices, such as the shredder roller only appeared at the end of the 17th century. Before that, hydraulic power

was used to operate mortars such as the one shown on the plate of the Kashmir manuscript.

Types of paper

The quality of the paper, that is to say its thickness, the fineness of its grain, its resistance to the reed pen or to water, are important selection criteria for the artist getting ready to work—'Ali Efendi describes, for example, the paper of Abyssinia or of Damascus, which he considers too rough. Calligraphy, like painting, requires solid paper with an extremely fine grain. That is why the finest ones are selected, sized and polished before they are put to use. After having launched into a tirade against Persian paper, Chardin says further on:

> "All their painting is in miniature: they work on a vellum paper which is admirable; it is a much finer card than any that we have; it is hard, firm, dry and smooth, on which the painting does not run".[90]

Paper is named generally after the place of its origin (names of places or of people); however, it may also designate some characteristic format, process or the raw material used for making the pulp. Thus, *hariri* paper is made of silk rags; *arwali** paper is made of hemp rags (in Lucknow; see earlier); *ashkhwari* paper from Samarkand mentioned by Simi is perhaps whitened with soda; *soltani* may designate a glossy paper, as we shall see later, but it is also the description by Simi of a type of paper from Bagdad, and by 'Ali Efendi[91] of a type of paper from Samarkand; decorated, dyed, marbled or gold-flecked, papers all have their own names, as we will see hereafter.

Other kinds of paper, for sketches and for pounced drawings, have to be practically transparent.

Paper called *daftari* is used for accountancy; the *vasli* is a cardboard made of old sheets pasted together[92] or of a pulp made of old paper.[93] O.P. Jaggi names other varieties of paper of which we have found no trace in texts; these are *sharbati*, *ruba-kari*, *balapuri*.[94]

Oiled paper (*kaghazliq*), which is referred to by Sadeqi as a protection for objects painted "in oil", should also be noted; it has also been mentioned by Mirza Haydar Dughlat.[95]

Formats

The format of the sheets is another important element in the codicological study of the manuscripts. Unfortunately, works which have kept their original size are very scarce in libraries; mostly they have been cut down in the process of binding or during successive repairs.

Most Persian texts only refer briefly to the format of the pages. Qalqashandi, on the other hand, has discussed this matter at length in his *Subh ul-a'sha.*[96] Here are the formats that he mentions:

- the standard format is the *qat' al-baghdadi al-kamil* (in-folio of Baghdad),
- *al-baghdadi al-naqes* (reduced folio),
- *al-salasain min waraq al-misri* (two-thirds of the Egyptian sheet),
- *al-nisf* (half-folio),
- *al-suls* (one-third folio)
- *al-ma'ruf bil-mansuri, rub'* ("*mansuri*", quarter folio),
- *al-saghir* or *al-'ada, sudus*, (one-sixth folio),
- *al-shami al-kamil* (Syrian in-folio),
- *al-shami al-saghir, min waraq al-tayr* (small sheet for carrier-pigeon).

These are the formats used by the Mameluk administration. Some research has been carried out on Arab sources to determine the size of the proposed formats, but this research still appears to be of a hypothetical nature.[97] The destination and the use of the paper determined its measurements. If we could have the dimensions of the entire sheet, as it was straight from the mould, this would give us some indications about the original formats of the folded sheets of the manuscripts. It is likely that the moulds for the manufacture of the paper were not standardized, varying by a centimetre here or there. However, although Bjorkman notes some fluctuating measurements, and the establishment of new formats depending on court fashion, some names remain significant, even in the Iranian world. Thus, Rashid al-din recommends that the Korans copied in the establishment should be done on *qat'-e hal-e bozorg-e baghdadi* (in-folio of Baghdad)[98] and the collections of *hadis, be qat'-i ke monaseb danand* (in the suitable format), which proves indeed that there is, in the sizes of paper, an accepted hierarchy and that each format is for a particular use. M.Bayani points out the names of twelve sizes of paper, whose dimensions he gives (*vaziri, soltani, rahli,* for instance). It should be noted that these names are still widely used by the authors of Iranian catalogues.[99]

The page format chosen for a manuscript (*qat'*) will condition the composition and the ruling (*mastar*) since the dimensions of the sheet provide the first ratio of proportions. That is why the format and the ruling are often related. When Soltan 'Ali, in his treatise, asks the student to copy out the lines of a master, he recommends that he follow the same format and the same ruling:

> *"ham bedan qat' mastar va qalamesh*
> *saz tartib ta koni raqamesh."*[100]

> "Examine the format, the ruling and the pen (writing),
> prepare the layout so that you may write (copy) it".

Similarly, Baysanqor, according to Dust Mohammad, got the album of Ahmad Jalayer copied *be haman dastur-e qat' va mastar* "in the same order of format and ruling".[101]

Sizing and polishing

Before it is used, the paper is sized and polished. Teflisi calls the sizing *gune dadan*; Simi uses this term just once, while referring to a marshmallow starch: "This process is highly appreciated, it softens the paper, and the calligraphy stands out well on it".[103] Teflisi describes sizing as follows:

> "If we want to size the paper in order to polish it, we must take some ripened rice and boil it, then pour the mush into a wide container and submerge the paper in it once or twice, then leave it to dry; once it had dried, polish it with (a polishing tool) made of glass (*abgine*).[102]"

Teflisi adds that we can also size the paper with gum tragacanth (*katira*) or with starch (*neshaste*). These three types of size are also mentioned in the '*Umdat*.[104] Apart from the sizing agents already noted, Simi mentions fish glue, psyllium glue, and melon juice as well as other glucosic extracts. He concludes by saying that with these processes we can make thin paper more resistant, so that any protuberances can be ironed out and the reed pen of the calligrapher can run across the paper as it should.[105]

We find in the *Resale-ye khoshnevisi* the following remark: "To size "*khata'i*" paper, whether it be meant for exercises or for calligraphy, if the starch is thick, we repeat the process two or three times."[106] As we may recall, Simi says that well-sized paper is better than *soltani* paper.[107] Similarly, in the *Majmu'at al-sanaye'*,[108] we find instructions for sizing paper in such a way that it becomes similar to the Baghdadi (the process described is similar to Teflisi's: a rice mush). The paper is thus known by different names depending on the manner in which it has been sized.

The *Bayaz-e khoshbu'i* also describes the sizing of paper: a rice paste is prepared with which the sheets are sized on both sides. Then they are covered with a cloth (*karbas*) and dried in the sun. The sheets are then polished (*mohre zadan*). H. Kh. Naqvi and, later O.P. Jaggi, who quotes her, translate these terms as "seals imprinted"; this is, of course, a mistranslation.[109]

At a later period (1221/1806), Gholam Dehlavi describes sizing in the following terms:

"Size the paper on the front but not on the back, with great care, like a fresh colourful flower.
Then polish the paper on the other side until it shines brighter than a mirror for writing."[110]

This relates perhaps to the sizing of a sheet meant for an album, as the pages of manuscripts are sized and polished on both sides.

2. Other grounds

Apart from mural painting (which we will examine later), other grounds have also been used for painting: wood,leather, terracotta, cloth. However, a detailed study of these various grounds would probably not bring in any new element as regards the technique itself. For this reason we will simply mention here some grounds other than paper, which also play a part in the arts of the book.

Cloth

Practically no technical information is available concerning this ground, which is rarely used in manuscripts. Teflisi says that if colours are to be used for painting on cloth, they must be mixed with *ab-e khun* (what could this be?);[111] in fact, Teflisi is referring here to printing with a block (*qaleb*) used for clothes and not for manuscript painting.

The technique of painting on silk is probably of Chinese origin; some fragments have been discovered in Xinjiang, among which there is a piece of a banner, found in Qotco dating from the 9th century.[112] In the Iranian world, some examples of painting on silk exist from the Timurid period, one of which shows Homay and Homayun.[113] Examples of Iranian paintings on cloth are nevertheless very rare. On the other hand, in India we find some traditional techniques of painting on cloth, such as the *pichhwai** of Rajasthan or the Orissa paintings on sized cloth (*pata-chitra**). In the field of Moghul painting, at least two important works on cloth were produced.

A well-known work on canvas is the painting showing the princes of the house of Timur, started probably for Homayun around the year 1550 and retouched at the time of Jahangir, around 1607.[114] The astonishing dimensions of this painting (108.5 cm by 108 cm in its present state), would perhaps explain the choice of the support, since rarely were sheets of paper made of such a large size; the eminently decorative objective of this painting and its light weight also lead us to think that it must have been meant to accompany the king during his travels.

As far as books are concerned, there is the colossal *Hamze-name,* commissioned by Akbar and executed between 1550 and 1575, an extensive work but the only one of its kind. We know from Abu al-Fazl[115] that this work was originally made up of twelve volumes containing 1400 illustrations. Unfortunately, there only remain to date, about a hundred of these paintings, distributed among several collections, the largest being that of the Museum of Decorative Arts in Vienna (61 paintings). These illustrations on canvas measure about 64 cm by 78 cm and are stuck onto the sheets of paper on which the text is written.[116]

Grounds for paintings using oil-based mediums (rang-o-rowghan).

Lacquer objects, which in Persian are called *rang-o-rowghan*, require specially prepared grounds. In manuscript art these types of lacquer are used particularly for bindings but also for casings (*jozdan*) and pen-boxes.

Sadeqi describes in his *Qanun al-sovar* the way to prepare the grounds (*batane*) for the lacquer.[117] The "oil colours" or lacquer are made on a ground composed of asphodel gum, collodion, plaster and grape juice. It is on this that the background (*bum*) and then the subject, are painted.

The term *batane* is also found again in the *Majmu'at al-sanaye'*.[118] In this text, several methods are suggested, all of which use *rowghan-e kaman*, a very resistant varnish explained also by Sadeqi.[119] The result of these formulae, which are long and difficult to makeup, is a paste which hardens and becomes like stone. However, the purpose of the result is not specified in this text. Fakhr al-din Nasiri Amini, in his article on binding, mentions however the cover of a manuscript which has a ground made of this substance. This is the Koran of the tomb of Sheykh Safi al-din Ardabili, now in the Iran Bastan Museum of Teheran.[120] This author subsequently gives a recipe for *laye* or *batane cini*, which seems to have come straight out of the *Majmu'at al-sanaye*, although he does not indicate the source.

Grounds for pen-boxes, *jozdan* and others :

The *Resale-ye jeld-sazi* explains how to make pen-boxes and other objects, meant probably to be covered with a lacquer decoration.[121] These objects are made with moulds (*kalbod*), and the base matter is paper, in the form of cardboard (*moqavva'*) or pulp (*bure-ye kaghaz*). The principle behind this technique is simple; pieces of paper are stuck one on top of the other, on a soaped mould until the desired thickness is obtained. For small objects or for details, paper pulp is used, mixed with gum. When the object is completed, it is covered with a glaze, then decorated and varnished. This technique is described by Chardin as follows:

> "They make their ordinary pen-cases in the form of a drawer. They make them on an iron mould, with sheets of paper which are stuck on top of each other applying some sheep's fat to the last one and a varnish on top which is resistant to water and is very fine (...) The glue that the Persians use is not made of flour, but of a crushed root which they call *serichom*, ground not finer than sawdust, between two millstones and made into a dough. It is soaked in cold water in which it immediately swells up, and it sticks marvelously well".[122]

This technique is also described by H. Wulff.[123]

NOTES

1. I. Afshar, *Seyr*, p.9, quotes Ebn Nadim in support of this; however, I have not found in the works of this author any specific mention of the Gondishapur

library, nor of a possible library of Ardashir, also mentioned by Afshar; as regards Gondishapur, it is important to refer to the work by H.H. Schoffler, *Die Akademie von Gondischapur.*

2. Danesh-Pazhuh, "*Moraqqa'* ", pp.152-153, gives an interesting study of sources in which these books are mentioned; unfortunatley, his references are often lacking in precision; it has therefore not always been possible for us to verify them; see Mas'udi, *Kitab al-tanbih va al-ashraf* (Bibl. Geogr. Arab., VIII) p.106; Hamze Esfahani, *Sani moluk al-arz*, transl. pp. 7, 13, 19 and 61; also *Mojmal al-tavarikh va al-qasas*, pp.33-37, no reference to edition.
3. Sa'alebi mentions a work called *Haftkhan* and says that the pictures in this book are found in the houses and in the books of Iranians (*Qarar al-sayyr*, pp.302 and 414., quoted by Danesh-Pazhuh, "*Moraqqa'*", p.154). This author also mentions the painted Zoroastrian books which survived Alexander's ravages and were recovered by Ardashir Papakan. Tabari, in the story of Afshin Asrushne'i writes that Mohammad b. 'Abd al-Malek Zayyat reproaches the latter with having a picture book in which the customs and rules of the Iranians were described (Danesh-Pazhuh, *id.*, p.151. Tabari, *Tarikh*, vol.3, p.1309, the edition is not specified).
4. A.Tafazzoli, p.195.
5. *Manichaische Miniaturen.*
6. Thus, Augustine exclaims admiration for the luxuriousness of the Manichaean manuscripts. *Contra Faustum*, Widengren, pp.111-112. Ebn al-Jowzi (*al-Montazam*, 6, p. 176 according to Danesh-Pazhuh, "*Moraqqa'* ", pp. 150-151) writes that in 311/923, at the 'Ama gate in Baghdad, some Manichaean manuscripts were burnt, and that the melted gold and silver flowed like streams from the pyres.
7. Chap. Cliv : 2; see G.Widengren, p.108.
8. Abu al-Ma'ali, *Bayan al-adyan*, p.17.
9. This is a fragment shown by the J.Soustiel Gallery in April 1988; see Soustiel, *Art musulman* (1988), pl.2 (see our plate no. 3).
10. Ebn Moqaffa, in the preface to his *Kalila wa Dimna* says that pictures are painted in his book in order to make it more pleasant; see Danesh-Pazhuh, "*Moraqqa'*", p.151, who quotes a Beirut edition of 1896 p.78. In the preface to the old *Shah-name* by Abu Mansur, completed in 346/957, it is said, of a *Kalila wa Dimna* by Rudaki, that this book was decorated with paintings executed by Chinese artists on the order of Nasr b. Ahmad; see again Danesh-Pazhuh, *id.*, p.152; see also H.Yaghma'i, *Ferdowsi va shah-name-ye u*, pp.263-264.
11. Danesh-Pazhuh, *id.*, p.153; these illustrations perhaps inspired the erotic figures in Mas'ud's tent, see Beyhaqi, *Tarikh*, pp.121-123.
12. *Rahat al-sodur*, ed. Iqbal p.57.
13. *Id.*, p.33. According to M.T. Danesh-Pazhuh, this person died in 588/1193 and was the same person as Jamal al-din Mohammad b. 'Abd al-Razzaq Esfahani; see Danesh-Pazhuh, "*Moraqqa'*", pp.155-156.

14. *Rahat al-sodur*, *id.*, p.44.
15. *Id.* p.336.
16. I. Afshar, *Seyr-e ketab dar Iran*, p.6.
17. I. Afshar, *id.*
18. A. von Gabain, p.615.
19. *Museum für Indische Kunst*, Berlin p. 110, no. 390.
20. Azarpay, "The development...", p.1139 and Mackenzie, p.1244.
21. *Serindia*, I, pp.224 and after.
22. Ph. Gignoux, pp.1212-1213.
23. J.P.Drege, p.23.
24. *Id.*, pp.24-27.
25. *Ibid.*
26. Le Coq, *Die manichaischen Miniaturen*.
27. *Ancient Khotan*, I, pp.306-309 and vol. 3 pl.CXIX; see also vol. 2, pp. 570-574.
28. A. von Gabain, p.615.
29. A.von Gabain, p.622.
30. Watson, W., p. 552 note.
31. *Lata'ef al-ma'aref*, ed. De Jong, p.126.
32. Ed. pp.107-108.
33. Huart, p.9.
34. Yaqut, ed. vol.2, p.422.
35. *Muqaddima*, transl. P.Gonabadi, II, p.851.
36. *al-Fihrist*, transl. B.Dodge, pp.39-40.
37. Huart, pp.9-10.
38. Transl. Sachau, chap.XVI, pp.170-171.
39. Ed. pp. 133 and 237; see also further "Formats".
40. See I.Afshar, "*Sahhafi az negah-e farhang*".
41. *Tuhfat al-albab*, p.202; Jaggi, p.171.
42. *Kashf al-mahjub*, p.8; Afshar, "*Sahhafi az negah-e farhang*", pp.80-81.
43. Simi, Ms. (London) fol. 43b, lines 2 to 7; see also Y.Porter, "Un traité de Simi", p.187.
44. It may be recalled that in the translation of the poem of Soltan 'Ali done by Minorsky, there is a confusion between *khata'i* paper = origin and *khata'i* (or *hana'i*) = colour; see transl. Minsorsky, p.113. We will also see further that the epithet *khata'i* may point not only to the origin but also to the quality of the paper. A *qat'e* of Mir 'Ali shows this distich, with a slight variation (Fogg Art Museum, Harvard), reproduced in A. Schimmel, *Calligraphy and Islamic Culture*, b & w. pl no. [4].
45. Transl. pp.81 and 305.
46. 'Ali Efendi, *Manaqeb-e honarvaran*, quoted by C.Huart, p.10.

47. Chardin, IV, 271.
48. Wulff, p.236.
49. Mirza Rafi'a, ed. p.93.
50. Barni, p.64.
51. See *e.g.*, K.M.Ashraf, p.103 and O.P.Jaggi, pp.170-171.
52. *Khateme* of the *Qeran al-sa'deyn*, B.N. ms. Sup. Pers 627; facsim. fol. 327.
53. The main quality of the paper is its whiteness, compared to the dawn, and its place of origin is Syria or the evening; see hereafter.
54. Jaggi, p. 170 and M. Chandra, p.8.
55. Ed. p.203.
56. I.Habib, "Capacity...", pp.7-8.
57. Aslah, *Tazkere-ye sho'ara-ye Kashmir*, pp.1326-1327.
58. Mirza Rafi'a, ed. p.93.
59. Razi, Amin, ed. Vol.I, pp.81-82.
60. Ms. (Patna) fol.10a; some versions of the treatise of Soltan 'Ali also point this out, see Mayel Heravi, *Loghat va estelahat* p.8, which points out that Dowlatabad paper belongs to the second category of *'adelshahi* paper.
61. Ms. fol. 121a.
62. 'Ali Mohammad Khan, p.12.
63. Ms. fol.10a.
64. Ethe no. 2784, fol.139a.
65. Ms I.O., fol. 138b.
66. Haig, p. 409.
67. 'Ali b. Aziz, pp.348-354 and 551-558.
68. Abu al-Fazl, *A'in*, I, p.582.
69. Ed. p.72.
70. Ms fol 121b.
71. Transl. p.12.
72. *A'in*, I, p.417.
73. Monshi Tek Chand, vol.II, p.286.
74. Karabacek, pp.82-83.
75. See Levey's transl. p.39.
76. Chardin, IV, 148. Du Mans makes similar observations, p.200; in fact, it is probable that Chardin's observations were in fact inspired by those of Du Mans (paper by Francis Richard, to be published).
77. Chardin, IV, 271.
78. Storey vol.II, part 3, p.431.
79. B.N.Sup. Pers. no. 1942 (*Traité dans lequel il est parlé...*).
80. B.L.Rieu, III, 1012a, *Tarkib-e tayyari-ye kaghaz-e Dehli.*
81. India Office Add Or. no. 1699. (*Album of the Crafts of Kashmir*); see our plate no. 4.

82. The name given on this plate, *hasre*, is perhaps a corruption of *hasir* (mat); this spelling is however not found in dictionaries.
83. Hoey, pp.127-128.
84. Anglo-Indian form of the Persian *man*; around 40 *sir*.
85. Hoey, *id.*
86. Transl. Levey, pp.41-42.
87. See Drege, pp.23-27.
88. *Vaqf-name*, ed. pp.204 and 207.
89. Transl. pp.81 and 303.
90. Chardin, V.203.
91. Simi, Ms. B.L. fol. 43b; 'Ali Efendi, Huart, p.11.
92. Vajed 'Ali, fol.278a.
93. Hoey, p.127.
94. See Jaggi p.172.
95. In the latter, this word undoubtedly means the oiled paper of windows; see Melikian, "Khwaje Mirak", pp.99-100, notes 7 and 9 (this latter probably by mistake). It cannot be ruled out that this "oiled paper" may also have been used as tracing paper.
96. Ed. VI.189-191.
97. See particularly W. Bjorkman, p.114 and EI 2., art. *kat'*.
98. Francis Richard has brought to my attention that the Bibliothèque Nationale, Paris, possesses a ms. originally from the library of Rashid al-din which has preserved its original format "*in-folio* of Baghdad" (Ar. 2324).
99. *Ketabshenasi-ye ketabha-ye khatti*, pp.13-15; Mayel Heravi, *Loghat va estelahat*, p.8.
100. Ed., p. 73; transl., in Minorski, p. 118.
101. Dust Mohammad, p. 198.
102. Ed. p. 354.
103. Simi, Ms. (London) fol. 45b.
104. Transl. Levey, p. 39-40.
105. Ms. (London) fol. 45; Y.Porter, "Un traité de Simi", p. 189.
106. Ms. fol. 10a.
107. See ed. "anonymous" version Golcin-e Ma'ani, p. 295.
108. *Bab* 29 *fasl* I, Ms. B.L. fol. 34b.
109. *Bayaz-e khoshbu'i* chap. 8, fol. 119a-120a; Jaggi, pp.174-175.
110. Ed. p.32.
111. Ed. p.345.
112. Bussagli, p.105.
113. Coll. al-Sabah (Kuweit), ill. Falk,T. ed. p.61 no.30.
114. British Museum (1913.2-8.1).
115. *A'in* I, p.115.

116. W.Staude, p.51.
117. Ed., lines 131-134.
118. *Bab* 10, fol. 17a-18a.
119. Ed., lines 192-205.
120. *Sahhafi-ye sonnati*, p.7; the date of this binding is not specified.
121. Ed., pp.123-130.
122. Chardin, IV, pp.145-146.
123. Wulff, pp.238-239.

2

DECORATED PAPERS

The paper of numerous manuscripts is often decorated. The pages may be dyed, flecked with gold or silver, or marbled. Yet other techniques have developed, with greater or lesser success depending on the regions, such as silhouetted paper, cut-outs or paper decorated with stencils. Depending on the case, the manuscript was written directly on the decorated sheets or mounted on margins of decorated paper.

Most of these techniques were executed on unsized paper. Indeed, soaking in dyes, or marbling, would remove the sizing. These types of paper are therefore sized after dyeing, and polished like white paper.

1. Dyeing

The oldest technique for the decoration of paper is undoubtedly that of dyeing. C. Huart mentions a letter from emperor Constantine VII Porphyrogenitus, addressed to the Caliph of Cordova 'Abd al-Rahman, written on violet parchment.[1] Other famous examples of dyed parchments are the Byzantian *Codex purpurissum*[2] and the blue Koran, probably Fatimid, from the 4th/10th century.[3] The Bibliothèque Nationale (Paris) possesses some Nasrid manuscripts on coloured paper from the 13th century;[4] F. Richard has moreover noted some Persian manuscripts from the end of the 13th century and the 14th century copied out on coloured paper.[5]

Several Persian treatises on the art of dyeing exist, applied, it is true, to textiles and not to paper. Among them are chapter 20 of the *Kholasat al-mojarrabat,* composed before 1766-67,[6] the *'Atr va rang* treatise, attributed to Tipu Sultan, dating from 1211/1797,[7] and the *Nomov al-sabbaghin* of Nasr-allah Khan b. Khurjavi, composed in 1280/

1863.[8] H.Wulff mentions a treatise on dyeing from which he quotes several recipes without indicating the original source.[9] It should be noted that all these texts have been written in India although some of their authors may be of Iranian origin. This is the reason why there are sometimes lexical difficulties due to the borrowing of indigenous terms, or to the same word having different meanings in Iran and in India. Although these texts do not mention the dyeing of the paper, they help us know about the dyes used and the names of the colours they produce.

As regards the dyeing of paper, several texts give us the recipes, among these being the *Jowhar-e Simi*[10], the *Resale-ye Khoshnevisi* of the pseudo-Seyrafi,[11] chapter 41 of the *Majmu'at al-sanaye'*[12] and chapter 8 of the *Bayaz-e Khoshbu'i.*[13]

Like the dyeing of cloth, paper undergoes several stages between its manufacture, its dyeing and its use. Paper meant to be dyed is not sized once it has been removed from the presses and dried. Some dyes,on the other hand, require a mordanting so that the colour penetrates more easily into the fibres.

Let us now see the different dyes in greater detail. Some are used after simple soaking (while cold) or decoction (boiled) such as turmeric, saffron, henna. Others undergo a more complicated process, such as indigo and safflower. Although the basic dyes are limited in number a very large range of nuances is achieved by a series of intricate mixing and dosing. Thus, soaking in a diluted solution and drying in the sun gives a very light colour, wheareas repeated soaking and drying in the shade give bright or dark colours.

About forty nuances are described in the various texts, obtained from the ten main dyes detailed below. Three mineral pigments are also used. A lexical difficulty arises from the fact that a colour may be obtained by means of different formulae, or, on the contrary, that the result of single formula may be called by different names depending on the texts (see below the table recapitulating the names of the dyes).

- Saffron *(Crocus sativus, za'faran)*

Known since ancient times, it is grown in Iran, notably in Khorasan (at Qa'en)[14] and in Kashmir,[15] particularly at Pampur and at Paraspur. Under Akbar, saffron was a state monopoly.[16] Jahangir describes it in his Memoirs, while saying that the saffron flower is of *susani* (iris blue)[17] colour. In these two cases, some details are given about how to grow and pick it. This highly prized and very expensive colour is used in textiles only for valuable cloth, particularly silk.

- Soaked in water, saffron, according to Simi, yields the colour *zard*, yellow, and the eponymous colour *za'farani*, according to *Khosh.*
- Mixed with (1) verdigris (Simi) or with blue vitriol (*Maj.*), it gives the colour of pistachio (*fostoqi*), (2) mixed with lac (Simi), the colour *golgun* (orange pink), (3) with safflower red (*shahab*), the colour orange (*naranji,* Simi).

It is also used in the composition of the colour *khata'i/hanna'i* (*Khosh.*, Soltan 'Ali[18]) and *zomorrod-e limu'i,* in fact a gold flecked paper (*zarafshan*) tinted with saffron (*Maj.*).

- Turmeric *(Curcuma domestica, zard-cube)*

Turmeric, like saffron, is an edible spice which is widely used in dyeing. Grown extensively in Iran and in India, it is described as being applied to paper only by *Khosh.* In the form of a decoction, and by adding soda, it gives the colour yellow (*zard*). Mixed with (1) safflower red, it gives orange (*naranji*), (2) indigo, it gives parrot green (*tutaki*).

- Safflower *(Carthamus tinctorius, gol-e mo'asfar or kajere)*

Safflower is widely grown in Iran and in India, not only for dyeing (flowers) but also as fodder (leaves) and for oil (seeds). For dyeing, only the flowers are used. Dried in the sun, the flowers have to undergo several operations before the red colour (*shahab*) is produced. In fact, safflower contains two colouring components: one is yellow, which is soluble, and the other one -red- is insoluble in water.

Safflower yellow: after several rinses in water containing soda a yellow coloured water (*zard-ab*) is obtained, which is collected and used for dyeing yellow:

When dried in the shade, the paper is a pale yellow (*kahi*: Simi, *Khosh*). Mixed with (1) safflower red, we obtain the colour *'onnabi* (jujube, *Maj.*), (2) indigo, depending on the proportions of the two ingredients, it gives shades of green: *sabz* (*Maj., Khosh.*), *fostoqi/bostani* (*Khosh.*), *sabz-e malh* (?) (*Khosh.*), *cini* (*Maj., Hamadan*[19]), *sabz-e barg-e ney* (*Maj.*). By adding vitriol blue and gallnut, the colour of aloe is obtained (*'udi, Maj.*)

Safflower red: it is obtained by adding an acid, particularly lemon juice which precipitates the yellow alkaline solution, turning it into an insoluble red dye, the *shahab*. Simi calls the paper coloured in this way *al*. In Hamadan version of Simi, we find, in addition to the description of this colour, another paragraph on safflower (*gol-e kajere esfahan*). The process described is similar to the first one but the colour obtained is called *zard-e la'li*.[20] However, in India, *al* is the name given to another substance, which is the *Morinda tinctoria*. This is mentioned for instance in the *Kholasat al-mojarrabat*[21] and it gives a colour similar to safflower. According to *Khosh.* safflower red gives the colour *sorkh* (red). This text also specifies that in the production of safflower red, we observe three stages of colour, from the purest to the most adulterated: *'ala'* (superior), *awsat* (medium), *adna* (inferior). Depending on the quality of the colour used, the nuances vary. Red is made with superior quality; with the inferior quality, a peach colour (*sheftalu*) is obtained. *Maj.* mentions several colours, obtained according to the number of soakings and the degree of purity of the dye: the *piyazi* (onion) is the least pure, and the colour *nokhodi* (chick-pea) is obtained without an acid bath.

Mixed with (1) safflower yellow, *'onnabi*, (2) turmeric, *naranji*, (3) saffron, *naranji*, (4) indigo, *banafshe* (violet, *Maj. Hamadan*), (5) superior safflower and indigo, *susani* (iris, *Khosh.*, *Hamadan*), (6) superior safflower and lighter indigo, *gol-e khar* (purple, *Khosh*), *lale* (tulip, *Hamadan*[22])

- Lac *(Tachardia lacca, lak)*

Several dyes are often grouped together under the name *lak*. Lac, strictly speaking, is an insect substance deposited on the exudation of certain trees (*lacciferae*); it is a dye that is well known and appreciated in Iran, although almost exclusively imported from India. During the Moghul period, it was found, among others, in the Panjab, in Awadh and in Bihar, as also in Gujarat and Kerala.[23] In fact, the epithet "lac" is a very vague one since, in everyday vocabulary, it connotes two different substances: it stands, on the one hand, for gum-lac, and on the other hand for coloured exudations. These red dyes of animal origin, such as cochineal (*Coccus lacca, qermez-dane*) or kermes, or other plant exudations, such as dragon's blood (*Dracaena cinnabari, khun-e siyavush*), imported from Zanzibar, are sometimes confused with lac (*Tachardia lacca*). What is common to these various dyes is that they all give the most beautiful reds, scarlets (old Persian *sakirlat*) and crimsons (*qermez*) and are very expensive. Of these dyes, only kermes and cochineal are found in Iran, in the North and in Armenia. A particular variety of cochineal (*Porphyrophora Hamelii*) is found in Armenia, which is called Armenian red.[24] The colour known as "Armeniac" used in the mediaeval West as a background for leaf gilding perhaps owes its name to this variety of cochineal. Chardin mentions it in the chapter on dyes.[25] We find in the *Mer'at al-estelah* a mention of a "red earth from Armenia" which refers perhaps to this dye, unless it really is some kind of earth.[26]

Widely mentioned for its use in cloth dyeing, lac is however mentioned just once for paper, by Simi. Among the various red dyes which he describes, this is the one he prefers.
Mixed with (1) croton blue, it becomes *'udi* (aloe), (2) saffron, *golgun* (orangish-pink).

- Sapanwood *(Caesalpinia sapan, baqam)*

This wood is produced in the Caspian forests and in the Deccan. When it is fresh, it has a pale colour which reddens when exposed to air. It gives a red (*sorkh*, Simi) and purple (*arghavani*, *Maj.*) colour. Mixed with (1) ceruse, it becomes pink (*golgun*, *Maj.*), (2) vitriol blue, it gives the colour of aubergine (*badañjani*, *Maj.*)

- Other red dyes

Other red dyes are also mentioned by Simi who considers them as being unstable, such as mulberry (*shahtut*) and amaranth (*bostan-afruz*). The latter is also mentioned by *Maj.* as composing, with henna, the eponymic colour *hanna'i*. Let us say a word about madder (*Rubia tinctoria*, *runas*) because, even though it is mentioned only occasionally here, it is undoubtedly the most abundantly used red dye in Iran. Extensively grown in Iran, in Fars and Isfahan, madder was imported into India by Iranian dyers who were working in that country.[27] Often mentioned in treatises on cloth dyeing, it is astonishing that mention is not made of it as being applied to paper (besides in *Maj.*, recipe for invisible ink).

- Henna *(Lawsonia alba, hanna)*

Henna is grown in Iran and in India, particularly for dyeing the hair, hands and feet. It gives an orange colour called *khodrang*, by Simi.

Mixed with (1) amaranth, it gives the *hanna'i* colour, (2) saffron and ink, the colour *khata'i/hanna'i*.

- Pomegranate bark (*Granata punica, pust-e anar* or *nasbal*)

Used since the Antiquity, this dye, which is very rich in tannins, gives a brown colour (*jowzi, Khosh.*)
Mixed with safflower red, it gives an orange colour (*naranji, Khosh.*)

- Indigo[28] (*Indigofera tinctoria, nil*)

Already mentioned by Pliny,[29] and known well before that, indigo is certainly the most appreciated and widely used dye, on account of its fast colour. In fact, like safflower, indigo has two colouring components, one a soluble yellow and the other a blue that is insoluble in water, with the result that once the blue colouring component has been fixed, it no longer runs. This colouring, indigotin, can be obtained from several varieties of indigo plants, the richest being the *Indigofera tinctoria*. Although basically imported from India, several varieties of indigo plants are found in Iran, particularly in Khuzistan (Shushtar, Dezful[30]). Tavernier gives a fairly complete description of the process of making indigo in India:[31]

> "The cut plants are placed in plaster vats and covered with water. The mixture is stirred every day, till it forms a mud. This is allowed to stand for a few days so that the paste settles at the bottom. The water is then drained out through orifices made in the vat; the paste is then put into baskets and made into small cakes which are left to dry in the sun."

The process of fermentation and the making of the small cakes is basically for export purposes. For local use, the method is a somewhat different one: after having soaked the indigo leaves in water and allowed them to ferment for a day, the water containing colourless indoxyl is recuperated and the fibres are soaked in it. Oxidization in the air fixes the indigotin and gives it its blue colour. It is probably this technique which is described by *Khosh.*:

> "The vat is prepared a day in advance. The sheets of paper are dipped into the water and drained out on a board. If the indigo

vat is far from the place of work, a damp cloth is placed on top of the sheets of paper. These must be inserted vertically into the vat and not laid out flat. Then they are removed, washed in water and put out to dry."

The colour thus obtained is a dark blue (*kabud*: *Khosh.*, Simi; *lajvardi, Maj.*). To obtain a lighter blue (*abi, Khosh.*), indigo is diluted in a larger volume of water; the amount of water added depends on the shade desired.

With the different shades obtained, other colours are made by mixtures:
(1)Reds

The darker shades of indigo, mixed with reds, give violets:
- safflower red and indigo: *qal'i* (?, *Khosh.*) *banafshe* (*Maj.*),
- "superior" safflower red and indigo: *susani* (*Khosh.*).
- the lighter shades give purples: *gol-e khar* (*Khosh.*).

(2)Yellows

The darker indigo shades mixed with yellow give dark greens:
- safflower yellow and indigo: *sabz-e malh* (*Khosh.*),
- turmeric and indigo: *tutaki* (*Khosh.*),
- *gol-e balas* (*Bhutea frondosa,* yellow colouring) and indigo: *marmari* (*malachite, Khosh.*),
- the lightest ones give light greens:
-safflower yellow and indigo: *bostani/fostoqi* (*Khosh.*); *cini/sabz-e barg-e ney* (*Maj.*)

(3)Mixed with red, then with safflower yellow, it gives the *tavusi* colour (peacock, *Maj.*)

(4)Mixed with ceruse, we get turquoise colour (*firuze'i Maj.*)

- Sunflower-croton (*Chrozophoria tinctoria, aftab-gardesh*)

The dye is extracted from leaves[32] or from seeds (Simi) through the action of ammonium chloride. This colour, which can give very bright blues, is only mentioned by Simi for making the colour *kabud* (blue).

Mixed with lac: *'udi* (aloe).

Mixed with gallnut: *farise* (blue-green).

We find in *Maj.* the description of a blue creeping plant similar to the convolvulus, and which is called *gol-e nile* (blue flower); the author of this text specifies that in Khorasan this plant is called *rangak* (colouring matter?). The juice that is extracted from it gives a blue dye. Simi also mentions some blue flowers (*golha-ye kabud*), but points out that their colour is not stable and changes to violet. The Calcutta version of the *Maj.* adds that we can obtain blue from morel (*tokhm-e buy, sag-angur*). Another dye which may be confused sometimes with indigo, is the woad (*Isatis tinctoria, vasme*), although its tinctorial qualities are less pronounced.

Some minerals are used for dyeing paper:

- Verdigris (copper acetate, *zengar*), gives the *zengari* colour (Simi, *Khosh.*) or *tuti* (*Maj.*).
Mixed with (1) saffron, it gives the colour pistachio (*fostoqi,* Simi), (2) ceruse, the colour *cini-ye rowshan* (light green, *Maj.*). Silver verdigris (*zengar-e noqre,* see this in pigments) gives meadow green (*sabze-ye daman, Maj.*[33]).
- Orpiment (yellow arsenic sulphide, *zarnikh*), mixed with gum arabic and indigo, gives the colour *sibaki* (apple green, *Maj.*)
- Ceruse (lead or tin carbonate, *sefidab*) is only mentioned by *Maj.*; mixed with dyes, it gives pastel shades: indigo: *firuze'i* (turquoise). sapanwood: *golgun* (pink).
- Blue vitriol (copper sulphate, *zaj-e kabud*) is only mentioned by *Maj.*; mixed with saffron it gives the colour pistachio (*fostoqi*); with safflower yellow and gallnut: *'udi* (aloe); with sapanwood, the colour aubergine (*badanjani*).

NAMES OF DYES

Name of colour	Source	Ingredients
abi light blue	*Khosh*	diluted indigo
al safflower red	*Simi, Maj*	red safflower (*'arusak, sorkh*)
arghavani purple	*Maj*	sapanwood
'arusak ruby red	*Maj*	red safflower (*al, sorkh*)
badanjani aubergine	*Maj*	sapanwood and blue vitriol
banafshe violet	*Maj, Ham*	indigo and red safflower
bostani green	*Khosh*	perhaps *fostoqi* ?
cini green	*Maj, Ham*	indigo and safflower yellow
cini rowshan (light)	*Maj*	verdigris and ceruse
do rang two colours	*Maj*	saffron and red safflower
farise green	*Simi*	gallnut and indigo/croton
firuze turquoise	*Maj*	indigo and ceruse
fostoqi pistachio	*Simi*	verdigris and saffron
golgun pink	*Simi*	lac and saffron
golgun "	*Maj*	sapanwood and ceruse
gol-e khar purple	*Khosh*	indigo and safflower red

.../...

../...

Name of colour	Source	Ingredients
hanna'i henna *khodrang*)	*Maj*	henna and amaranth (*khatai,*
jowzi brown	*Khosh*	pomegranate bark
kabud blue	*Simi*	indigo or croton
kahi straw	*Simi, Khosh*	yellow safflower
khata'i	*Khosh, S.'A.*	henna, saffron, ink (*hanna'i*)
khodrang (flesh ?)	Simi	henna (*khata'i hanna'i*)
lale tulip	*Ham*	indigo and safflower red
lajvardi lapis lazuli	*Maj*	indigo
la'li ruby	*Maj*	see *'arusak*
limu'i lemon	*Maj*	saffron
marmari malachite	*Khosh*	Bhutea and indigo
naranji orange	*Khosh*	turmeric or pomegranate bark and red safflower
" "	*Maj, Simi*	saffron and red safflower
nokhodi chick pea	*Maj*	red safflower without acid
'onnabi jujube	*Maj*	yellow and red safflower
piazi onion	*Maj*	red safflower (2 soaking)
qal'i violet ?	*Khosh*	indigo and safflower red
" turquoise ?	*Maj*	indigo and ceruse (firuze'i)
sabz green	*Simi, Maj*	safflower yellow and indigo/croton
sabz barg-e ney reed	"	" "
sabz dahi (yoghurt ?)	*Maj*	" "
sabze-ye daman	*Maj*	silver verdigris
sheftalu peach	*Khosh*	safflower red (inferior)
sibaki apple green	*Maj*	orpiment and indigo
sorkh red	*Simi*	lac, amaranth, mulberry or sapanwood
sorkh "	*Khosh*	red safflower
susani iris	*Khosh, Ham*	indigo and safflower red
tavusi peacock	*Maj*	safflower yellow and red and indigo
tutaki parrot	*Khosh*	turmeric and indigo
'udi aloe	*Simi*	lac and croton
" "	*Maj*	yellow safflower, indigo, vitriol, gallnut
za'farani	*Khosh*	saffron
zard yellow	*Simi, Maj*	saffron
" "	*Khosh*	turmeric
zengari greyish-green	*Simi, Khosh*	verdigris
zomorrod-e limu'i citrine	*Maj*	saffron and gold

After dyeing, some colours need to be fixed with an acid. This is the case for the colours described by *Khosh,* turmeric, red safflower and derived colours (*susani, gol-e khar*), the green mixtures (*marmari, tutaki, bostani*) and orange.

The next operation consists in rinsing the paper in clear water. The ways of drying vary according to the desired shades. If a light shade is desired, the paper is dried in the sun; for bright shades, the paper is dried in the shade. It is then sized and polished. Some texts suggest coloured sizing agents (Teflisi, *'Umdat*).

Mordants and acids :

We saw, when studying the above mentioned recipes, that several acidic and mordant substances are required during dyeing to fix the colours. Here is a summary:

Acids: pomegranate, lemon and tamarind juice are used before the safflower dyeing described in *Maj.*; similarly, on paper dyed with safflower, the writing in lemon juice turns red (*Maj.*). *Khosh.* describes the three vats required for dyeing: one for dyeing, one for water containing lemon juice, then one for clear water. Here the acid fixes the colour after dyeing.

Mordants: Alum (alumina sulphate, *zaj* or *shabb*) is the mordant par excellence. It is generally used for dyeing cloth but also for marbled paper as we shall see later. *Maj.* recommends it before dyeing with sapanwood, with saffron on gold flecked paper, and with safflower, to obtain orange. Alum is also required for mordanting dyeing produced by pomegranate bark (*Khosh.*).

2. Marbling

Despite the recent discovery of several virtually unkown texts on marbling,[34] the place and date of origin of this technique still remain uncertain. M.T. Danesh-Pazhuh asserts that the oldest mention of marbled paper (*kaghaz-e abri*) appears in the biography of Shahab al-Din 'Abdallah Morvarid (844/1441-906/1501[35]) about whom it has been written that "he was a maker of (paper) flecked with (gold) dust and of marbled paper" (*sazande-ye afshan-e ghobar va rang-amizi-ye abri kaghaz*). The Iranian scholar then gives several bibliographic references in which one might hope to find this quotation. However, the words cited by Danesh-Pazhuh have not been traced in any of these references, whether it be the *Habib al-siyar* by Khwandamir,[36] the *Kholasat al-akhbar* by the same author,[37] the *Tazkerat al-sho'ara* by Dowlatshah,[38] the *Tohfe-ye Sami* by Sam Mirza[39] or the *Babur-name* by the Emperor Babur.[40]

It would therefore seem more correct to advance the date of the first appearance of marbled paper by almost a century; this theory seems to be backed by more concrete facts. A.Soheyli Khwansari asserts that it was Mir Mohammad Taher who invented the *abri*;[41] according to him, this Iranian illuminator lived during the time of Shah Tahmasp and he went to settle in India where he invented marbled paper. Again according to this same author, Mir Mohammad Taher sent some samples of his productions to Iran; these were highly appreciated and were imitated by artists such as Yahya Qazvini. Soheyli Khwansari unfortunately mentions no source, but it appears likely that his information came from letters referred to by Danesh-Pazhuh, preserved in the Malek library in Teheran.[42] One of these letters is addressed to Yahya Qazvini, illuminator and marbler mentioned in the *Golestan-e honar*.[43] On the other hand, Mir Mohammad Taher is unknown in the *tazkere* of the time. Qazi Ahmad names another artist Mohammad Amin Jadvalkesh from Mashhad who was famous for his marbling [44] This talented man was the master of Qazi Ahmad himself. The "late" version of the *Golestan* relates his death which occurred probably between 1596 (date of the first edition) and 1606 (presumed date of the second edition[45]). It is probably by coincidence that there appears, in the court of 'Abd al-Rahim Khan-e Khanan (Akbar's general), a person by the name of Mohammad Amin Jadval, also from Mashhad and also a marbler.[46] The work in which this second Mohammad Amin Mashhadi is mentioned was completed in 1025/1616; it cannot therefore relate to the same person who was the master of Qazi Ahmad. There is, on the other hand, a person of this name, who was young and promising, during the first publication of the *Golestan*, and who left for India.[47] The marbler of the Khan-e Khanan is probably this young calligrapher. According to Nahavandi, it was this person who invented marbled paper.[48] This last assertion appears questionable. It seems certain, at any rate, that marbled paper was much in fashion in India at the end of the 16th century. The data available to us at present do not enable us to pinpoint the exact place and date of its first appearance.

The relatively recent interest in codicology means that authors of catalogues have paid little attention to the nature and characteristics of the paper which decorates the margins of albums and manuscripts. That is why it is still difficult to date and to situate the examples of marbled paper that we occasionally encounter.[49]

The margins of a page calligraphed by Shah Mahmud Neyshapuri (Iran, around 1540-50), from an album which has unfortunately been broken up,[50] some margins of a *Khamse* by Nezami copied by Qasem 'Ali Soltan Darqat-oglu for Khayr-allah b. Hoseyn Golabi Shushtari in 967-8/1560-1,[51] and one page of calligraphy on marbled paper signed by Ekhtiyar Monshi in Herat in 970/1563-4,[52] are among the oldest examples of marbled paper in the Iranian world, known to this day.

In the 17th century, album pages framed in marbled paper, are quite frequent.[53] However, no systematic study on marbled paper exists to give us an overall view of the subject. We could probably discover other examples, perhaps earlier than these.

Among the oldest examples of Indian marbled paper, available to us, mention can be made of the pages of a *divan* of Anvari dated 1588, produced in Lahore[54] and some paintings from a *divan* by Mohammad Quli Qutab Shah of Golconda, dating from the end of the 16th century.[55]

It appears that in the Topkapi Museum, there is a sheet of marbled paper dating from 1447, and Ugur Derman[56] is said to have a sheet dating from 1554 in his collection. If these examples are genuine we should have no more doubt as to the origins of marbled paper. We have pointed out that until now the Turkish treatise by Shebek *Tartib-e resale-ye abri* dating from 1017/1608, was considered as being the oldest known text on marbling.[57] The discovery of the pseudo-Seyrafi treatise, the *Resale-ye Khoshnevisi*, means we can present it as, if not an earlier text, at least one contemporary with the Turkish treatise.[58] Other texts on marbling exist, such as Chapter 21 of the *Kholasat al-mojarrabat*, one copy of which is dated 1180/1766,[59] and the treatise on binding, *Resale-ye jeld-sazi*, the oldest copy of which is dated 1228/1812.[60] M.T. Danesh-Pazhuh points out yet another text in which marbling appears: it is the *Ganj-e bad-avard-e saheb qerani*, by Mirza Aman-allah Hoseyni Amani, composed in 1040/1631, at the beginning of the reign of Shah Jahan;[61] we have unfortunately not succeeded in laying our hands on any of the copies of this text.[62] It should be noted that these four Persian texts were all written in India.

Marbling techniques: some colours that are lighter than water are poured, drop by drop, into a vat containing mucilaginous water; they then spread out on the surface. Depending on the designs he desires, the marbler then acts on the drops of colour by modifying their shapes and creating new ones. If he contents himself with simply putting drops of colour into the vat, these will form regular spots like pebbles; this is the origin of what is called the "pebbled" design. The design can be printed on paper by placing a sheet on the vat, or it can be modified with the help of a rod or combs, creating an infinite variety of designs.

Here are some pieces of information given in the treatises:[63]

Material :

- A wooden vat about 90 cm long and half the width, or, according to another text, 90 cm on all sides. The shape of the vat should have dimensions slightly larger than those of a full sheet of paper.

- Paper. Only one text (*Kholasat al-mojarrabat*) specifies the qualities of paper suited to marbling; these are the *khata'i*, *Kashmiri* paper and *Qasem Beygi* paper.

- Colours. The *Resale-ye Khoshnevisi* distinguishes two types of colours, depending on the results desired: some dyes such as safflower, turmeric and indigo give *abi* (diluted in water) colours, and some mineral pigments, cinnabar, orpiment, lapis-lazuli, ceruse, lamp black give *ahari* colours (with starch). I had ventured to suggest that these colours "with starch" were used for making marbled paintings such as those produced in the Deccan during the first quarter of the 17th century. However, this is still a hypothesis that remains difficult to confirm. This particular technique will be explained in greater detail later. The pigments are ground as fine as possible.

- The flotation additive (*bosteman*).[64] This is the element which enables the colours to remain in a state of suspension on the surface of the water; several recipes are suggested in the texts. The *Resale-ye jeld-sazi* suggests (1) gum-lac boiled in water, (2) myrrh mixed with soap-berry in water, (3) a mixture of gum-lac, borax and milk, (4) the juice of onions mixed with gum-lac, soap and borax, (5) gum-lac mixed with myrrh, soap-berry and Egyptian soap, (6) Egyptian soap. The *Kholasat al-mojarrabat* describes only one formula for flotation additive, made of a decoction of soap-berry.

Operations :

- Mordanting of the paper with alum; as in dyeing, mordanting facilitates the penetration of the colours into the fibres of the paper; it is done in a solution of alum.

- Preparation of the mucilage. This is done with fenugreek seeds soaked overnight, then boiled till the desired consistency has been obtained. The seeds are then passed through a piece of cloth, and the liquid recuperated is used as mucilage. The *Resale-ye jeld-sazi* also suggests some mucilages made of boiled white onions or of flax seeds.

- Dosing of the colours. Before putting the colours, drop by drop, into the vat, their flotation capacity should be verified. To do this, the colours are tested in a plate full of mucilage; the flotation agent or the colour is added depending on whether the latter spreads out or retracts on the mucilage.

- Placing of the colours. After testing, the colours are added in small drops on to the mucilage, care being taken to distribute them over the entire surface. At this stage the sheet can be printed or designs can be drawn. Arabesques or flowers and other shapes can be drawn with the help of a rod. To obtain combed paper, the colours have first of all to be stretched out in zig-zag fashion from top to bottom and from right to left; then a comb made of pins implanted in a wooden ruler is passed over the surface from the top to the bottom of the vat.

- Laying of the paper. When the design made on the vat is satisfactory, a sheet of paper, the size of the vat is held at two corners, and placed gently on the surface of the water. If some bubbles appear, in the form of air pockets under the paper, they should be pushed away towards the edges, otherwise a white spot will appear at this place. Then the paper is raised by drawing it towards the edge of the vat; it is carefully rinsed and put to dry. Once sized and polished, it is ready for use.

Marbled paintings :

This particular technique produces, with starched reserves, marbled designs with clearly defined contours which can then be completed with a brush. Around 1625, these paintings were in fashion at Bijapur, in Deccan. About twenty of these paintings have been listed up to now, all appearing to have originated from the same workshop.[65] Once he has drawn the contours of the parts to be marbled, the painter applies some starch, with his brush, on the parts which he wants to reserve. He then marbles the sheet and rinses it; the water washes away the starch and the reserved areas appear in white. It is also possible to achieve these spaces by sticking some cut-out paper with starch on the areas to be reserved.

Till recently, marbled paper continued to be made in India. W.Hoey mentions this in connection with bindings; he tells us that in Lucknow the price of a "quire" (sheet folded into four) of marbled paper (*abri*) was 5 1/4 anas.[66] Today, the making of marbled paper on mucilage has practically disappeared in India. This is not the case in Turkey, where this technique remains alive (see our plate no. 6).

3. Gold flecked paper

Gold flecked paper (*zarafshan*) probably appeared in the 15th century. According to Qazi Ahmad, its inventor was probably Ghiyas al-din Mohammad Mozahheb of Mashhad, who died in 942/1537;[67] Sam Mirza on the other hand, credits its invention to 'Abd-allah Morvarid (died in 922/1516.[68] It is difficult to consider these two artists as being the inventors of the *zarafshan* since, according to Dowlatshah, it was one of the techniques practiced by Simi almost a century earlier.[69] Some examples, such as the pages of a *divan* from Hafez, dated 1451, display gold flecked motifs on a paper that is dyed blue and painted with a design in gold lines, in Chinese style. That probably is why N.Titley wonders whether this gold-flecked paper could be of Chinese origin.[70] In an anthology copied at Shamakha (Shirvan) in 1468, the pages are dyed in colour (blue, pink, mauve) and are gold-flecked.[71] Ivanow and Akimushkin point out that the *Hal-name* from 'Arefi copied in 901/ 1495 by Zeyn al-din Mahmud al-Kateb in Herat is the first manuscript copied on coloured paper.[72] The illustration that they present from this manuscript shows a white sheet with gold flecks and not a coloured sheet.[73] The authors no doubt meant that this *Hal-name* was the first manuscript on *zarafshan* paper; however, in either case, this is incorrect. In the *Bayaz-e Khoshbu'i*, dyed paper which is then flecked with gold is mentioned several times.[74]

Several types of *zarafshan* are found, depending on the size of the particles of gold and on whether it is in sheets or in a solution. In the biography of Mohammad Amin Jadvalkesh in the *Golestan-e honar*,[75] four types of flecks are specified: *line* (?); *miane* (medium); *ghobar* (dust); *hall karde* (in solution). While the last three seem to be self-evident, the first term is totally obscure.[76] This term also appears in the *Resale-ye jeld-sazi*;[77] the editor gives it the written form *tate* or *paste* in different places, but the manuscripts (Madras and Calcutta, see Bibliography) use the written form *l-h*, which could be read as *line* or *late*; the latter term may mean "pieces".[78]

Here are the techniques for "gold flecks", as described in this text.

The paper is first of all starched, either to make "*late*", or *afshan*. *Afshan* is made with gold in solution; this is put on a horsehair brush and sprayed onto the sheet of paper; it is possible to create designs with the help of stencils, for instance in trellis form (*moshabbak*). When the flecking is complete, the contours of the stencil can be outlined with a brush (*band-e tahrir*). The *late* is made from sheets of gold placed in a little canvas sieve; threads are pulled out of the canvas so that some particles of gold can pass through and the gold sheets are sieved above freshly starched paper. When the starch is dry, the paper is polished.

This last process gives different results depending on the spacing of the threads of the sieve; a tightly woven sieve will give very tiny pieces of gold leaf while a loose strainer will allow larger pieces to pass through. This is perhaps the grading suggested by Qazi Ahmad (see above).

As regards the term *moshabbak* (trellis), I found the following quotation in the *Borhan-e Ma'aser*:[79]

moshabbak shod in gonbad-e gerd gard
zarafshan shod in safhe-ye lajvard.

"This dome which turns round has become a trellis.
This page of lapis-lazuli has become flecked with gold".

The word *moshabbak* is used here as a metaphor to describe the sky; it is followed by *zarafshan*, which shows that it is indeed a related term. In fact, both words come from the arts of the book and they illustrate in poetry the fiery colouring of the sky at sunrise or the starry night. As for the configuration of this "trellis", we can simply conjecture. It relates perhaps to a sort of stencilled decoration (*'aks*, see below), withdrawn in contours (*tahrir*).

Qazi Ahmad adds, again on the subject of *zarafshan*, that Mowlana Kepek of Herat, who was very gifted in *'aks*, made gold-flecked paper unnecessary.[80] Indeed, we have seen, in connection with *moshabbak* that gold in solution has something in common with *'aks*. This same author notes that the calligrapher Bulbul used to write on *hall-kari* paper (with gold solution).[81]

4. Other decorated papers

- *'Aks*, stencilled and silhouetted paper. It would seem that there were two techniques of the same name, one using a stencil on which the colours were lightly sprayed, and the other using cut-out stamps soaked in colour.

The first technique is not described explicitly in any text and is only the result of observations. This technique consists in cutting out a stencil which is placed on the sheet to be painted; some colours are sprayed with a horsehair brush in such a way as to deposit them in small regular drops over the entire surface. When the stencil is removed, the reserved portions appear in white. In the same way as the *moshabbak* or the tampon-stencil described below, examples of stencilled margins in which the contours of the designs are drawn, are not rare, as for instance the wide margins of a copy of the *Salaman va Absal* by Jami, executed perhaps in Qazvin, in 959/1581.[82] These margins may be of many colours. Beautiful examples of these coloured stencils are found in some pages of two anthologies preserved in the Bibliothèque Nationale (Paris).[83] Mohammad Amin Mashhadi "Junior", invented some *'aks-e haft rang* for the Khan-e Khanan. that is to say some paintings for which seven stencils are required, one per colour.[84] It should be noted that the term *'aks* has been erroneously translated by Mahfuz ul-Haq (in 1931), then by Rahmat Ali Khan (in 1986) as "tracing paper" and "tracing work".[85] *'Aksi* paper is mentioned in the *Mer'at al-estelah*, at the same time as marbled paper, as being paper painted without a brush.[86]

The second technique of the *'aks* is described in the *Resale-ye jeld-sazi*.[87] This technique requires a sort of tampon made of cloth soaked in safflower dye (*kasambhi**[88]), which is cut out in the desired shapes and placed between two sheets of paper; the sheets are then dampened and the tampon deposits its dye on the paper; only those parts covered by the tampons get coloured, and the rest of the sheet therefore remains white. Once dry, the contours of the design are drawn again with the brush (*tahrir*); the sheets are then polished. It should be noted that the only colours produced by this safflower tampon are yellow and red *(rang-e sorkh va zard)*. This stencil-tampon process seems quite similar to the one for Turkish silhouetted paper. For this, the designs to be reproduced are cut out in felt which is soaked in colour. These cut-out designs are pressed between two sheets of paper dipped in alum; then they are pasted together at the edges after the tampons are removed. The designs appear through the paper, in subtle colours.

- Paper cut-outs. No technical information is given in the texts about paper cut-outs. Apart from some examples preserved in collections, in calligraphed material or in decorative designs, the only data available to us are of a biographical nature.

Thus we know for instance that 'Abd al-Rashid, Khan of Kashghar (1533-1570) cut out a tree in paper and painted it in colours, and he did it so well that the masters of this arts were astounded.[89] C. Huart suggests several names of paper cutters, without giving the references to Persian texts:[90]

- 'Abd-allah Heravi, son of the calligrapher Mir 'Ali, was reportedly the inventor of this art. Minorsky associates this person mentioned by Huart with the son of Mir 'Ali *Tabrizi*, inventor of the nasta'liq; who lived in the 8th/14th century.[91] Does he not confuse him with Mir 'Ali

of Herat, who lived just around 951/1544?[92]
- Dust Mohammad Qate' (different from Dust Mohammad Gushvani[93]) son of Mir 'Abd-allah Shekarin-qalam; this artist is apparently not mentioned in biographies except in the *Manaqeb-e honarvaran*; Huart must have mentioned him after consulting this work.[94]
- Sang 'Ali Badakhshani was a student of Dust Mohammad. Qazi Ahmad calls him Mowlana Nazar 'Ali Qate' of Badakhshan, and says that he won renown by cutting out some calligraphy from models made by Mir 'Ali. It should be noted moreover that Qazi Ahmad plays on the dual meaning of the word *qat'e* which implies both "cut out" and "piece"; this latter meaning is applied to small poetic compositions or to pages of calligraphy. Thus Nazar 'Ali makes some *qat'e* (cut outs) of *qat'e* (calligraphic extracts)[95].
- Fakhri of Bursa is also among the paper-cutters mentionned by C. Huart, and was one of the best artists of the kind in the Ottoman empire.

NOTES

1. Huart, p.12.
2. Among these we can cite the *Genesis* of Vienna and the *Gospels* of Sinope and of Rossano
3. J. Bloom, "The blue Koran".
4. Information given by Mme Yvette Sauvan.
5. See F. Richard, "Un lectionnaire".
6. (ETHE no.2346) fol. 114b-135a.
7. (ETHE no.2785) fol. 8a-30b.
8. Ms. Hyderabad, 10 fol.
9. Wulff, pp.192-3.
10. Simi, see Y. Porter, "Un traité de Simi", pp.188-189
11. Ms. Patna no.1076; abbrev. = *Khosh.*
12. Ms. fol. 49b-51a. References to these three treatises will be given in the text, in abbreviated forms, as Simi, *Khosh.* and *Maj.*
13. (ETHE 2784) Fol. 111a-126b.
14. Wulff, p.191.
15. Abu al-Fazl, *A'in,* I, pp.89-90; II, p.358.
16. *Id.* I, pp.452 and 535.
17. Jahangir, *Tuzuk,* I, p.93.
18. See transl. Minorsky, p.113.
19. A variation of the treatise of Simi, see ed. in Bibliography.
20. *Id.*
21. Fol.134a-b.
22. The compiler of the Hamadan version of the treatise by Simi was definitely

mistaken as regards the violet, iris and tulip colours, since he says they should be mixed with safflower yellow instead of red, this would naturally result in greens.

23. I. Habib, *Atlas,* 4B, 7B, 10B, 11B. (the numbers refer to the maps; their commentaries follow the same numbering); see also O. P. Jaggi, p.162.
24. Wulff, p.189.
25. Chardin, IV, p.143.
26. Anand Ram, Ms. fol. 228a.
27. Wulff, p.190.
28. The importance of this dye was such as to justify an entire exhibition being devoted to indigo, *Sublime Indigo.* See Bibliography.
29. Pliny (book 35, 27) calls it *indicum* which has become our "indigo" and he describes it as being a blue mud coming from the marshes of India.
30. *Flora Iranica,* no. 157, pp.51-60.
31. *Voyages,* II, p.10-11.
32. Wulff, p.192.
33. We also find this "silver verdigris" and the colour *sabze-ye 'dahan'* in the *Bayaz-e Khoshbu'i,* fol.117a-b.
34. Y. Porter, "*Kaqaz-e abri*".
35. These are the dates suggested by Danesh-Pazhuh, "*Rang-sazi*", p.21, Sam Mirza and A. Beveridge (see following notes), give 922/1516 as the date of his death.
36. Ed., IV, p.113 (and not "13", to be corrected in the article) and pp.250, 254-255, 325-326, 329.
37. Ed. Kabul (1324) pp.56-57; Danesh-Pazhuh mentions for this text the ms. of Teheran University no. 5583 fol. 33b.
38. Ed. Browne, pp.515-517.
39. Transl. Mahfuz ul-Haq, *J.A.S.B.* 1932 p.245; Danesh-Pazhuh refers to the Dastgerdi edition, pp.120.
40. Transl. A. Beveridge, pp.278-279 and 291; Danesh-Pazhuh refers to a lithographed edition, p.111.
41. Preface to the ed. of Qazi Ahmad's *Golestan-e honar,* p. *cehel o do* (xlii).
42. "*Rang-sazi,*" pp.21-22; mss. no 64/3846 fol. 119b to 120b, letter from Mohammad Yahya Qazvini to Mir Mohammad Taher and no. 73/3846 fol. 155a-156b, letter from Molla Khalil Veqari to Mir Mohammed Taher.
43. Qazi Ahmad, transl. p.194; this passage represents the end of the ms. that Minorsky made use of for the translation and does not appear in the edition by Soheyli Khvansari; it appears, on the other hand, in its entirety in the autograph ms. (Salar Jang no.598; see Y. Porter, "*Kaqaz-e abri*").
44. Transl. p.189; ed. p.148.
45. Y. Porter, "Notes sur le *Golestan*".
46. 'Abd al-Baqi Nahavandi, ed. vol.III, pp.1682-1688.
47. Qazi Ahmad, transl. p.153; ed. p.104.
48. *Ma'aser,* III, p.1688.
49. An attempt is being made at the Bibliothèque Nationale (Paris) by F.Richard

and A.Berthier, to draw up a list of marbled papers.

50. Falk, *Trésors de l'Islam*, p.103, no.68; the margins were mounted perhaps after the execution of the calligraphy.
51. B. N. Suppl. Pers no. 1956; for this work, on the other hand, it seems that the margins were mounted at the time of the transcript, perhaps in Shiraz.
52. Museum of Turkish and Islamic Arts, Istanbul, Env. no. 2179; the latter two examples have been brought to my attention by Francis Richard.
53. For instance B. N. Arabic ms.6076.
54. Harvard Univ. Art Museum no. 1960.115.2; the calligraphy on the marbled paper proves that it was contemporary with the transcript.
55. Salar Jang Library, Hyderabad. J. Mittal was the first to indicate the presence of pieces of marbled paper on some paintings of this *divan*, see *India*, ed. S. C. Welch, pp.296-297. These paintings are reproduced by K. Khandalavala and Rahmat Ali Khan, fig.28 and 29; however, these authors do not believe that these are marbled papers.
56. Doizy and Ipert, p.26.
57. Y. Porter, "*Kaqaz-e abri*", p.50.
58. See Y. Porter, "Traité attribué à 'Abd-allah Seyrafi"; this treatise dates from the reign of Akbar.
59. (ETHE no.2346) fol. 135b-138b.
60. Mss. Madras and Calcutta; ed I. Afshar in *Sahhafi-ye sonnati.*
61. "*Rang-sazi*", p.31.
62. A. Monzavi, *Fehrest,* vol. III, p.590 indicates three copies:
    - Najaf 5:414; -*Elahiyat* 7/187 J and -Hendustan (?) 8951.
63. We are repeating here the operations already mentioned in the article "*Kaqaz-e abri*".
64. This is the term used by Sadeqi to designate medium material (see below).
65. J. Mittal, in *India*, ed. S.C.Welch, pp.296-297.
66. Hoey, p.122.
67. Ed. 145; transl. 189.
68. Transl. Mahfuz ul-Haq p.245.
69. Dowlatshah, ed. Browne, p.412.
70. N. Titley, pp.241-242 and fig.82.
71. *Id.* pl.6 p.69. See our plate no.5.
72. O. F. Akimushkin and A. A. Ivanov, "The Art of Illumination", in B. Gray *The Art of the Book in Central Asia*, p.56.
73. *Id.* ill., p.49.
74. Fol. 116b and 117b; see also *Majmu'at al-sanaye'*, fol.50b.
75. Qazi Ahmad, ed. p.148 and autograph ms. fol.46a.
76. Steingass proposes for *linat:* leathern cushion, being smooth; *lina,* a kind of palm.
77. Ed. pp. 136-137.
78. This is therefore the written form that we are adopting.
79. 'Ali b. Aziz, ed. p.448.
80. Qazi Ahmad, ed. p.157, transl. p.193.

81. Qazi Ahmad, ed. p.41, transl. p.83.
82. *Salaman va Absal* by Jami, ms. dated 959/1581; also contains a marbled sheet (fol.30a); the same stencils are found from one page to the next. See the ed. of Ayni, pp.22-23; see also Qazi Ahmad, ed. Soheyli, ill. p.142.
83. Suppl. Pers. no.1425 and 1789.
84. ᶜAbd al-Baqi Nahavandi, vol.III, p.1688.
85. Mahfuz ul-Haq. (1931) and Rahmat Ali Khan, (1986); see also review of this article in *Abst. Ir. 10.*
86. Anand Ram, fol.216b.
87. Ed. pp.145-146.
88. This Indian word is defined by Platts as cloth dyed with safflower.
89. Mirza Haydar Dughlat, transl. D. Ross, p.147.
90. pp.325-326.
91. Qazi Ahmad, transl., p.100.
92. *Id.*, p.131, his note 441.
93. See Y. Zoka, "*Dust Mohammad Mosavver*".
94. See Zoka, p.250.
95. Ed. 155-156; transl., p.193.

3

LAYOUT AND COMPOSITION

A striking fact with Moghul manuscripts, is that their illustrations are often the result of collective work. There are three main operations usually referred to as:

(1) *tarh* ("design");

(2) *'amal* (the "main part" of the work), or *-rang-amizi* (colouring);

(3) *cehre* (faces).

This functional division corresponds to various successive or parallel stages which will be examined here, in their technical aspect. In Part Two we will return to the collective organisation of the production of illustrated manuscripts within the workshop.

1. Ruling and layout

As C. Adle has shown for the manuscript of the *Fotuhat-e-Homayuni*,[1] a module was used in the Iranian world for the production of manuscripts, which served to rule not only the pages but also the illustrations, and gave the manuscript its unity. While in Persian technical literature, we find no precise reference to this module (the quotation which C. Adle has relied on is, in fact, borrowed from a poem by 'Abdi Beyg Shirazi 950/1544[2]), there is, on the other hand, in the West, a tradition of the golden number applied to the manuscript, which dates back to at least the first century A.D.

L. Gilissen has shown that some modules are discernible in papyruses of the end of the 2nd century, or the beginning of the 3rd century A.D.;[3] he also mentions a formula given in a Latin manuscript of the 9th century[4] which reads:

> "The form of the quaternion should be such that there are five parts lengthwise and four widthwise. Reserve one-fifth part of the lower and front margins; divide this fifth part into three and reserve two portions for the upper margin; divide the two portions into three and reserve them for the back margin. The half-way margin will be equal to this one. Space the lines according to the size of the writing, as larger writing will require wider spaced lines, and a smaller requires narrower lines".

L. Gilissen observes that these instructions seem to guide the craftsman in the fairly accurate production of a layout in which the columns correspond to the superimposition of two golden rectangles.

Despite evidence of the module of the *Fotuhat*, we have found no detailed sources in the Iranian world, concerning modular proportions in layout. However, a systematic study of the layout of manuscripts of a particular school and for a given period, would undoubtedly show some preferences or choices in layouts of a similar module. Little research has been done till now in this matter. Paola Orsatti has shown, on the basis of examples, that some variations in layout were possible from the same ruling (*mastar*, see hereafter) and that one could perhaps establish a typology of the rulings of the different schools.[5]

Ruling

Once the sheets of paper have been starched and cut to the desired size, the calligrapher or the supervisor decides on the *mastar* or ruling. This ruling will determine the whole work, that is to say the spacing of the lines and the columns, and on this basis, the variations in layout, the position of the illustrations and illuminations and even the form of the binding.

The *Resale-ye jeld sazi*[6] describes how to make the *mastar*: the cardboard matrix on which silk threads are stretched is placed under a folded sheet of paper which is rubbed lightly in such a way that the threads stretched on the cardboard get printed in relief on the sheet.

The *mastar* gives unity and harmony to a manuscript -some *mastar* were so perfect that they were copied, such as that of the album of Ahmad Jalayer which Baysanqor had copied for his own album "*be haman dastur-e qat' va mastar*" "in the same order of format and ruling"[7]. In his treatise, Soltan 'Ali Mashhadi urges the copyist to practise by taking a small well-written manuscript, copying it in the same format (*qat'*), the same ruling (*mastar*), and even the same style of calligraphy.[8]

Babur relates in his *Memoirs* that he made a *mastar* of eleven lines for the calligraphy of his Indian *Divan*.[9]

In the *Mer'at al estelah*, Anand Ram quotes a verse of Mohammad Sa'id Ashraf:[10]

> "*khame-ye jadval-keshi ra mastar dar kar nist*"
> "There is no need for a *mastar* when using a framing pen".

This quotation leads the author to remark:

> "The akhund says that the *mastar* is not necessary for the framing pen but that is incorrect as the *mastar* cannot be used without the framing pen; the *mastar* is made of iron or wood, so that it remains straight; it is called *setare-ye jadval*; lines are drawn on starched paper, with the framing pen and this is impossible without (the *mastar*)".

It is obvious that the object described here under the name *mastar* is in fact a ruler (also called *khatt-kesh*) and not the cardboard slab used for ruling. Indeed, the arabic *mistara* generally has the meaning of "ruler". It is quite possible, therefore, that Anand Ram misinterpreted the verse by Mohammad Sa'id Ashraf by translating *mastar* as "ruler" and not "ruling". Indeed, it is only if we choose the sense of "ruling" that the verse has any meaning: "there is no need for a ruling-board when using a framing pen"; the framing pen, in fact, draws several lines at a time like the ruling-board (see below). Moreover, the ruler is called *mastara* more often than *mastar*.

Once the ruling is over, we go on with the layout, that is to say the positioning of the calligraphy, the illuminations and the illustrations. The *jadval* will frame the pages, with variations, but always according to the same ruling; the *jadval* remain the same for the entire manuscript.

Jadval

The *jadval* are the coloured lines which frame the pages of manuscripts. The large variety of combinations of thicknesses and colour of the lines makes it possible to carry out a typological study. The examination of the number of lines and spaces and the frequency of the colours, helps us to establish criteria by which workshops could be identified. F.Richard has shown for example that the brown lines of a *Khamse* by Nezami, copied in 1565 by a certain Shams al-din Mohammad Kateb - as well as the quality of the paper - seem to indicate its Indian origin.[11]

Jadval are successive bands of colour and blank spaces outlined in black. Some descriptions of examples are given in the *khateme* of the *Golestan-e honar.*[12] The first example is given in verse and is particularly confusing:

> "Draw three lines close together, the golden line being the last (inner or outer?); mark the three corners in such a way that the lines are properly aligned. The space between these two lines (it was *three* just a little earlier !) should be less than the blunt edge of a knife, so that blanks do not appear everywhere. After which, make use of the polisher (this would imply other golden lines, as gold is polished before the other colours; therefore are the other two lines also golden ?) Make two outlines (*tahrir*)[13] of the first two lines and three outlines of the third; between the two, divide (the space) into two by making four outlines; in the middle one, draw two lines of lapis; between the two, draw yet another line of lapis; lower down (towards the inside ?) draw a green line".

A calculation would lead us to understand that there are three golden lines, three in lapis and one in green, each colour band being outlined with one or several black lines (*tahrir*).

The other examples are simpler to understand:

> "- *jadval-e avval* (or *davale*): draw a first line in gold, then another thicker one; polish them. Around the first one, draw two *tahrir*; around the second, draw four (two on each side?) and colour them in with lapis.
> - *jadval-e mosanna* (double): draw two lines in gold, polish them, then draw for each golden line two *tahrir* and colour in with lapis.
> - *jadval-e se tahrir* (with three contours): draw a line of gold and polish it, then draw two *tahrir*, one on each side; on the latter, place lapis (this "latter" must be a third *tahrir*, as the name of this *jadval* would lead one to assume)".

M. T. Danesh-Pazhuh[14] has noted that in the text of the Iranian edition of the *Golestan-e honar*, the first of these three *jadval* is called *davale*, while in the manuscript no. 599 of Hyderababd, we read *avval* (first). However, one would expect that a "first" *jadval* would be simpler than the second (*mosanna*, double) and the third (*se tahrir*, with three contours); now, the complexity of the *jadval* described, is, on the contrary, on a decreasing scale. The term *davale* hardly enlightens us further. Dust Mohammad notes that the illuminator Qavvam al-din Mas'ud makes the *davale* from the *jadval* with the ray of a shooting star (*az sho'a'-e shahab saqeb davale-ye jadval karde*).[15] Steingass suggests for the word *davale* the meaning of "leather strap used in a game"; *daval* also has this meaning of "leather strap"; this written form *daval* (or *davale*) could therefore, by comparison, suggest the colour bands of the *jadval*.

Simi points out that with the colours that he describes, borders can be made, and that if the *jadval* is made in gold solution, it will give a most beautiful effect.[16]

We find similarly, in the *Resale-ye jeld-sazi*, a brief description of the outline of the *jadval*.[17] More interesting than this is the description, accompanied by a drawing of the *qalam-e jadval* or pen for borders.[18] This device is also mentioned by Anand Ram (see earlier). The *qalam-e jadval* is described as a pen or metal drawing-pen in the form of a fork or a trident; some *jadval* compasses also exist (see our plate no.10).

The word *jadval* which, originally, meant a stream, was the subject of many poetic metaphors. In his *Perikhane*,[19] Anand Ram compares the gold of the *jadval* to a ray of the sun: "*tala-ye jadvalesh ra ba khatt-e sho'a-ye khorshid sanjidan ast*" (The gold of his *jadval* can be compared to the beam of a ray of sunlight).

Mohammad Saleh Kanbuh, in his *'Amal-e. Saleh*,[20] compares the water of the canals of the gardens of Delhi to the silver border on a page of stone:

> "*ab-e simab-e san-e an gu'i jadvalist az sim-e kham ke bar alvah-e sang ghaltan ast*".
>
> "It would seem as if its water, like mercury, was a *jadval* (border/stream) of pure silver running over a page of stone."

2. Calligraphy and black inks

Once the ruling and the *jadval* have been completed, the sheets are entrusted to the calligrapher who, following the general plan of the work, starts to copy the text. In the case of illuminated manuscripts, the text starts on the second page (folio 1 verso), or on the fourth page (folio 2 verso), depending on the space given to the preliminary illuminations (*shamse, dibace*, see these words). The first written page starts generally towards the end of the first third of the length of the page, thus leaving space for the *sar lowh*. However, there again, the position of the illuminations is defined in accordance with the *mastar* and is therefore subject to its modular variations.

There is no need to dwell at length here on calligraphic styles or on other aspects of this art, the most valued of the Muslim world. Indeed, not only does calligraphy overstep the bounds of our study, but it has also given rise to a great deal of technical literature, on the part of both Eastern and Western authors, far greater than that of painting. Calligraphy is of importance to us here only because it is an integral part of a whole, *i.e.* the book, and must be included in its illustration. However, it often happens in art history studies, that the analysis of the painting and calligraphy in a single work are separated. How can the modular construction of the whole then be justified if half the work is missing? There are numerous cases of manuscripts that have been split up, in which the text and the illustrations have been separated, probably forever, making it impossible to study the whole.

The treatises on calligraphy are also of interest for us because they provide a large quantity of technical information about some points concerning both calligraphy and painting.

The calligraphy of the text is generally done in black ink. Sometimes titles, some words or just some letters, are drawn in red ink. Other colours also used in the text are blue, gold and white (on a dark background). The latter are often found inserted in illuminated title panels (*'onvan*). Coloured inks are made in the same way as paints, the only difference being in the degree of fluidity. Indeed, ink has to be more fluid than paints, in order to adhere to the reed pen and flow from it on the paper. The formulae for the colours will be given in the following chapter.

Black inks

There are numerous recipes for black inks in treatises on calligraphy. These are divided, depending on the black colouring constituent, into three main groups:

(1) carbon inks (lamp black);

(2) metallo-gallic inks (black precipitate of tannin and a metallic salt);

(3) mixed inks (carbon and metallo-gallic).

In all three cases, a binding element is necessary, which is generally gum arabic. Some recipes are more or less complete.

The oldest recipes describe the metallo-gallic inks.[21] According to 'Abd-allah Kuhdezi, "until the time of Ebn Moqla (272/866-328/939) who is the inventor of the *naskh*, all calligraphers used metallo-gallic inks (*medad-e ab-e mazu va zag*). It was he who added lamp black and gum to them"[22].

The *'Umdat al-kuttab* gives eleven recipes for carbon inks and twenty-six gallic and metallo-gallic inks.[23] Teflisi[24] gives the following recipes:

- *hebr* three recipes of variable proportions, made up of a decoction of gallnut (*ab-e mazu*), iron sulphate (*zag-e sorkh*) and gum (*samgh*).
- *hebr-e neshaste*: charred wheat flour mixed with gallnut water and iron sulphate.
- *medad*: two recipes. (1) decoction of madder, added to gum and charred gallnut; (2) lamp black, gum, sugar, salt, rose water and saffron.
- *medad-e hendi*: carbonised and finely-ground pine wood; no solvent is mentioned.
- *enqas-e parsi*: gourd charcoal, egg-white, gum, gallnut water.

These recipes show that the metallo-gallic inks are called by Teflisi "*hebr*" and the carbon inks "*medad*". The ink called *enqas* is an incomplete mixed ink (a metallic salt is missing for precipitating the tannin).

An interesting text on the manufacture of inks is the one by 'Abd-allah Kuhdezi, *Adat al-kateb*, written probably during the reign of Akbar. The author, a calligrapher from Iran, found that the inks being used in India were not of good quality. He therefore decided to write a treatise based on the recipes of the master calligraphers, notably Soltan 'Ali Mashhadi and Majnun Chapnevis (d. 945/1538). This is an interesting treatise because it not only shows the classical recipes but also their adaptations to other environments. The formulae are as follows (the proportions are indicated in brackets):

1- Lamp black (2), gum arabic (not specified), gallnut (8), Turkish alum (4).

2- The famous *do beyti* "*Ham sang-e dude zaj ast...*" also mentioned by Simi:[25] lamp black and vitriol (1), gallnut (2), gum (3).

3- The formula of Soltan 'Ali Mashhadi:[26] lamp black (1), gum (4), alum (1), gallnut (2).

4- The formula of Majnun Chapnevis.[27] Here the author adds some comments on the proportions of alum, gallnut, lamp black and gum, and he makes particular mention of the difficulty in procuring good gallnut in India. These four formulae therefore describe the complete mixed inks.

5- The peacock ink. Also described by Simi, it is composed of: lamp black (10), Kerman alum (10), gallnut (20), gum (40). Additives are given below, in comparison with those suggested by Simi:

'Abd-allah Kuhdezi	*Simi*
-epitymum (20)	-
-ammonia	-
-saffron (3)	-saffron
-henna (3)	-henna
-woad (3)	-woad
-charred marcasite (3)	-
-hyacinth petals (3)	-
-yellow weed (3)	-
-sugar (2)	-
-aloe (3)	-aloe
-rock salt (1)	-rock salt

Simi suggests the use of some additives which are not mentioned by 'Abd-allah Kuhdezi (myrtle, rose water and wild rose water, in addition to infinitely small quantities of pearl, coral, musk, amber, gold, silver, copper, brass, cinnabar and lapis).

6- The ink of the pupil of Yaqut Mosta'sami. It is also mentioned by Simi, and almost literally, in the *khateme* of the *Golestan-e honar*;[28] It is moreover described in the *Majmu'at al-sanaye'*:[29] lamp black (6), gum (3), saffron (2), aloe (3), indigo (2), verdigris (2), rose water, wildrose water (not specified).

In the unpublished manuscript of R. Du Mans *De Persia*,[30] one way of mixing ink is to attach it to a camel setting off for Mecca!

3. Preparatory sketch and modular composition

Sketch

Before starting to paint a subject, the painter works on scrap paper to get into practice or to work out the position and details of a subject.

Several hundreds of outline drawings made on these pieces of paper and stuck on to pages of albums have been preserved in many collections. We also find in these some simple sketches, and some designs traced with stencils (which can be recognised by their pin hole contours), as well as some preparatory sketches or unfinished paintings;[31] these designs and sketches must have been used not only for painting but also for binding and probably for other products of the royal workshops, as we shall see further on.

Several terms exist for designating the preparatory designs, sketches and pounced drawings, which the painter makes use of before starting to paint.

Using the *Borhan-e qate'* as his source, A. Sakisian calls the sketch *nirang*;[32] however Dehkhoda contests this designation (see this entry).

Pounced drawings (*gerde-ye tasvir, kaghaz suzan zadan*[33]) are made on very fine paper or goat skins (*carbe*[34]). The design is copied from an already existing work, or from a sketch, in black lines (*be siyah qalam*). Then the lines of the design are pierced with pin holes. When one wants to reproduce the pounced drawing, it is placed on a white sheet, and a tampon of canvas full of powdered charcoal is rubbed on it in such a way that the charcoal passes through the holes on to the sheet. The design is thus reproduced (see our plate no.8).

Tarh means first and foremost "design"; in the marginal attributions of the Akbarid miniatures, *tarh* has the meaning of "composition" (see below), as opposed to *'amal* (the larger part of the work), to *rang-amizi* (colouring) and to *cehre-gosha'i* (faces; for a study of the division of tasks in the workshop, see Part Two); we find in the *Mer'at al-estelah*, under the heading *ostokhvan-bandi* (composition[35]) the term *tarh-e mosavvede* (design in black), which designates the sketch of the guidelines and *angare*, which is the rough sketch. This can be drawn in charcoal (*negar-e zoghal*[36], *zoghal gereftan*[37]) or in ink (*qalam-e siyahi*[38]).

The composition, strictly speaking, (*ostokhvan-bandi*) is mentioned by Mirza Haydar Dughlat on the subject of Behzad:

"*qalam-e vey mohkamtar ast, tarh va ostokhvan-e an az vey behtar ast*"

"His pen (his brush) is firmer, his design and his composition are better than those (of Shah Mozaffar)".[39]

Referring to Khvaje Mirak Naqqash, Mirza Haydar Dughlat says:

"*Asl-e tarh-e vey pokhtetar az Behzad ast, agarce pardakht-e vey meqdar-e Behzad nist*" "The basis of his compositions (*asl-e tarh*) displays a greater maturity (*pokhtetar)* than those of Behzad, although his production is not as large"[40].

Mirza Haydar Dughlat notes the harmonious qualities (*endam*) of Behzad, but remarks, on the other hand, that Qasem 'Ali or Baba Hajji do not possess them:

"Qasem 'Ali is a student of Behzad. His works are very different from those of Behzad, but any expert can recognise from his style (*oslub*) that they are much heavier (*doroshtar*) than those of Behzad and that his composition is less harmonious (*asl-e tarh-e u bi andamtar ast*).[41]

Here is what Anand Ram says about composition:

> "*Ostokhvan-bandi* means preparing the sketch (*angare*) and making the composition (*tarkib bastan*); for instance, if we want to calligraph a small piece (*qat*') or make a drawing, we first of all prepare the composition (the layout of the guidelines) in black lines (*be tarh-e mosavvede*), then we execute the main part of the work."[42]

Several possibilities are offered to the painter at the beginning of his work, but a glance at the Iranian or Indian pictorial production as a whole shows that there is a certain permanence in the compositions, on the basis of which one can attribute them to a specific artist or a school.[43] The artist, for example, resorts to freehand drawing, or uses a pouncing pattern; some examples are shown by N. Titley.[44] The more inventive artists, naturally, do not make use of this kind of procedure.

Practically nothing has come down to us concerning the rules of composition. While it is empirically possible, on the basis of examples such as the one studied by C. Adle, to retrace the guidelines of a composition, we do not have enough information in the texts to restore a theoretical "set of instructions".

Sadeqi[45] gives some vague instructions about animal design:

"Lifelessness has to be guarded against (...)
Repetition is not appreciated either,
Variety, on the other hand, is pleasant.
Repetition, even if it sometimes has charm,
Becomes boring in nature."

These few facts are indeed of little use, and they do not permit us to formulate theories about the notions of composition in Persian painting.

Modular composition

In calligraphy, the diacritic dot determines the module. It is a square whose side is equal to the length of the nib of the reed pen; for a reed pen of a given size, the dot is invariable. It is therefore on this invariable modular basis that the composition of the text is constructed. However, while this calligraphic module is borne out by numerous treatises, from Ravandi to Reza 'Alishah Qaderi,[46] this is not so for painting. C. Adle believed he had found, in some lines of the poet 'Abdi Beyg Shirazi, a formula defining the module for paintings. Here are the verses:

> "*kelid-e kherad ra honar shod 'alam/ kelid-e honar cist nuk-e qalam/ qalam naqshband ast o cehre-goshay/qalam bar do now' afaride khoday*".
> "Art has become the banner of the key to intelligence
> What is the key to art? It is the nib of the reed pen.
> The reed pen links the designs and unveils faces
> God has created two types of reed pen."[47]

While we may feel tempted to apply the lines of 'Abdi Beyg Shirazi to the composition of painting, by considering the "two reed pens", the pen and the brush, as instruments for the same writing, these lines are the work of a poet and not of a technician, and it appears difficult to use them as directions. Nonetheless, C. Adle's discovery of a module is convincing even if no literature on this matter is yet known to us.

As C. Adle points out, some art historians, including E. Wellesz and K. Blauensteiner, and then Grace D. Guest, have already focused their attention, if not directly on the problem of the module, at least on the importance of proportions in the composition of the illustrated manuscripts of the Shiraz school in the 16th century.[48] At the end of his first article on the module, C. Adle wondered whether this module might be found in other art forms, fresco, architecture, monumental epigraphy, *kashi*, textiles. This author has partially answered his question by demonstrating the existence of a module for two twin ceramic tiles.[49] Similarly, H. Halimi has shown that the *mehrab* of Oljaytu Khodabande in the Friday Mosque of Isfahan was designed and composed on the basis of a golden number.[50]

By way of example, the study of some illustrations of an *Anvar-e Soheyli*, probably commissioned by Akbar,[51] has shown that, on the one hand, the lines of the *mastar* are present in the composition of the painting and mark some important points of this composition and, on the other hand, that a construction based on the parallel diagonals of several squares is superimposed on this ruling. A detailed study of the module of this manuscript is presently underway to show that the ruling has been constructed according to a golden number. The spacing between the lines of the ruling gives the basis of the module. This being so, it is not surprising, as we saw earlier, that some particularly harmonious *mastar* have been copied. Nevertheless, it is only through a comparative study of different manuscripts produced by a single workshop that we can hope to throw light on this system of modular construction.

From a study of this particularly important phase of ruling and layout in the production of the manuscript, it is clear that the work of the painter, like that of the illuminator, is closely linked with that of the calligrapher. In other words, as we shall see in Part Two, the making of an illuminated manuscript, particularly in the royal workshops, is a collective task, made possible by specialisation and division of labour.

NOTES

1. See "Module et tracé correcteur, 1".
2. Danesh-Pazhuh, "*Rang-sazi*", p.25.
3. *Archéologie du livre mediéval*, p.53.
4. Paris, B. N. Lat. 11884 fol.2b.; transl. L. Gilissen, *id.*
5. "Epigraphes poétiques dans des manuscrits persans du XVe et XVIe siècle" in F. Deroche, ed. *Manuscrits du Moyen-Orient*, pp.72-75.
6. Ed., p.130.
7. Dust Mohammad, p.198, already quoted in the part on *qat'* (format of paper).
8. Ed., p.73; transl., p.118.
9. Transl. p.643.
10. Fol.211b.
11. "Les manuscrits persans d'origine indienne", p.44.
12. Ed. pp.161-164; transl. pp 195-196.
13. *Tahrir*, the black line which outlines a colour.
14. "*Rang-sazi*" pp.19-20.
15. Ed., p.202
16. Only in the "anonymous" version, ed. Golcin Ma'ani, pp.300-301.
17. Ed., p.137.
18. *Id.*, p.134; for the illustration, it would be advisable to refer to the manuscript, as the drawings of the edition are quite different from the original.
19. Ms. Patna no.882, fol.52b.

20. Vol.III, p.34.
21. Levey, p.7. These recipes date back to the Egypt of the Pharaohs.
22. *Adat al-kateb*, fol. 8a; see Qazi Ahmad, transl. p.56 for biographical details.
23. Levey, pp.15-21.
24. Ed., pp.351-354.
25. See Y. Porter, "Un traité de Simi Neyshapuri", p.186.
26. Ed. 69, transl. p.112.
27. Ed. R. Mayel-e Heravi, pp.*i* and 5-6; these texts by Majnun Rafiqi owe much to those of Simi.
28. Qazi Ahmad, ed. p.168, transl. pp.199-200.
29. *Bab* 29 *fasl* 3, fol. 35a-b.
30. Ms. British Library; pointed out by F. Richard.
31. See for example the pages of the Diez (Berlin) and Fatih (Topkapi) albums, reproduced in Lowry and Lentz, *Timur*., pp. 164 and 171-204.
32. "Esthétique et terminologie persanes", p.146.
33. Anand Ram, *Mer'at,* fol. 215a and 225b.
34. *Jeld-sazi;* ed. p.146; Anand Ram, *Camanestan* fol.93a.
35. Anand Ram, *Mer'at, fol. 11b.*
36. Qazi Ahmad, ed. p.134, transl. 9.180.
37. Mirza Haydar Dughlat, transl. *B.W.G.* p.190.
38. Dust Mohammad, p.197; Mirza Haydar, *B.W.G.* p.190.
39. Mirza Haydar, *B.W.G. p.*190; see also Sakisian, "Esthétique...", which contests Arnold's translation.
40. As A. S. Melikian-Chirvani points out, Mirza Haydar's text has yet to be edited. I am quoting this passage from the version he gives in his article "Khwaja Mirak Naqqash", p.100; Melikian also tells us that Sam Mirza admired the composition (*tarrahi*) of the painter Aqa Mirak (see his note 24).
41. This passage is quoted from the transl. of *B.W.G.*, pp.190-191, retranslating the Persian quotations mentioned in a note of this translation; see also Sakisian, "Esthétique".
42. *Mer'at al-estelah*, fol.11b.
43. See for example Titley p.70 pl.8 and p.75 fig.35.
44. *Id.* p.217. fig.68 and p.219 fig.71.
45. *Qanun al-sovar*, lines 121-125.
46. See Huart p.21 ss.
47. C. Adle, "Module, 1", p.96, Qazi Ahmad, ed. p.9; Danesh-Pazhuh, "*Rang-sazi*", p.25.
48. C. Adle, "Module et tracé correcteur, 1", p.102.
49. C. Adle, "Module et tracé correcteur, 2".
50. H. Halimi, "Le *mihrab* d' Uljaytu Khodabande et le nombre d'or" in *Luqman* 2,2 (1986) pp.53-79, 9 fig.
51. The starting point of this study was our review (*Abs. Ir.* 11) of the article by John Seyller, "The School of Oriental and African Studies *Anvar-i Suhayli:* the illustration of a *de luxe* Mughal manuscript", *Ars Orientalis,* 16 (1986), pp.119-151, 20 fig.

4

PAINTING

1. Colours, perception and symbolism

The world of colours is very vast; those of perception and symbolism are equally so. M. Pastoureau remarks that "colour is a strictly cultural phenomenon, which it is impossible to consider outside time and space".[1] This would imply that the perception of colours is not a universal phenomenon. We will therefore try to study in the following pages the specific case of the perception of colours in the Iranian world.

As far as language is concerned, C. Levi-Strauss notes that "A language which possesses a word for "red" necessarily has two for "white" and "black", or "light" and "dark"; the presence of a word for "yellow" implies that of a word for "red" etc."[2]

There is no denying that a certain distance exists between the semantic level of the names of colours and their poetic concept. Thus, "the eye of the poet who admires nature therefore sees forms and figures in a multiplicity of colours which, when they take shape, become garments and adornments, the face of the ideal beloved, Paradise or a meeting place. The radiance of shapes lies in their colours."[3] The poet will describe the colour of a single object by different names. The cheeks of the beloved may therefore be, in turn, the colour of wine, of cinnabar, of pomegranate, of amaranth, of fire, of blood, "all these comparisons do not appear to be a search into the variety of reds, but varied ways of saying the same thing: the colour red."[4] The painter, on the other hand, makes a distinction between the names of each colour: the names of pure colours (yellow, red, green, blue) as well as the names of their shades (purple, amaranth, sky blue).

Let us see what the texts say on the theory of colours. Tusi, in his *Tansuq name*[5] says that colours all emanate from the mixture of white and black in different proportions; white is the origin and black the end result of colours. It should be noted that this observation, repeated by Abu al-Fazl,[6] corresponds exactly to the modern theory of colour defined as a phenomenon of light; this concept was unknown in Europe in mediaeval times.[7] The idea of colour associated with light is again found in the attribution of colours to the planets. Thus, we know that the ziggurat of Birs Nimrud in Babylon had seven storeys of different colours, each dedicated to a planet:[8]

-Saturn	-black
-Jupiter	-reddish brown
-Mars	-red
-Sun	-yellow
-Venus	-light yellow
-Mercury	-blue
-Moon	-white

Among the Sabaeans, the order of the planets is the same, but with some colour variations:[9]

-Saturn	-lead	-black
-Jupiter	-tin	-green
-Mars	-iron	-red
-Sun	-gold	-yellow
-Venus	-copper	-blue
-Mercury	-*kharsini*	-brown
-Moon	-silver	-white

During the Muslim era, these associations of colours persist, as can be seen in Nezami, for instance. Thus, in the colour of the seven pavilions described in his *Haft Peykar,*[10] the order of the colours follows that of the days of the week and of the planets which rule over these days:

-black	-Saturn	-Saturday
-yellow	-Sun	-Sunday
-green	-Moon	-Monday
-red	-Mars	-Tuesday
-blue	-Mercury	-Wednesday
-grey	-Jupiter	-Thursday
-white	-Venus	-Friday

Similarly, we find lists of colours on two occasions in the *Qanun-e homayuni* by Khvandamir. The first gives a description of the clothes to be worn according to the day of the week and the corresponding colour.[11] This description follows closely the order given by Nezami. Some discrepancy is however to be noted in the colour of the moon (white or green), of Jupiter (brown-grey) and of Venus (green or white). The second list of colours is given on the occasion of the description of a carpet showing a cosmological design[12] and, naturally, follows the order of the planets. Two colour classifications therefore appear:

Planets:	Saturn	Jupiter	Mars	Sun	Venus	Mercury	Moon
Colours:	black	grey	red	yellow	green	blue	white

Day:	Saturday	Sunday	Monday	Tuesday	Wednesday	Thursday	Friday
Colours:	black	yellow	green	red	blue	grey	white

Both classifications however follow the white/black axis.

A last example is given in the *Makhzan al-adviye* by Mohammad Hoseyn,[13] which does not provide the names of colours but of the elements associated with the planets:

Planet	metals	stones	colour deduced
Saturn	-lead	-black stones	-black
Jupiter	-tin	-diamond	-grey
Mars	-iron	-haematite, cinnabar	-red
Sun	-gold	-ruby, sulphur	-yellow
Venus	-copper	-pearls, emerald	-green
Mercury	-zinc(?)	-turquoise	-blue
Moon	-silver	-pearl, crystal	-white

While some variations can be observed in the colours of some planets, it appears on the other hand that the cosmographic arrangement follows a horizontal line which extends from the white of the moon, representing the East, to the black of Saturn, which is the West, passing through the yellow of the noonday sun.

The discrepancy in the colours of the Moon and Venus is found again in the classification of colours according to the days of the week. The week starts on Saturday (black) and ends on Friday (white), which, in Nezami, is represented by Venus in white and not in green; this confusion of white and green is found again in Khvandamir for the same planets. While it is certain that in the chromatic circle, green borders on white, this confusion is also found in poetry and is seen again in the objects likened to these stars: copper, pearls, and emeralds for Venus, and silver, pearls, and crystal for the moon. The colour of pearl, like that of mother of pearl, is therefore likened to green (Venus, copper, emerald); the sky is sometimes compared in poetry to green mother of pearl.[14] It should be noted that Venus and the Moon are the brightest "stars" and that their very brightness makes it difficult to identify their colour.

Mercury, on the other hand, has a less bright colour which fluctuates between blue, brown and violet. Khvandamir specifies that the colour of Mercury is a mixture of blue and pink which comes next to black (violet), and corresponds to the bottom of the chromatic circle. Jupiter, similarly, has an ill-defined colour.

I have not found in Persian texts any description of a chromatic circle comparable to that of Oswald or of Goethe.[15] It is, at any rate, evident from this brief study, that the theoretical perception of colours is more cosmological than chromatic in nature. Indeed, the colours move along a horizontal axis, from white to black, in a linear fashion which does not allow for relationships between the colours themselves. The beginning is white, the end is black, but between the two, the colours do not follow a chromatic evolution of values. In the chromatic circle, the base is provided by the three primary colours (yellow, red, blue) which, through binary relations, give the first three secondary colours (orange, violet, green) which in turn give other tertiary combinations (golden yellow, vermilion, purple, indigo, turquoise, lemon); in this circle, the colours are contrasted by their complements: yellow/violet, orange/blue, red/green...

Symbolism or convention?

In addition to the cosmological aspect, what could be the symbolic value of the colours? To denote abstract concepts, as in the West where white is the symbol for purity, green for hope, red for passion and black for mourning? However some colours which seem conventional in the West, have more than symbolic significance: for example the cloak of the Virgin is also blue on account of the price of ultramarine. The colours of the Immaculate Conception, for their part, only date back to Bernadette Soubirous. One might think that in addition to abstract concepts, colours, particularly in the illustration of poetic texts, could translate metaphors. However, it does not take long to realize that most poetic metaphors are impossible to translate into painting.

While the use of some colours seems compulsory, laid down by the texts, such as the colour of the pavilions of the *Haft peykar*, the black colour of the horse Shabdiz in *Khosrow va Shirin*, the white colour of the *Div-e sefid* (the white demon) in the *Shahname*, the red colour of the bonnets of the *qizilbash* (lit. "red-heads"), these are perhaps the only cases of rigid colour symbolism. True, there are some conventional colours, such as skies of gold or of lapis in certain miniatures, which literally translate some metaphors, or streams of silver - which have become black only due to oxidization. However, counter-examples are far more numerous: the cheeks of the faces shown are rarely red, the entire face being of the same colour; the darkness of the night is not shown in Persian painting till the end of the Safavid period. Thus, the scene of the *Shahname* of Shah Tahmasp showing Barbad hidden in Khosrow's garden, is supposed to have taken place at night; this is shown not by the absence of light (dark sky, people in shadowy light) but only by the fact that some people are carrying torches. The dark figures (African or other slaves) have features similar to the "whites", but their faces are painted grey. That is all that distinguishes them from the others. There are practically no variations in the pigmentation of the skins. The differentiation is made through other features, such as the beard, the turban or the clothes; but even the colours of garments probably correspond more to the demands of rhythm and harmony of composition than to any kind of symbolism.

On the other hand, it is not uncommon in Persian miniatures to find horses that are orange, red, violet or blue, which shows that their natural colour is less important than the general impression which has to be conveyed by the play of colours and composition. It is not the work of the painter to be a poet or a photographer. Starting from a palette which is very limited compared to the infinity of colours found in nature, he does not paint a reproduction of what he sees, but his conceptualised version of it. C.Levi-Strauss has this to say about the painting of Max Ernst, which is equally applicable to the Iranian painter: "Both of them (Max Ernst and Merleau-Ponty) consider painting successful when it transgresses the border between the external and the internal world, and gives access to this intermediary zone, *mundus imaginalis* of ancient Iranian philosophy, described by Henry Corbin."[16]

The colours described in the treatises are not the result of calculations of light frequency, but the product of human experiments on materials of variable quality. Consequently, it is practically impossible to have a perfect gauge by which to define them. That is why the pigments have been classified in groups of colours and not in exact shades which are difficult to name. It should be noted, finally, that the Persian language often designates several different pigments by the name of a single colour:

sefidab, ceruse of lead, of tin or perhaps of zinc;
lajvard, lapis-lazuli, azurite, cobalt;
zarnikh, orpiment and realgar.

2. Pigments

- ***Whites***

Two main kinds of white pigments are mentioned in the texts: ceruses (*sefidab*, lead or tin, and perhaps zinc carbonates) and talc (*talq*, pure magnesium silicate). No white earth is ever mentioned.[17]

-*Sefidab*. Teflisi explains[18] how to make tin ceruse (*sepidab-e arziz*) by oxidization and calcination. In his chapter on colours,[19] he does not specify whether the ceruse is of tin or of lead, but he describes how to prepare it for painting: after it has been washed and strained through a cloth, the white is mixed with gum arabic if it is to be used on paper; if it is to be used on other grounds, it is mixed with egg white. This recipe is also mentioned in the *khateme* of the *Golestan-e honar*.[20]

Kashani[21] describes the preparation of lead oxide in the following manner:

> "When lead is calcinated, it becomes red (through oxidization); it is called *asranj* or *shangarf*[22] and this is the colour that painters use on paper, walls, wood, etc...; when it is calcinated yet again, it becomes ceruse (carbonate), which is also a colour used by painters, and this is called *sefide-ye kamangaran* (the white of makers of bows).[23]"

Tusi gives an entirely similar description.[24] Sadeqi too describes the dual operation, oxidization and reduction of the lead, to obtain minium, then ceruse.[25]

Simi only mentions tin ceruse (*esfidaj*) and points out that when washing the pigment, the top of the deposit is called *ruh* (spirit, essence[26]).

The *Majmu'at al-sanaye'* gives several recipes for ceruse[27]:

> "-ceruse from Kashghar. Grind some lead and reduce it to powder; put it into a varnished earthen container, seal it and place it in an oven; when calcination is complete, pour vinegar over it and leave it for a week, till everything becomes white.
> -tin and lead ceruse. Heat lead and tin in a cauldron; add two leaves of aloe (*kanwar**), some anethum (*ajva'in*) and thirty leaves of *Calotropis gigantea* (*ak**) which is to be burnt and added to the metals; cook the mixture till ceruse is obtained.
> -*sefidab-e farsi* (Persian ceruse). Put pure tin in a cauldron with a little salt; heat it over a low flame, then grind and reduce it to powder; then put the tin into a sealed container and this into a glass oven; a *deram* of this ceruse is worth at least three *deram* of any other type".

-Zinc. There is no evidence of the use of zinc oxide in painting, in the treatises. However, this metal was well known in Iran, from at least the 10th century, as Ebn al-Faqih described the zinc mines of Dunbawand, near Kerman.[28] In a recipe for making imitation silver, the *'Umdat* mentions *tutiya*, which could be zinc oxide (see below).
-Talc. Several treatises on calligraphy including the *Golzar-e safa* and the treatise by Simi[29] mention talc in solution (*talq-e mahlul*), used as a white ink; it is also mentioned in the *Majmu'at al-sanaye'* but only in the recipe for *batane* (ground for lacquer). The *'Umdat al-kuttab* mentions it in a recipe for white ink (*liqe-ye sefid-e khub*[30]). There is, therefore, *a priori* no evidence of the use of talc solution in painting.

- ***Yellows***

The colour yellow comes mainly from orpiment (yellow arsenic sulphide, *zarnikh-e zard*). It can also be obtained by mixing saffron to a white base (ceruse or talc). Other yellow pigments have been used in painting, among these being ochres and the Indian *peori**, but these are not mentioned in the texts.
-Orpiment. The stone in its natural state is ground, washed and mixed with gum arabic; this very simple recipe is the one that is the most frequently mentioned.[31]
-Saffron and white. Teflisi gives a recipe of ink "similar to gold", made of a mixture of tin oxide and saffron to which gum arabic is added.[32] Simi suggests the mixing of saffron with a talc solution.[33]

Jamali-ye Yazdi has a recipe for ink "similar to gold" without a white base:

> "Cook some turmeric in water till it has given out all its colour, then filter it; add some saffron and boil once again; filter a second time. Add gallnut water and gum arabic before the mixture cools down and stir well."[34]

-Yellow ochres are not mentioned in the texts. However, Chardin mentions a yellow earth ("*zerd guil*", *zard gel*), which the Persians use for plastering their walls.[35]

-*Peori** or *goguli** (*gav-geli*) is not mentioned in any text. It is a typically Indian pigment, which C. Huart says is "a sort of yellow earth found in India; this yellow is brighter than that of orpiment."[36] Platts dictionary defines it as "yellow chalk, yellow colour said to be obtained from the urine of a cow fed on the flowers of the *Buthea frondosa*, or, according to others, on the leaves of the mango tree". This pigment is still found occasionally in India.

-Jamali-ye Yazdi suggests yet another recipe for "gold" ink, made with fish blubber (!).[37]

- ***Oranges***

Orange colours are obtained from minium (lead oxide, *soranj* or *asranj*) and from realgar (red arsenic sulphide, *zarnikh-e sorkh*). Cinnabar also can, depending on the proportions of sulphur and of mercury, give an orangish colour. Well known since Antiquity, these three pigments give rise, nevertheless, to numerous confusions in the Latin texts. In fact, Pliny[38] confuses three different pigments, sometimes calling them *cinnabaris*, sometimes *minium*. These are:

-cinnabar,
-minium,
-dragon's blood (red exudation of the *Pterocarpus draco* or of the *Dracaena cinnabaris*).

Minium :

Pliny[39] and Vitruvius mention this as do also the Silpa (*sindura*). The way we obtain minium, like ceruse, is through oxidization, by heating first the lead and then adding some acids to it (Kashani, Tusi, Sadeqi). The *Majmu'at al-sanaye*[40] has a formula for minium, called *shangarf-e zavoli* (cinnabar from Zavol; note once again the shift in meaning of minium/cinnabar):

"bleach the lead in a new cauldron; for ten parts of lead, add

> one part of *shangarf-e zavoli* to the lead oxide; leave (on the heat) for a night and a day, and keep a check on the colour, which should be a ruby red".

Realgar :

Called *sandarac* by Graeco-Latin authors, this red arsenic sulphide appears to be found, according to these authors, only in the Pontus region.[41] Teflisi claims that if orpiment (*zarnikh-e zard*) is ground while dry, the more it is ground, the redder it becomes.[42] Tusi, on the other hand, specifically states that "there are two kinds of *zarnikh*, red or yellow; when *zarnikh* is crushed and mixed with gum arabic, it becomes a colour which is used for painting on paper and other (grounds)".[43] This pigment is also mentioned in the *Majmu'at al-sanaye'*:

> "grind realgar (*zarnikh-e shakh-shakh-e sorkh*, realgar in thin sheets -orpiment and realgar are found in this sheets) on a stone; when it has been finely ground, mix it with diluted gum, then leave it to dry in the sun; just before using it add a little diluted gum".[44]

- *Cinnabar*

Possessing astonishing properties and essential to alchemy, cinnabar has played an important role in the history of science. Unfortunately, the study of its use in painting is a difficult subject because, although its presence can be easily detected by analyses, these reveal nothing, on the other hand, about its mode of preparation.

Vitruvius as well as Pliny[45] call it *minium*. This term now refers to lead oxide, no doubt on account of a very old confusion. The etymology of this word suggests its origin: it is extracted near the river Minius (Menjo) in Spain.[46] Vitruvius adds: "Large reserves of minium/ cinnabar have been discovered in Spain and its manufacture has been shifted to Rome". The discovery of deposits of Spanish cinnabar is important as it continues to be exploited even today, particularly at Almaden.

Tusi says on the subject of cinnabar: "The majority of mercury mines are to be found within Europe (*hodud-e farang*; could these be the Spanish mines?); the mercury stone is red, like unground cinnabar; some call it "mineral cinnabar" (*shangarf-e kani*); the cinnabar that painters use for colour, is made of mercury and sulphur."[47] Simi[48] and Mir 'Ali Heravi[49] also say that the best cinnabar comes from Europe (Mir 'Ali also adds *Rum*; Byzantium?)

The principle behind the making of cinnabar is a simple one: mercury is mixed with sulphur and raised to a high temperature; the result is a mercury sulphide. The proportions of the two elements vary according to the sources.

Perhaps the oldest explanation of the separation of mineral cinnabar into sulphur and mercury is the one given by Zosimus, in the 3rd century A.D. However, the reverse operation, which consists in reconstituting cinnabar from sulphur and mercury, is not explained by this author. We have to wait perhaps for the great alchemists such as Jabir (8th century) to at last find the formula. In the *'Umdat al-kuttab*,[50] composed around 1025, cinnabar was apparently used in its mineral state, although at this time, its chemical preparation was already known. Around 1122-23, Theophilus, in his treatise on the arts,[51] describes the chemical manufacture of cinnabar. Could this be the oldest formula specifically applied to painting?

Cinnabar is mentioned in the *Silpa*[52] also, again without any clarification about its mineral or chemical nature.

Here, summarised in the form of a table, are the proportions of sulphur and mercury, such as they are given in the texts:

Source	Proportions	
	Mercury	**Sulphur**
- Teflisi[53]	4 or 6 parts	1 part of sulphur
- Razi[54]	1	1
- Sadeqi[55]	3 or 4	3
- *Majmu'at*[56]		
rumi	12	8
(*forsi*?)	10	1
mosaffa	17	1 (or the opposite)
(*farangi*?)	20	12 (and 2 of realgar)

The last formula suggested by the *Majmu'at* (*shanjarf-e romani*) does not include sulphur, but some *ruy sakht*. This element has proved difficult to identify (it is perhaps antimony oxysulphide (Steingass) or copper oxide.[57]

Generally, the proportions of mercury are higher (or equal). The methods of preparation vary, though the principle remains the same, particularly as regards the method of calcinating. Razi points out that the ideal temperature for calcinating is found by experiment.[58] The usual method consists in putting the ingredients into a clay container covered with lute (*gel-e hekmat*). The *Majmu'at*[59] as well as Mir 'Ali Heravi[60] describe some formulae for making the lute. This is made of mud or plaster, hair and marshmallow flowers according to Mir 'Ali. The *Majmu'at* adds horse dung, rice bran, salt and pottery crushed into powder. This paste is used to cover the containers meant to withstand very high temperatures.

The *Majmu'at al-sanaye'* also describes some material used for the calcination of cinnabar.[61] Once the cinnabar has been obtained, it is finely crushed, rinsed in water[62] or in pomegranate juice,[63] then mixed with gum arabic or glue (*serishom*, Mir 'Ali). Teflisi specifies that if the colour is meant for painting, the mixture should be thick, and if it is for writing with the reed pen, it should be more fluid (see also the "cinnabar test" in "Mediums").

- ***Non mineral reds***

We have seen, in the case of dyes, that several elements are given the name *lak* (or *lok*). In painting, texts show that this is essentially *tachardia lacca*. Indeed, in the *'Umdat*[64] as well as in Sadeqi,[65] it is specified that the lac has to be separated from its wood, in other words that the coloured exudation of the insect has to be separated from its natural ground. In both cases (*'Umdat* and Sadeqi) the lac is boiled in saponaria juice (*ashnan*); in the *'Umdat*, some borax (*buraq*) is added; Sadeqi first of all adds the unidentified element *lotr*, then alum (*zamj*); he thus obtains the ruby red colour (*la'li*). The term *lotr* has been translated by Dickson[66] as "lime", by comparison with a process described by C. Cennini. However, it could perhaps refer to something else: indeed, O.P. Jaggi describes the preparation of lac by specifying that it is mixed with curdled milk.[67] The curdled milk may have some connection with the word *luk* which we find in a formula for a binding agent based on gum-lac, for marbled paper.[68]

Teflisi makes use of lac only in mixtures: the colour *golgun* (pink) is made of lac and ceruse, while violet (*banafshe*) is made of lapis, cinnabar and lac.[69]

The *'Umdat* suggests a number of recipes in which some plant pigments are involved, particularly for reds, sometimes with a mineral base,[70] sometimes mixed with other dyes or tannic elements.[71] These plant pigments are produced by anemone, sapanwood, *Althea rosea* (*khir-e sorkh*) and safflower.

Simi also gives a recipe for colour with safflower (*'arusak*).[72]

- ***Greens***

Very few green pigments are described in the texts. The rare greens present in pre-Islamic paintings are a mixture of orpiment and indigo.[73] Malachite, a natural green-coloured carbonate of copper, is not mentioned in any source,[74] nor is chrysocolla (copper silicate).[75] Vitruvius mentions three other green pigments:[76] Appian green, or green chalk; green earth, (terra verde) from Smyrna; verdigris.

None of these seems to have been used in Central Asia, at least according to the data available to us. It is astonishing that terra verde (*harabhata**) does not appear in the *Silpa*, considering how easily it is obtained in India, how simple it is to prepare and how widely it is used even today. The same remark applies to verdigris.

Verdigris (copper acetate, *zengar*) is about the only green pigment described in the texts. However, as Simi and Mir 'Ali Heravi have pointed out, it has the disadvantage of making holes in the paper.[77] Painters must certainly have noticed this, and must have been keen to use other greens, among these being the indigo/orpiment mixture. Unfortunately, there are a large number of pages of manuscripts which have been damaged as a result of the use of verdigris: the *jadval* painted in this colour have literally cut the pages.

The description of this colour in the anonymous version of the treatise of Simi is less explicit than the "signed" version. Here it is:

> "There are two types of verdigris. One is (obtained) with copper filings and vinegar which are put into a container suspended in a well; after forty days it becomes verdigris. The other kind is (obtained) by taking the water from sheep blood and proceeding in the same manner (as with vinegar). The verdigris is then passed through a piece of cloth, poured into a porcelain bowl and mixed with sarcocolla juice (*'anzarut*). It is then mixed with gum arabic and after that anything can be written with it. But after some time, the paper develops holes; the remedy for this is to mix a little saffron (to the verdigris), which produces the colour pistachio (*fostoqi*)."[78]

Another very similar formula is suggested by Mir 'Ali. As regards sarcocolla, he tells us: "*Anzarut* is the name of the tree in Pars which has several skins on top of each other, like the onion; everything that comes from this tree is white at night and red in sunlight (!)."[79]

The *Majmu'at* suggests eight formulae for verdigris;[80] the principle is always the same, since it involves the oxidization of copper by acid:

(1) *Zengar-e sabze-ye daman*. Strangely enough, silver and not copper, is used, with ammonia salt; the colour obtained is that of the young shoots growing on the slopes of hills (*daman*). I do not know however if silver can produce any kind of green colour.[81]
(2) *Fara'uni*: copper filings and green grape juice or vinegar.
(3) *Tarsa'i*: copper and ammonia salt.
(4) *Farise*[82]: copper and vinegar heated.
(5) *Mosaffa*: *fara'uni* verdigris and distilled white vinegar. This verdigris is the best and is used for colouring turquoises.
(6) *Firuze'i*: copper in sheets, distilled vinegar and ammonia.
(7) Other: *tarsa'i* verdigris, copper, ammonia, vinegar, buried in horse dung.[83]
(8) *Khamesi*: brass (*berenj-e demashqi*), juice of bitter oranges, ammonia, heated in a water-bath.

- ***Blues***

The blue par excellence, which corresponds to the metaphor of the lapis sky, is lapis-lazuli itself. Known since at least the 3rd millenium B.C.,[84] it was not necessarily used in painting as early as this. Being a rare and precious substance, since it came almost exclusively from the mountains of the Badakhshan (a proto-historic mine has however been found in Baluchistan[85]), lapis-lazuli is one of the materials used in the construction of Darius I's palace in Susa.[86] It is possible that it may have been used for the Susa frescoes,[87] but R.J. Forbes thinks that the methods known in antiquity for washing the lapis were too rudimentary to obtain a pigment of a satisfactory quality:

> "We have no evidence of the refining and washing of ground lapis-lazuli in order to prepare ultramarine (free from silica and calcite particles) before the 6th and 7th c. A.D. in Afghanistan, and its use in Byzantine times is established, but not earlier."[88]

As we shall see later, the method for washing lapis described by Teflisi at the end of the 12th century makes it difficult to obtain ultramarine. This observation about a much later date backs up the remark made by R.J.Forbes. Yet, lapis is seen in analyses, in Pendzhikent as well as in Dilberdzhin. Unfortunately, the presence of lapis in these analyses tells us nothing about the methods employed to obtain it, and therefore for its colouring. Theophilus mentions the colour *lazur*, but we do not know if he was referring to lapis or to azurite.[89]

Lapis-lazuli is, with gold, the most precious colour for miniatures. However, as we have already noted, Persian names of colours may include several pigments. Thus, while the generally accepted meaning of *lazhvard* (or *lajvard*) is lapis-lazuli, other blue pigments are also called by this name.

Descriptions of lapis[90]

According to Razi (*Serr al-asrar*) there is only one kind of lapis, deep blue verging on red, in which some tiny golden eyes can be seen. Tifashi describes it as a stone that is soft and crumbly (characteristic of azurite!); the best is the one which shines the most and is a dark blue. Kashani[91] says that lapis is of two kinds, with or without golden dots; the purest and the most beautiful colour is the one which has the least white.[92] Biruni[93] says that in Greek it is called *arminaqun*, a corrupt form of Latin *armenicus*, which in fact means azurite.

Origins

Although it is considered as being certain that lapis originates exclusively in Badakhshan, some sources indicate other deposits. Kashani and Dastaki mention, apart from Badakhshan, Karaj, Dezmar and Kerman. M.Zavesh has verified that lapis is not found in any of these regions. He also points out that Hamd-allah Mostowfi, in his *Nuzhat al-qolub*, mentions some lapis in Mazanderan, which is quite unlikely.[94] The lapis of Badakhshan is mentioned often in texts.[95] M.Zavesh quotes a *Javaher-name* attributed to a Khvaje Nasir[96] which points out: "There are no lapis mines outside Badakhshan; there are, near Kashan, some mines from which a black stone is extracted; this kind of stone is used in Arabia, Azerbaidjan, Shiraz; it is imitation *kashi* lapis, which is obtained by calcinating this black stone, which becomes blue.... in painting it can only be used to decorate buildings, and after a certain time it becomes black". This is a most astonishing passage as it obviously describes cobalt which, as we shall see further on, is also called *lajvard*. This passage could be related to the description of lapis given by Kashani, were it not for the fact that this latter mentions lapis as originating in places other than Badakhshan. It is therefore all the more unfortunate that M. Zavesh does not give a more precise reference about his source. From these descriptions and origins, it follows that the word *lajvard* covers here three minerals: (1) lapis-lazuli (alumina silicate and sodium + sulphur); (2) azurite (copper carbonate); (3) cobalt. Since the only established source of lapis is Badakhshan, the other presumed deposits must in fact be producing copper (and therefore blue carbonates, azurites and some malachites), or cobalt (Kashan).

Techniques for washing lapis

Several methods more or less sophisticated are suggested in the various texts. Indeed, crushed and unwashed lapis gives a bluish-grey colour, which is very far from ultramarine. The long and delicate process of washing lapis kept a whole body of professionals (*lajvard-shuyan*) occupied within the workshops. Several painters also became famous for this technique (see Part Two).

Teflisi[97] recommends that lapis be crushed on a stone, then very pure vinegar and gum arabic solution added to it. After that, it should be washed the same way as cinnabar, that is to say, once it is finely ground, like collyrium *(sorme)*, it is put into a container full of water, stirred and left to stand till the water is clear. The water is then poured out and the operation is repeated two or three times. It is then left to dry. Once dried, the colour is crushed again and gum arabic is added. He specifies that washed colour is better and purer than unwashed colour.

Simi[98] says that the lapis has first of all to be ground, then mixed with water, and what remains on the surface (*shamt*) is removed; what is left is full of colour and is mixed with gum. The author of the *Golzar-e Safa*[99] specifies that there are three kinds of washed lapis: the top, the middle and the deposit (*shamt*). In fact, in all cases, *shamt* signifies the greyish residue which has to be separated from the ultramarine.

In the *khateme* of the *Golestan-e honar,*[100] the method is slightly different: the stones are broken into little pieces; the most colourful among them are separated from the others. Each kind is ground in different mortars, then strained and washed with *'eraqi* soap.[101] To wash the lapis with soap, water must be put in a pot with soap and beaten to make it frothy. The crushed stone must be poured into the water and stirred, then left to stand for an hour. The water is poured into several containers. The deposit is reground and re-washed; this water is poured into another container. The operation is repeated till the lapis has entirely come out. When it is dry, it is wrapped in paper.

In the *Majmu'at al sanaye'*,[102] we find two methods for washing *lajvard*. In both, the kind of *lajvard* being referred to is not specified at any time. Although it might relate to lapis, there is never any mention of crushing, which leads us to believe that it is not lapis but indigo. Indeed, this text calls dyeing with indigo[103] by the name *lajvardi*. Let

us examine these methods:
(1) Put the *lajvard* in an iron container, or even better, a copper one; pour vinegar into it in such a way as to cover it; then boil it and remove the scum till none remains; then boil it again with some new vinegar. If some vinegar still remains (after repeating the operation), boil it again adding some water; then remove the water and dry in the sun. When it is to be dissolved, take a little and mix with gum arabic.
(2) Take some good *lajvard*, that is to say the kind whose colour borders on green (?) and put it in a container over heat; bring it to boiling point, then leave it to cool; remove the water which remains on top. Add salted water and stir with the finger so that the salt gets diluted; add a little water and stir to the consistency of plaster; wash in water, leave to stand, then remove the salt water. Just before use, put it in a shell with diluted gum and stir with the finger.

In both recipes, it is clear that the colour obtained is meant for painting, as it is mixed with gum, and put into a shell (in the second recipe), which is characteristic of colours used by painters.

Imitation of lapis

According to R.J. Forbes, in Antiquity the usual pigment for frescoes was either based on azurite or on an imitation lapis made of silica, malachite (natural copper carbonate) and calcium carbonate.[104]

Vitruvius[105] gives a recipe for blue (*coeruleum*) based on silica, aluminate of copper (natron) and copper filings, all of them ground together and heated in a furnace. This formula is very akin to that of frit, mentioned by R.J. Forbes.[106]

In the Muslim era, only one text gives a formula for making imitation lapis-lazuli, applied very definitely to painting: this is the *lajvard-e 'amali* described by Simi, made from indigo and ceruse.[107] As we have already noted, indigo is sometimes called *lajvard*.

We have seen from description of lapis/*lajvard* that most formulae for painting seem to include lapis-lazuli. It is however not impossible that, in some cases, azurite, which is less costly, and easier to find, but which produces a less beautiful colour, may also have been used.

A formula for imitating lapis-lazuli was discovered in France in the 18th century, made of soda, kaolin and sulphur. To the naked eye, this colour is a perfect imitation of lapis. It is only under the microscope that the absence of colourless crystals, present in natural lapis, is detected.[108] Indeed, kaolin (hydrated alumina silicate), soda and sulphur are the constituent elements of lapis and undoubtedly its basic colouring components -chemical analysis can therefore differentiate with difficulty a natural pigment from an artificial one. Nevertheless, no mention of this pigment being imported to the East is available in texts.

Two texts mention *lajvard*/cobalt: the one by the "pseudo-Tusi" and the *'Arayes al-javaher* by Kashani. Kashani suggests that "for making imitation lapis, one *man* of *shekar sang* (lapis arabicus, quartz?), 100 *deram* of salt of soda (*malh-e shakhar*[109]) and 40 *deram* of (?) *soleymani* (one word is missing in the manuscript of the edition) be taken, and all finely crushed with senna, and put into vessels of varnished clay in a *kashi* furnace. Once cooked, the product is crushed again and produces an excellent colour."

There are two unknown factors in this formula: the element called *soleymani* and the use of the result. It would appear, according to J.A.Pope,[110] that the Chinese word for cobalt comes from the Persian *soleymani*.[111] Kashani, in his formulae for making ceramics, mentions *lajvard-e soleymani*,[112] which has been identified by J.W. Allan as cobalt.[113] However, the word *soleymani* by itself probably does not designate any particular stone, and it is found only as an adjective. Tusi calls the third category of turquoise by this name.[114] Zavesh gives the name *sang-e soleymani* to the variety of onyx also known as *babaquri*.[115] Lastly, the *Majmu'at al-sanaye'* mentions, in a formula for the ground for lacquer (*batane-ye tavusi*[116]) and in a formula for colouring glass turquoise blue,[117] the element called *sang-e soleymaṇi*. This word is explained in the margin when it first appears, as *maghniśa*. Steingass defines it as follows: "a black earth brought from a mountain in Kashan; a coloured stone, very soft, used by glass-maker". This definition could as well be a description of cobalt. Thus, if we accept the hypothesis *(x) soleymani* = cobalt, there only remains to explain what the recipe was used for.

Let us return to the context in which this formula appears. Kashani talks of imitation lapis (*lajvard-e 'amali,* the same word as the one earlier used by Simi to describe the mixture of indigo and ceruse). He has just described the characteristics of lapis and how to wash it (this part is missing in the edition). It is apparent that the washing of the lapis is for its use in painting, since it cannot be used in ceramics. The substance produced by his formula is a solid that has to be recrushed. It has therefore to be used in the form of a powder, which excludes the idea of imitation lapis for jewellery. We do not know whether this powder is meant to be heated again, for ceramics, or whether it can produce an acceptable blue pigment. This latter possibility seems ruled out by the text by the "pseudo-Tusi" who, as we saw earlier, says that this colour is not suited to painting. However, although there is no proof in the texts, it is not impossible that other forms of cobalt have been used, such as smalt (blue potassium and cobalt silicate) used in painting in Europe from the 16th century, as the Elizabethan painter Nicholas Hilliard[118] points out.

Experimentation

The risky matter of experimenting with formulae has nevertheless enabled me to make an assessment of the extent of difficulty experienced in washing lapis. It appears from these experiments that the simplest formula, the one which consists in washing in successive amounts of water, does not produce the ultramarine colour, but a much lighter and more impure pigment. The process which consists in decanting the ground lapis in soapy water gives better results. The formula which provides the best pigment is, however, the one given by Cennino Cennini:[119] the lapis powder is mixed with wax and oil and this paste is washed in water; the pigment mixes with the water while the impurities remain in the paste. However, this method involves a great deal of wastage. The other formulae have not yet been tested.

The conducting of experiments shows to what degree the formulae proposed in the texts are vague and insufficient for obtaining satisfactory results. They serve mostly as reminders, and cannot in any way replace the advice of a master. In the case of lapis, unfortunately, the artisans that I met, only paid lip service to the process. None of them undertook the washing of lapis any more, on account of its high price, the difficulty involved in the operations, and the fact that it is easier to buy the synthesized product. The existence of a professional group, specialised in this task, therefore seems fully justified in the royal workshops!

Azurite

This natural blue coloured copper carbonate is called *armenium* by Pliny,[120] on account of its origin. We have seen that according to Forbes, it often replaces lapis in mural painting.[121] Azurite corresponds perhaps to the *syama* of the *Silpạ-sastra.*[122]

- *Red and brown earths*

Red and brown earths are ferruginous pigments which were used in abundance during the Antiquity. Red chalk is perhaps the best known of these pigments which has been described by Pliny and Vitruvius.[123]

Apart from one mention of red earth in the *ᶜUmdat*,[124] only one earth is described in the texts, the *gel-e hormuz*, or Ormuz mud, by Simi and by Seyrafi.[125] We find in the *Mer'at al-estelah*[126] mention being made of a marine mud (*gel-e bahri*) perhaps similar to the Ormuz mud. Mention is also made of the Armenian earth (*gel-e armani*), whose nature is not specified (see also "lac" in Dyes). It is however very likely that ochres (ferruginous earths) were also used in painting, considering that they are still found easily to this day, in shops and in nature, and their manufacture is very simple. Moreover, several mixtures of pigments can easily provide browns: orpiment and black; cinnabar, green and black, for instance.

- ***Blacks***

Black pigments applied to painting are not described in the texts, probably because their nature is obvious: made from carbons (animal, mineral or plant), their manufacture is very easy. The carbon -some lamp black, an animal or vegetable fat, some charcoal or crushed kernels- is mixed with gum, in the same way as for ink, but in such a way as to obtain a thicker liquid.

- ***Metals***

Gold and silver have been abundantly used as pigments in painting. Occasionally we find mention of brass and copper (Simi). Their preparation is similar to that of other metals. Tin is still used to this day in India, giving some very shiny, slightly silvery greys, but this metal is not mentioned anywhere in the texts. The method for dissolving is the same for all metals, but the authors of treatises have described it particularly with reference to gold. Teflisi explains how to dissolve gold only in the chapter devoted to the preparation of elements for alchemy. This preparation is unsuitable for painting.[127]

Before being dissolved, the gold is beaten into leaves: "Out of a piece of pure gold of one *mesqal*, the *zarkuban* (gold beaters) make a hundred leaves"[128]. I have had the opportunity of watching this process in Jaipur. The gold beaters place the piece of gold between two skins, then into a leather bag and hammer it during the entire day (almost eight hours). The piece of gold is cut exactly into two, then into four, then into eight, thus creating more and more leaves of increasing fineness. At each division, finer and finer skins are placed between the gold leaves. When the hammering is over, each gold foil is placed between two sheets of silk paper. It is in this state that the gold is turned into a solution.

Simi[129] suggests that we take some gold leaves (experience shows that at least ten leaves are required) and some liquified black gum. A little of this gum is poured into a porcelain container and the leaves are dropped in one by one. With hands washed in *raqi*[130] soap, the mixture is kneaded using the tips of the index and middle fingers of the right hand, till it is well mixed. A lot of clear water is then poured in and the hands and container are washed clean. The mixture is left to stand till the gold settles at the bottom. The superfluous water is thrown out.[131]

The method suggested by Sadeqi[132] is almost identical to the one that I was able to observe in Jaipur. Sadeqi suggests we take some gum (*serishòm,* animal gum) and add a little salt during the kneading. The Jaipur craftsman used acacia gum (*mimosa arabica*) and not salt. Some drops of gum are put on an enamelled metal tray and spread with the hand. The fold leaves are lifted up by sticking them to the side of the hand, and they are placed on the tray, two by two where they stick to the gum. They are worked with the side of the hand, then some more leaves are added. When all the gold leaves have been mixed with the gum, it is all kneaded with the palm of the hand, and moistened very slightly so that it slides well on the tray. This operation (for ten gold leaves) lasts around half an hour. Then the tray and the hand are rinsed in water and the gold is allowed to settle. The top of this water is then poured out and left again to decant. The deposit is quickly washed again and passed through a piece of cloth in a porcelain cupel. The tray is then rinsed and the water poured into the same cloth. The solution is left to settle down in the cupel and all the surface water is progressively thrown out. Just before use, a drop of gum is added to the gold and mixed with a brush.

Although this is not indicated in the treatises, it is customary to use one brush exclusively for gold, as well as a special mug for the water so as to recuperate the gold particles which get deposited each time the brush is dipped in the water. This is understandable, considering the price of gold.

As was seen earlier, some "imitations of gold" are suggested in the treatises. These are made of a white base (talc or tin ceruse) and saffron in a gum solution. The result however must be closer to yellow than to gold!

The *'Umdat*[133] suggests an imitation of silver made of talc, tutty (zinc sulphide?[134]) and vinegar.

- ***Mixtures of colours***

The treatises rarely give indications about the mixing of colours, probably because this is more a matter determined by the sensitivity of each artist, and it does not necessitate any particular technique. However, it is only through experience that we discover that some colours, depending on their nature and their preparation, do not mix together, or give unhoped for results. Nevertheless, Teflisi suggests the following mixtures:

-ceruse and indigo	= light blue (*lajvardi-ye sefid*),
- " " minium	= skin pink (*gune-ye mardom*),
- " " lac	= pink (*golgun*)
- " " cinnabar	= pink (?) (*ogar-gun* ?)
- " " verdigris	= pale green (*zengari-ye sefid*)
-lapis, cinnabar and lac	= violet (*banafshe*),
-realgar and indigo	= mid night blue (*nilgun*)

Sadeqi sums up the mixing of colours[135] in a very poetic way:

"When you want to mix colours,
You need clean and pure pigments.
Whatever much or little you do with them,
Mix two colours, the lover and the beloved"[136]

While in present day Iran, the technique of "traditional" or *miniyatur* (!) painting has practically disappeared, in India, on the contrary, it remains relatively alive, particularly as far as the making of colours is concerned. It should be noted here that research on pigments based on 19th century documents in Hindi[137] has revealed some formulae very similar to those used at present, for example, in Jaipur. It is interesting that already in the 19th century, the greens and the blues particularly were imported (*angrezi*) colours.

3. Mediums

Once the pigments have been prepared and before they are used, it is necessary to mix them with a medium. This enables them to adhere to the ground. Teflisi remarks on this subject:

"Know that the colours which we want to put on paper have to be mixed with gum arabic; if we want (colours) that are more oily, that is to say for objects made of wood, they have to be mixed with egg yolk, so that they become bright; the colours that we would like to use for the matrix design (*qaleb*) on cloth, have to be mixed with *ab-e khun* (blood water?[138])."

He adds further on:

"For each colour that we want to mix, we must first make a gum (*asrash*), then the "substance" (*owre*) of the colour."[139]

Sadeqi says about glue colours (*rangha-ye serishomi*):[140]

"If you make a binding element (*bosteman*) in proportion,
the glue should be within the norms
If your colour does not have enough binding agent (*cashni*)
it will come unstuck when dry
If on the contrary there is too much, it will crackle;
experiments with these proportions have to be carried out."

The word *bosteman* is found again in the *khateme* of the *Golestan-e honar*:[141]
"agar bosteman-e tala kam ast, digar bosteman kon"
"If the binding element of gold is insufficient, add some more".

This same word is found again in the *Resale-ye jeld-sazi*, as a binding or flotation agent in colours for marbled paper.[142] It is the Madras manuscript of this text which specifies the vocalisation *bosteman* (and not *basteman*).

- *Gum Arabic*

This is the binding agent par excellence both for inks and for paints. Apart from metals which are sometimes mixed with glues (see Simi about gold), the colours are all mixed with gum arabic in the descriptions by Simi.

Sadeqi, on the other hand, mentions no gum. In fact, apart from "oil colours" (*rang-o-rowghan*) the formulae that he gives for colours concern only their production and not their dissolving (see below "colours with glue").

In the *'Umdat*, most of the recipes for inks and for *liq* give gum arabic as the medium. In chapter VI (description of colours), several recipes mention no binding agent. However, out of thirty recipes, fifteen use gum, either alone or mixed with other binding agents. Out of twenty-nine recipes for coloured inks, twenty-one make use of gum. This is also the case for twenty-three out of the twenty-five recipes for *liq*.[143]

The *Resale-ye khoshnevisi*[144] suggests a way of testing colours to know whether they contain enough gum:

> "Once the colour has been spread out and dried, it is rubbed with a piece of cloth: if the colour comes off, that means there is not enough gum in it."

- *Glue*

There are plant or animal glues. Plant glues (*serish*, asphodel glue) are mentioned only by Sadeqi, and only applied to the preparation of the ground for lacquer (*batane*). In his paragraph on "colours with glue" (*rangha-ye serishomi*), Sadeqi is not explicit about the glue he is talking about. It is probably goat glue (collodion). It is probably also the one that Simi uses for gold and silver solutions, and which he calls *serishom-e siyah*.[145] Mir 'Ali suggests vaguely for cinnabar that glue or gum be used:

"*shangarf be ab-e serishom ya samgh besereshand.*"[146]

In the *'Umdat*, mention is being made of the use of fish glue as a medium, in a recipe for *liq* and in one for lapis, but in neither case is it used along.[147]

- *Other binding agents*

Sarcocolla (*'anzarut*) is used in the preparation of verdigris, but gum is also added (see "verdigris"). Sadeqi also mentions sarcocolla but not as a binding agent (see below "Corrections").

Saponaria (*ashnan*) is used in the production of the colour ruby red (see "Lacs") and is apparently the only "binding agent" added to this recipe.

Gum-lac, combined with gum arabic in one recipe, and alone in another, is mentioned in the *'Umdat*.[148]

The white or egg yolk are used in some recipes. Teflisi insists on it as a binding agent for all painting on wood.[149] The egg yolk serves as a binding in a recipe for a gold solution in the *Majmu'at al-sanaye'*.[150]

Naptha (*naft-e eskandari*) is mentioned in the same text as a binding agent for orpiment.[151] Chardin says moreover that the Persians use naptha oil for painting and for varnish.[152]

Binding agents for special techniques

While the basic pigments remain the same for the different techniques of painting, the medium changes according to its use. Thus, oil paints, lacquers and colours for marbling require mediums that are not soluble in water. We have already seen the binding/flotation agent for colours in the case of marbled paper (see above). Let us now look at other techniques.

Colours for lacquer

In his treatise Sadeqi describes the colours for making lacquer (*rang-o-rowghan*[153]). On the ground (*batane*, see "Grounds"), the colours mixed with oil (probably linseed oil but it is not specified), are applied flat. This is what Sadeqi calls *rang-e jasmi* (see below "Application of colours"). Another solution for the background is to cover it with silver leaf (*noqre-push*). After the background and the painting of details, a varnish covers the painting, the *rowghan-e kaman*, or literally, the "oil of the bow". Undoubtedly this name is due to the fact that this varnish was used for bows, as Chardin also points out. He mentions these Persian varnishes on two occasions:

> "The bows of Persia are the most beautiful and the most prized in the entire East. The material is wood and horn placed one on top of the other and covered with ribs, and on the top with the very smooth and uniform bark of a tree; then it is painted and varnished. They do this admirably well as they take great pride in these bows which are found in the brightest colours."[154]
>
> "This varnish which is so beautiful and which our masters admire so much is made only of sandarac and of linseed oil, mixed together and reduced to the consistency of a paste or an ointment. When they want to use it, they dissolve it with naptha, or failing that, with spirits of wine rectified several times."[155]

Sadeqi describes the way to make this oil[156] with sandarac and linseed oil, which are boiled to the required consistency. It may be recalled that this *rowghan-e kaman* is also mentioned in the *Majmu'at al-sanaye'* for lacquer grounds (see earlier). A detailed description of the manufacture of these colours is also given, much later, in the *Matla' al-'olum* of Vajed 'Ali (1261/1845):[157]

> "Painters who want to paint objects on wood or other grounds, must first of all prepare oil colours. This is done by a mixture of resin of *Shorea robusta* (*ral**) and linseed oil (*alsi**); the resin is melted over heat and linseed oil is added; some people use sandarac instead, which is preferable as resin takes three or four days to dry; others replace linseed oil with turpentine (*tarpin**)".

According to H.Wulff,[158] a coat of this oil is painted on the ground before the colours, and another one after, on top. In the chapter on pen-cases and other objects in the *Resale-ye jeld-sazi*, the medium and the varnish are not specified; the colours mentioned are gold, silver, black, red, yellow.[159]

Oil colours

What we understand as oil colours in the West, appeared at a relatively late date in the Indo-Iranian world. Probably the large compositions of the *Cehel-sotun* palace in Isfahan and the paintings in the Armenian houses in Jolfa are their forerunners. That is undoubtedly why this technique is never mentioned in the texts. Nevertheless, all the ingredients required for oil painting "in the European way" are mentioned in some later texts, such as the *Matla' al-'olum* which we have just referred to.

4. Application of colours and polishing

Once the preparatory drawing has been completed, the colouring of the composition starts. Some unfinished miniatures enable us to study the progressive arrangement of the colours. N.Titley, for instance, shows a miniature in which only the silvers have been placed.[160] This example enables us to verify some points: the calligraphy is already done; it has been executed on a page ruled with silk thread (*mastar*), and the border (*jadval*) is already painted. The general composition appears clearly drawn with a brush. The silvers, darkened through oxidisation, appear in flat tints. Another painting, also incomplete, is reproduced by A.-M. Kevorkian and J.P. Sicre,[161] and shows a painting in a more advanced stage: all the background colours are in place, juxtaposed as in a mosaic, without the outlines drawn. But let us return to the texts.

Teflisi indicates that, once the drawing has been made (*rasm*), the background (*astar*) has to be coloured, then the "stuff" (*owre*) has to be drawn and the desired colours applied.[162] It should be noted that *astar* normally indicates the lining of a dress or a hat and can therefore be placed very naturally under "stuff".

These words, which may appear to be replete with imagery, must actually have had a technical meaning known to those in the profession. In fact, we find Sadeqi using the term *astar* to indicate the priming of the lacquer ground on which the *jasmi* (i.e. "consistent") colours are placed, forming the *rukesh*, the binding board.[163]

Sadeqi divides "oil colours" into two categories: *jasmi* and *noqre-push*.[164] These words which describe the flat surfaces which serve as a background to lacquered paintings, do not appear in other texts, as far as I know. One can therefore wonder whether they are used only for lacquered paintings. In an article on "The art of making pen-boxes", A.Zabeh sets the *jasmi* ("corporeal") colours in contrast with the *ruhi* ("spiritual") colours.[165] The former could be explained as "opaque colours" and the latter as "transparent ones". However, this author does not mention his sources. It is likely that he may have been inspired by the text of Sadeqi, the only one, as far as I know, which has mentioned the *jasmi* colours (unless perhaps this word continues to be used as a technical term ?). This opposition is therefore a mere hypothesis, particularly since in Sadeqi, these *jasmi* colours, which we could consider as "opaque", are not contrasted with "spiritual" or "transparent" colours, but with the *noqre-push*, or silver foil surface, which is just as opaque. It is against these "opaque" or "consistent" (*jasmi*) or silver foil (*noqre-push*) background that the details are painted.[166]

- *Shosteman*

Another stage of the colouring described by Sadeqi is called *shosteman*.[167] This word appears in the beginning of the 15th century, in the *'urze-dasht* of the Baysanqor workshop:

> "*naqqashan (...) haftad-o panj cub-e kharqah-ha be rang-amiz va shosteman mashghul and*"[168]

"The painters are busy painting and making the *shosteman* of 75 tent poles". Dust Mohammad also uses this word in his Preface when talking about the painter Ghiyas al-din:

> *"Be alvan-e fetne angiz rang amiz nemud va be khun-e jegar va ab-e dide-ye pakize-ye abr shosteman farmude be etmam resanid."*[169]

"He coloured with the colours of delight and he ensured that the *shosteman* was executed with the blood of the heart and the pure tears of the cloud".

Although this lyrical context does not tell us much about the meaning of the word *shosteman*, we should probably, here again, consider it as having a technical meaning, used in a metaphorical sense.

Let us recall the context in which this word appears, in Sadeqi:

I will now describe the method of *shosteman* (...)
There are two types of *shosteman*, one as good as the other,
One is *dam-shu*, the other *mian-shu*.
If you make your drawing on the "full-blown" colour
Then don't deviate from the rules of the *dam-shu*.
If on the contrary, you are executing the background (*bum*),
Then make use of the *mian-shu*.
After which spread a good coat of oil...."[170]

The expression *dam-shu* presupposes an operation on colour that has already been applied, whereas *mian-shu* is the background itself. Probably these words apply only to the technique of "oil colours" or lacquer. Dickson[171] translates verses 88-91 of Sadeqi, on the subject of the *shosteman*, as "On the art of tinting with washes" and uses a passage from Cennini to support this (see his note 11). However, the passage from the Italian treatise refers to drawing on tinted paper. The French translation of Cennini text (chap. XXXI) is: "How you should draw and shade on tinted paper with water colour and highlight with white."[172] Dickson's interpretation, based on Cennini, which seems to suggest a sort of relief technique, appears inappropriate in the context of "oil colours".

It seems to me, from the three passages mentioned above, and considering that the term *shosteman* (for Sadeqi's *dam-shu*, and certainly in the two earlier cases) refers to an operation carried out on the painting, that its most likely meaning would be that of a varnish. This appears probable for the tent poles mentioned in the *'arze-dasht*, but also for Dust Mohammad's metaphor. In the case of the *miyan-shu*, it could relate to a preliminary layer of varnish (or lacquer) applied to the background.[173]

- *Finishing touches and "relief"*

After applying the colours in flat tints, there remains a last stage: the final drawing. This concerns the details of each figure, the features of the face, the design of the clothing, the details of flowers, of animals, of the landscape, the ornamental designs on the clothes and the architecture, and the last outlining of the contours. In Western painting, at this stage, the details of relief would also be executed, giving volume to the painted objects through the play of light and shade. Depending on the techniques (oil or water colour, charcoal and chalk...), this relief can be achieved by adding paint, or, on the contrary, by removing some pigment at places. In general, the Iranian painter prefers to add on some touches of paint with an almost dry brush, in such a way as to show the folds of clothes, the down of a beard, or the uneven forms of rocks. The other process, which is much rarer, and only possible with water colours, consists in making furrows in the pictorial surface with the end of the brush, working it in such a way as to obtain the desired roundness. This is a kind of tinting which is, however, extremely rare in Iranian painting. This could perhaps be the process used by the painter of a miniature in the *Shah-name* of Shah Tahmasp, to make some rocks.[174] It seems to me that most of the rocks of the Shah Tahmasp school owe their smoothness to a technique of this kind, similar therefore to a wash (see also "The court of Kayumars" painted by Soltan Mohammad). However, it would be necessary to carry out some study under low-angled light and with a magnifying glass to estimate the variations in the level of the pictorial surface. This is therefore just a hypothesis.

Generally, however, Iranian painting can be distinguished by its absence of relief at least till the time of Mohammad Zaman, in the second half of the 17th century. Iranian painting, as we noted for colours, pays no attention to light: night is shown as bright daylight. The notion of relief is therefore limited, restricted to drapery folds and some details. An enlargement of a face in profile, depicting Iblis, with his hooked nose, shows indeed that it is not just flat -outlined by a line marking the nose, the eyes and the mouth-, but made up of a large number of brush strokes of different colours which accentuate certain parts and suggest, if not relief, at least expression.[175] What a far-cry from the roundness of Western painting of the same period!

- *Polishing*

Once the painting is completely finished, it has to be polished (*jala dadan*[176]). This is not the first polishing that the ground undergoes: we have seen that white paper is first polished after being starched. A second polishing is done after the gold or silver have been applied. These are painted before the other colours and polished on the right side up, with a small polishing instrument of hard stone or ivory. Simi recommends, after gold calligraphy, that it be polished very gently with jade or with onyx.[177] Similarly the golden line of the *jadval* is polished before other colours are applied (see earlier). Sadeqi points out an intermediary polishing of the painting with a "Bagdad brick" (*khesht-e Baghdadi*). But this relates perhaps to a process which only concerns "oil colours"?[178]

In general, the final polishing is done on the back of the paper, on a slab of marble or glass. However, for manuscript paintings, and particularly if the paintings are on both sides of the page, a thin paper is placed over the painting before polishing, so as to protect it from the direct rubbing of the polishing instrument. The polishing is done with the right side up.

NOTES

1. M. Pastoureau, in *Sublime indigo*, p.20.
2. Levi-Strauss, p.61.
3. C.-H. de Fouchécour, p.170.
4. C.-H. de Fouchécour, p.171.
5. Ed. pp.23-25.
6. *A'in*, I, 96.
7. Pastoureau, *id.*
8. H.E. Stapleton *et al.*, p.403.
9. *Id.*; it is interesting to note that a metal corresponds to each planet, and therefore to each colour.
10. Ed. Vahid-e Dastgerdi, according to the order of the colours, pp.180-181; 196-197; 214; 234; 266-267; 291; 315.
11. Ed. pp.73-76.
12. *Id.* pp.110-112.
13. Stapleton, p.404.
14. Seyrafi Sha'er, ed. p.30.
15. *De la théorie des couleurs*, published in 1810.
16. C. Levi-Strauss, p.329; see also Henry Corbin, "*Mundus imaginalis* ou l'imaginaire et l'imaginal".
17. On the other hand, gypsum, which gives greyish white, is found in Pendzhikent and in Dilberdzhin. Purer whites are obtained from clays or from kaolin and from natural or artifical calcium carbonate (plaster). Pliny mentions some white earths such as *paraetonium* and *melinum* (Pliny, book 35, 19, p.468). The *Silpa sastra* mention white clay, *sitamrad*; see Gunasinghe, p.43.
18. *Bayan*, p.303.
19. *Id.*, p.346.
20. See Y.Porter, "Notes sur le *Golestan-e honar*".
21. *'Arayes*, ed., chap.5, p.,234.
22. There is a common confusion between minium and cinnabar; see below.
23. As a reminder Khvaje Mirak was a descendant of the *kamangar* of Herat

and he practised this art; see Dust Mohammad, ed. Bayani I, p.199.

24. *Tansuq name*, p.219.
25. Ed. lines 163-176.
26. Ed. "anonymous", p.300.
27. *Bab* 27, fol. 33b-34a.
28. Laufer, *Sino-Iranica*, p.512.
29. Ed. "anonymous", pp.299-300.
30. Transl. Levey, p.29; *Buqalamun*, fol.138b.
31. Teflisi (p.346) and *Golestan*, which mentions it; Simi (fol. 138b); *Majmu'at*, *bab* 22, *fasl* 5, fol. 26a and *bab* 29 *fasl* 11, fol.37a; *Matla' al-'olum*, fol.309b; *Kholasat al-mojarrabat*, fol. 137a (*harital**).
32. *Bayan*, text p.353.
33. Ed. p.300.
34. Jamali Yazdi, p.360.
35. Chardin, IV, 114.
36. *Calligraphes*, p.20.
37. *Farrokh-name*, p.360.
38. Pliny, book 35, 39.
39. *Id.*
40. *Bab* 16, *fasl* 2, fol. 21a.
41. Pliny, book 34, 35; Vitruvius, p.248; Forbes, p.214.
42. *Bayan*, p.346.
43. *Tansuq-name*, pp. 178-179.
44. *Bab*, 29 *fasl* 11, fol.37a.
45. Vitruvius, pp.245-247; Pliny, book 33, 118.
46. Vitruvius, *id.*
47. *Tansuq-name*, pp.207-209.
48. Ed. pp.298-299.
49. *Medad al-khotut*, p.121.
50. Transl. Levey, pp.25-26.
51. *De artibus*, transl. chap.34, pp.40-41.
52. Gunasinghe, p.45.
53. *Bayan*, p.304.
54. Stapleton, p.365
55. Ed. lines 181-184.
56. *Bab* 16, fol. 20b-22b; seven recipes for cinnabar are given, (1) *rumi*, (2) *zavoli*, in fact, minium, see earlier, (3) *forsi* (? doubtful spelling), (4) *mosaffa*, (5) *rumi* (mentioned for the second time, perhaps standing for *farangi*, mentioned in the title), (6) cinnabar for colouring glass, (7) *romani*.
57. See Maqbul Ahmad, p.429.
58. Stapleton p.365,
59. *Bab* 20, *fasl* 7, fol. 25b.
60. *Medad al-khotut*, p.121.
61. *Bab* 20 *fasl* 1, fol. 25a.

62. Teflisi, p.345.
63. Simi, ed. p.298; Mir Ali, p.121.
64. Transl. Levey, p.30.
65. Ed. lines 185-190.
66. See this transl. of the *Qanun* by Sadeqi, in S.C. Welch, *The Houghton Shahnama*, pp.259-270, verses 183-188 and his note 43.
67. *Science and technology*, p.160.
68. In *Jeld-sazi* see our "*Kaqaz-e abri*, notes sur la marbrure", note 34.
69. Ed. p.347; the recipe for violet is defective in the *khateme* of the *Golestan*, ed. p.167. transl. p.198.
70. See Y.Porter, "Une traduction persane", table 1 nos. 7, 9, 13.
71. *Id.* nos. 2, 10, 18, 56.
72. Ed. p. 300.
73. This is also mentioned in the *Silpa* which also suggests a mixture of orpiment and azurite: Gunasinghe, pp.46 and 48.
74. It has however also been found at Shahrestan, see G. Azarpay, *Sogdian painting*, p.165.
75. It is however found in Dilberdzhin. R.J. Forbes also points out that from the VIth dynasty in Egypt, artificial chrysocolla was manufactured; see Forbes, p.222.
76. Vitruvius, pp.245, 248 and 250.
77. Ed. p.299 and *Medad al-khotut*, p.121.
78. Simi, Ms., fol. 47a; the anonymous version of Hamadan (ed. p.35) is, here, the closest to that of the London. ms.
79. Mir 'Ali, ed. p.121.
80. *Bab* 17, *fasl* 1 to 7, fol. 22b-23b.
81. See this name also in Dyes.
82. See this dye; this name appears also elsewhere in the *Majmu'at* concerning a dye for the hands (*khazab*), *bab* 15 *fasl* 5, fol. 20b.
83. This process of oxidization with dung is well known to alchemists, see Maqbul Ahmad p.443.
84. M.Tosi, "The lapis-lazuli trade...".
85. According to R.Besenval (unpublished).
86. F.Vallat, p.57.
87. A. Labrousse. and R. Boucharlat, p.83.
88. Forbes, III, p.214.
89. *De Artibus*, pp.21-25.
90. See Zavesh, pp. 245-253; the texts quoted without references are those mentioned by this author.
91. *'Arayes al-javaher*, p.137.
92. Mohammad b. Mansur Dastaki, *Javaher-name-ye soltani* gives an absolutely identical description (see Zavesh); same for Tusi, *Tansuq-name*, pp.116-117.
93. *al-Jamaher*, see Zavesh *op.cit.*
94. Zavesh, pp.249-250.
95. See Biruni, Kashani, *op.cit.*; Simi ed. p.298.

96. Zavesh, pp.251-152, could it be Tusi? However, this text is reportedly different from the *Tansuq-name*, in which this passage does not appear.
97. *Bayan*, p.346.
98. Ed. p.298.
99. Seyrafi Sha'er, ed. p.39.
100. Qazi Ahmad, ed. p.165, transl. pp.196-197.
101. The "Iraqi soap" is mentioned in the *Mer'at al-estelah* (fol. 189a) as a soap used for bleaching; Simi mentions *raqi* soap in gold solution (see below); Chardin (IV, p.149-150) mentions the one from Alep as being the best.
102. *Bab* 18 *fasl* 3, fol. 24a.
103. See this in Dyes.
104. Forbes, p.224. He specifies that the manufacture of this false lapis or Egyptian frit goes back to the IVth dynasty and that frit furnaces have been discovered at El-Amarna.
105. p.248.
106. See also the article by C.Kiefer and Allibert, "Les céramiques bleues pharaoniques".
107. Ed. p.298; this formula does not appear in the manuscript.
108. M.Chandra, p.26; Doerner, p.78.
109. *Shekar-sang* and *malh-e shakhar* are mentioned later by Kashani for making ceramics; see *'Arayes*, p.439 and Allan, pp.111-112.
110. (*Su-ni-po*), see *Chinese porcelain from Ardabil*, p.84.
111. Laufer, *Sino-Iranica*, however does not mention this.
112. Ed. p.339.
113. Allan, pp.111-120
114. *Tansuq-name*, p.77.
115. *Kani shenasi*, pp.208-213 and Index.
116. *Bab* 10 *fasl*. 4, fol.18a.
117. *Bab* 9 *fasl*. 4, fol.16a.
118. See, N. Hilliard, pp.93-94.
119. Transl. D.V. Thompson, pp.37-38.
120. Pliny, book 35, 28.
121. Forbes, p.214.
122. Gunasinge, p.48.
123. Pliny, book 35, 13.
124. Transl. Levey, p.31.
125. Simi (anonymous) ed. p.300; Seyrafi Sha'er, *Golzar-e Safa*, ed. pp.40-41.
126. Anand Ram, fol.228a.
127. *Bayan*, p.307.
128. Simi, ed.297.
129. *Id.*
130. See this word with relation to the washing of lapis; the B.L. ms. and the Hamadan version give *sabus* (bran) instead of *sabun* (soap), the adjective *raqi* or *'eraqi* is not mentioned; the use of bran however seems inappropriate

here.

131. Some similar formulae are suggested in Seyrafi's *Golzar-e Safa*, ed. p.38; Mir Ali Heravi, p.122.
132. Ed. lines 95-108.
133. Transl. Levey, p.28; *Resale-ye buqalamun*, fol. 125b-126a.
134. See Laufer, pp.511-514 and "Whites", zinc.
135. As we shall see in Part Two, *rang-amizi* does not only mean the action of "mixing colours", but it is also an attribute of the painter, which we would then be more inclined to translate as "colourer" (*rang-amiz*).
136. Ed. lines 85-86.
137. Agar Chand Nahatta, "*Chitra aur rang banane*", an approximate translation in English is found in Srivastava, *Punjab Painting*, pp.70-71.
138. This word is not clear; it should perhaps be likened to the *khun-ab* Simi uses for making verdigiris (see above).
139. *Bayan*, p.347; the term *owre* is also used in connection with the application of the colours, see later.
140. *Qanun*, lines 155-157; the same remarks on the proportions of the binding element in the pigment are made in the *Silpa*, see Gunasinghe, p.54.
141. Qazi Ahmad, ed. p.166; transl. p.197.
142. Ed. p.142; see also earlier, "Marbled paper".
143. See transl. Levey and Y.Porter, "Une traduction persane du traité d'Ibn Badis", tabl. 2 and 3.
144. Ms. Patna, fol. 14a.
145. Ed. p.297.
146. *Medad al-khotut*, p.121.
147. Transl Levey, pp.29 and 32.
148. *Id.* p.23.
149. Ed. p.345.
150. *Bab* 5, *fasl.* 2, fol. 13a.
151. *Bab* 22, *fasl* 5, fol. 26a.
152. *Voyages*, IV, 87.
153. Ed. lines 126-134.
154. *Voyages*, IV, 136.
155. *Id.* V, 204.
156. Ed. lines 191-204.
157. Ms. fol. 309a-310a.
158. p.239.
159. See ed. p.126 and our "Grounds for oil-based mediums".
160. p.220, fig.72; see also our plate no7.
161. p.74.
162. *Bayan*, p.348.
163. *Qanun*, line 132, see also "Grounds".
164. *Id.*, ed. lines 135-148.
165. A. Zabeh, p.25.

166. *Qanun*, lines 140 and 148.
167. *Id.*, lines 88-95.
168. *Fac-sim.* in Lowry, *Timur*, p.160; see also transl. Thackston, *id*, p.364; the latter uses the translation of the word suggested by Dickson, see below.
169. Ed. p.199.
170. Ed. lines 87-94.
171. See S.C. Welch, *The Houghton Shahnama*, I, pp.259-270.
172. French transl. pp.21-22; transl. Thompson pp.17-18.
173. For an insight into the technique of Iranian lacquer, see G.Fehervari, "The Near East, the Middle East and India", in J.Bourne *et al.*, pp.150-169.
174. S.C. Welch, *Wonders of the Age*, p.78 and colour detail p.81; this author attributes the painting to Aqa Mirak.
175. Welch, *id*, p.55, pl.10.
176. Sadeqi, *Qanun*, line 94b.
177. Ed. p.297.
178. *Qanun*, line 92; "Baghdad brick" must be a sort of polishing device about which we have no knowledge.

5

SUBJECTS OF THE PAINTINGS

We shall now attempt to discover what names Persian painters and poets give to the subjects of their paintings or their descriptions. The first part of the chapter will be devoted to figurative painting, and the other to non-figurative or decorative painting. We must begin with a definition of both these kinds of painting, and then analyse the words used to describe them.

In fact, a word understood in its technical sense, may stand for a very precise object, but, used in a poetic context, it may lose its technical value. Similarly, as we saw in the case of the perception of colours, a poetic description is often inappropriate to define a real object.

1. The portrait

Form and meaning

A portrait is most of the time called *surat*, that is to say, literally, "form". While, in painting, this word or its synonyms are clear, in poetry, on the contrary, the ambiguous meaning of *surat* leaves the field open to the interpretation of the poet. Several epics, in Persian literature, relate the story of a portrait of such grace and attraction as to steal the heart of whoever looked at it. Such was the case of the portrait of Khosrow painted by Shapur,[1] or Hosn painted by Khiyal.[2] Just like a dream, the portrait is capable of causing enchantment and giving rise to passion. The perfection of such portraits even enable Nushabe to recognise Alexander, despite his disguise.[3] That is because the portrait goes beyond the imitation of nature: it is not just the reproduction of a form but it bears within it the very meaning (essence) of the form.[4]

Here is what Sadeqi says about the portraits painted by his master,

Mozaffar Ali:

> "If he desired to paint someone's portrait,
> He did in such a way that it was like the original image.
> None could find a difference,
> Except as regards movement and rising."[5]

Similar descriptions are common in poetry; now when we look at the portraits of the Safavid period, nothing seems farther from a "realistic" portrait. A line from Sadeqi enlightens us on this matter:

> "I have become so skilled in the art of portraiture,
> that I have taken the path away from the formal image (*surat*)
> towards the inner meaning (*ma'ni*)."[6]

It becomes clear thereafter that what is sought, is not a duplication of the "real", original image (*surat*), but a higher vision of reality, which transcends the object (*ma'ni*, the "meaning" par excellence). Sadeqi adds, about the "art of portraiture":

> "No one will ever be free from error
> Not even Mani or Behzad"[7]

It shows that, beyond photographic perfection, it is the emotion or the hidden meaning of reality that is sought after.

A lot more could be said on this matter, which would undoubtedly overstep the bounds of our study. It appears that the adoption of a conceptual pictorial language such as that of "miniature", which takes such little account of "realism" is, in a way, a manner of defence against a taboo placed on the image. At any rate, the fear of this taboo discouraged the formation of a concept of "realistic" art. Proof of this lies in the rarity of the sculpture in the round in Islamic countries, and also the superstition with which the photography is viewed by the general public.

Moreover, the preference given to "meaning" over "form" is also one of the most profound aspects of Sufism. Thus, in connection with painting from the reign of Akbar, M. Brand[8] quotes the following lines by Amir Beyg Saveji "Peyrovi":

> "O God! I cannot reach the world of the ideal,
> Forgive me if I worship form."[9]

These lines which seem in total contradiction with those of Sadeqi, are used by M. Brand to explain that the painting of Akbar's time is more "realistic" than the Safavid or pre-Akbarian paintings. However, while Peyrovi's idea is acceptable in poetry, it is -contrary to what M. Brand thinks- very different from Akbarian concept of art, which is guided more by these lines of Abu al-Fazl, inspired undoubtedly by Ebn Arabi's[10] notion of *vahdat al-vojud*:

"What we call form (*sovar*) leads us to recognise a body; the body itself leads us to what we call a notion, an idea (*ma'ni*). Thus on seeing the form of a letter, we recognise the letter, and this again will lead us to some idea. Similarly, in the case of what people term a picture."[11]

Surat-gari, the portrait

This term is mentioned by Teflisi,[12] probably in a larger context (i.e.drawing; like, *tasvir* is used without, for all that, meaning a portrait, but any drawing whatsoever), Several words refer to the portrait and are, in fact, synonymous, such as *cehre-gosha'i*, *cehre* (or *surat*) *pardazi*, *shabi-keshi*, and other compound nouns, often used in texts more for their assonance and play of doublets than to indicate a particular technical reality (see "Painting and literature", Part Two Introduction). On the other hand, the terms used in painting to indicate the different poses of the subject, portrait, bust, full-length portrait, and other words used in the West, are almost unknown. The term *yeke surati* indicates the portrait of a single person, and is set against the *majles-sazi*, a group portrait or scène de genre (see below). Most Iranian portraits show three-quarter faces; the profile (*nimrokh*), rarely executed in Iran, is mentioned, as far as I know, in a technical context, only in some Indian texts.[13] It may therefore appear surprising to read in Chardin:

> "It is true that the faces represented give quite a good resemblance; they are generally shown in profile because these are most easily painted; they also paint them in three-quarters; but for full or frontal faces, they are highly unsuccessful, as they don't know how to shade them well."[14]

Several texts, apart from novels, mention some portraits. As we saw earlier, the Sasanid *Khoday-name*, included portraits of kings and queens. Similarly, during the Muslim era, Nezami 'Aruzi relates in his *Cahar maqale* the story of the portrait of Avicenna which Mahmud of Ghazni supposedly commissioned from the painter Abu Nasr 'Eraq

Naqqash.[15] These references, however, tell us nothing about the style of these portraits. On the other hand, what does Eskandar Beyg mean when he reports that Seykh Mohammad Sabzevari "introduced the *farangi* portrait into Iran ('Ajam)"?[16] Similarly, Qazi Ahmad says that Soltan Mohammad "depicted better than the others (painters) the demeanor (*ravesh*) of the Qizilbash."[17] Both these cases relate probably to matters of aesthetic appreciation which we have difficulty in grasping but which also perhaps designate particular types of subjects: the *farangi* portrait perhaps shows the first depiction of Europeans; the demeanor of the Qizilbash is perhaps a way of painting the gallantry of the "red caps". As we have seen with composition, the notions of "art criticism" and the vocabulary which goes with it remain an area still obscure for the Western art historian.

Majles-sazi, group portraits and "scènes de genre"

The word *majles-sazi* indicates paintings in which several persons are shown; there are several types of conventional representations, often meant to decorate the frontispiece of a work, such as banquet scenes (*majles-e bazm*), battle scenes (*sepah pardazi*), hunting scenes (*shekar-gah*). Eskandar Beyg says of Mozaffar 'Ali:

> "*Tasvirat-e dowlat-e dowlatkhane-ye homayun va majles-e eyvan-e cehel sotun tarahi moshar aleyhe.*"[18]

"The figures of fortune of the royal palace and the scenes de genre in the pavilion of the Forty columns have been drawn by the above mentioned (Mozaffar 'Ali)."[19]

The same word is used by Qazi Ahmad to describe the scenes de genre that Shah Tahmasp drew in the palace of Cehel Sotun of Qazvin.[20] This passage about the qualities of Shah Tahmasp as a painter is certainly borrowed from the work of 'Abdi Beyg Shirazi, *Dowhat al-azhar*.[21] In this the author describes the paintings in the palaces of Qazvin, among these being: *Majles-e bazm va shekargah* (scenes of feasting and hunting), *Majles-e Yusuf va Zoleykha va dast boridan-e zanan-e mesr* (scene of Yusuf and Zoleykha: the Egyptian women cut their own hands), *Majles-e qabaq andazi va cabok savaran* (scene of a game of *qabaq*, "bow and arrow", and agile horsemen).[22]

Eskandar Beyg says that Siyavush Beyg excelled in battle scenes (*sepah pardazi*) and scenes de genre (*majles-sazi*).[23]

To describe the scene showing the court of Kayumars painted by Soltan Mohammad, Dust Mohammad uses the word *mowze'*: "*mowze'-*

e palang-pushan ast"[24] (subject depicting some figures clothed in panther skins); similarly,this word is used several times in the *'arze-dasht* of the Baysanqor workshop in relation with the painters Amir Khalil and Khvaje Ghiyas al-din.[25]

2. Landscapes, animals

Paintings of landscapes, without figures, are very rare in Persian miniatures. However, details of landscapes, mountain for instance, have been noted by authors such as Eskandar Beyg, who says that Siyavush and 'Ali Asghar Kashi were excellent at *kuh-pardazi* (drawing mountains).[26]

Janevar-sazi, animal drawing, is not only a common design in miniatures, but it also constitutes an essential part of the illumination of margins. The description of this kind of painting is however only found in some lines by Sadeqi.[27] This author first of all gives the names of the animals: the *simorgh*, the dragon, the lion, the *gav-e ganj*. This list is not exhaustive; it is, in fact, common to see animals other than those mentioned by Sadeqi. He goes on to describe the *gereft-o-gir*, "animals fighting", a typical theme in Iranian art, starting with the reliefs at Persepolis where animals are shown fighting. He adds that Aqa Mirak is the master of this art, an example of which can be admired in the painting, attributed to him, showing Majnun in the desert, surrounded by animals.[28] Jahangir's painter Mansur, who is mentioned several times by this sovereign for his painting from life of animals and flowers and who is known to us through several signed works shows a style which is much close to our own animal artists.[29]

Other expressions are used by present day Iranian authors to describe composition of animals and of foliage, such as *shakh-o morgh* (branches and birds); as a technical expression, this does not appear in the texts. However, 'Abdi Beyg uses these words to describe the paintings of Qazvin:

"*Neshaste morgh bar shakh-e khata'i*"
(the bird seated on an arabesque/branch in Chinese style) and:
"*ze shakh o barg o morgh-e gune gune*"[30]
(branches, leaves and birds of all kinds and colours).

Yet others,such as *shakh-o barg* (branches and leaves), *gol-o bolbol* (rose and nightingale) are also expressions commonly used by modern Iranian authors.[31]

3. Illumination designs

Most of the animal designs that we have just seen are widely used to decorate margins or the frontispieces of manuscripts. We will therefore confine ourselves here to a study of non-figurative designs only.

The bigoted taboo imposed on the image, during certain periods and in certain regions of the Muslim world, is an obvious factor in the development of non-figurative decorative painting. Thus 'Afif tells us that Firuz Shah Tughluq prohibited the depiction of figures in the paintings of his palace; some non-figurative designs were therefore painted instead:

"*be jay-e suratgari, naqsh-e bustan negarand.*"[32] (in place of portraits, drawings of gardens will be painted).

A "basic system" seems to govern the designs used in illuminations; these are the *haft asl-e naqqashi* (seven basic principles of painting). Appearing in literature probably in the middle of the 16th century, these "seven principles" are mentioned by Sadeqi[33] as well as by other authors, such as Qotb al-din Qesse Khvan and Qazi Ahmad who quotes him.[34] Perhaps the oldest mention of these *haft asl* is the one we find in Qotb al-din Qesse Khvan (964/1557) who names these "seven principles":

"*hamcenan ke dar khatt shesh qalam-e asl ast, dar in fann niz haft qalam mo'tabar ast: eslami, khata'i, farangi, fassali, abr, dagh, gere.*"[35] (as in calligraphy where there are six styles (principles) of writing, similarly in this technique (painting), seven "brushes" can be recognised).

Let us recall the seven names mentioned by Sadeqi:[36] *eslimi, khata'i, abr, vaq, nilufar, farangi, band-e rumi.*

We find in the *Rowzat al-safat* by 'Abdi Beyg Shirazi, composed in 967/1559:[37]

"*Naqsh be haft asl dar u fasl o vasl/hamco sepehrist dar u haft asl*" (the drawing has seven principles attached to it/it is like the sky, which has seven principles).

'Abdi Beyg does not mention here what these "seven principles" are. Nevertheless one could imagine that, since Qotb al-din borrowed the theory of the two reed pens from the *A'in-e eskandari* by 'Abdi Beyg composed in 950/1544,[38] it was the latter who also influenced the idea of associating seven principles with painting to imitate the six basic styles of writing. The origin of this idea is not yet well defined; on the other hand, some of the names of these "seven principles" were known well before the middle of the 16th century. The existence and the meaning of

these words have been the subject of a detailed study.[39] Let us however explore certain details:
-*eslimi* or *eslami*: this design, already mentioned in the *'arze-dasht* of the workshop of Baysanqor (around 1427-28) in relation to the binder Qavvam al-din,[40] was invented by 'Ali himself, according to Dust Mohammad (951/1544):

> "*Dar akhbar cenin amade ast ke avval kasi ke be naqsh va tazhib-e zeynat afzay-e ketabat-e kalam lazem al-tarhib shodand, Hazrat 'Ali b. Abi Taleb al-salam budand (...) va cand barg ke dar 'orf-e naqqashan be "eslami" ma'ruf ast, an hazrat ekhtera' farmude-and.*"[41]

"It is related in the tradition that the first person who encouraged painting and illumination to add to the decoration of the Word was 'Ali son of Abi Taleb...it is he who invented the foliage called "*eslami*" in the language of painters".

The attribution of the invention of an "Islamic" design to 'Ali is of significance. It comes at a historic moment during which the "disciples of 'Ali", the shi'ite Safavids, were in power in Iran. Indeed, the *eslami* is opposed to two other concepts, the Turkish or Byzantian *rumi* and the Chinese *khata'i* (which also means "at fault"). A *beyt* by the poet Omidi is mentioned in the *Mer'at al-estelah*[42] to explain the doublet *eslimi/ khata'i*:

> "*Qaza' dar kargah-e kebria'i/fekande tarh-e eslimi khata'i*"

"Destiny in the divine workshop/has sketched some arabesques (*eslimi*) (in) the *khata'i*".
However, this line is incomprehensible if it is not placed in its proper context: the battle of Chaldiran fought between Shah Esma'il, whose pen name was "Khata'i", and the Ottoman Sultan Selim. This therefore causes confusion, if *eslimi*, the invention of 'Ali, is identified with the Turk!
-*Khata'i*: originally, this word refers to China, Cathay. The Persian taste for a certain literary "exoticism" which turns Mani into a Chinese painter and makes Chinese painted silks the paragon of beauty, is well known.[43] This word also plays on ambiguity: *Khata'i* not only means "Chinese" but also "guilty" and can therefore be opposed to *eslami* or *eslimi* which means "islamic"; for without doubt *eslimi* originally stood for a perfectly non-figurative one, in which not only leaves and branches (*shakh-o-barg*) but also animals are absent. However, this dichotomy gradually disappears (if it ever really existed), and is transformed into a doublet: thereafter *eslimi-khata'i* is used to express every kind of arabesque, as

Anand Ram Mokhles says in 1157/1744, in his definition of this doublet:

> "*Khotuti ke gerd-e noqush keshand va anra gere bandi sazand va dar 'avam be band-e rumi shohrat darad.*"[44]

"The lines that are drawn around designs and from which arabesques are made; the common people call them "*band-e rumi*"."

This late definition is interesting as it brings together three concepts which are, originally, dissociated in the list of the "seven principles": *eslimi, khata'i* and *band-e rumi*. It should be noted that this same definition is given in the *Ceragh-e Hedayat* dictionary, mentioned by Danesh-Pazhuh.[45]

-*Band-e rumi* or *gere-bandi*: This term is used in the *Ma'aser-e Mahmudshahi*, dated 872/1467,[46] to describe the tile decorations made by the Persian craftsmen at the *Bam-e behesht madrasa* in Mandu, in 845/1442:

> "*dar ta'qid-e gere-bandi sefati ejtehad nemude-and*"

"They deployed their best efforts to draw the decorative tracery".

Apart from Sadeqi, 'Abdi Beyg, Qotb al-din and Anand Ram, as we have just seen, this term is used by Dust Mohammad,[47] with regard to Kamal al-din Hoseyn:

> "*va har band-e rumi va katreme ke u sakhte...*"

(and each tracery motif and *katreme* (?[48]) that he made...)

In the translation by Minorsky,[49] *gere* is read as *akrah*, probably on account of the defective writing of the manuscript. However, I think that it is out of the question to consider the suggestion made by Zakhoder that it is the name for Agra. We find *gere* mentioned numerous times in the descriptions of Shahjahanabad, by Mohammad Saleh. For example:

> "*dar taz'in-e saqf-e zarrin-e eyvan-e ghoslkhane ke be tariq bandha-ye delgosha-ye khater-e pasand-e farangi va gereha-ye khosh tarh-e rumi sarasar be sarf-e noh lak rupiye be enjam resanid.*"[50]

"For the decoration of the gilded roof of the palace of the baths, which displays lovely tracery in the style of the Franks, and foliage of beautiful "Byzantian" lines, 9 *lak* rupees were spent".

-*Farangi*: this word probably stands for a foliage of European origin, perhaps similar to the acanthus, which was used later under Louis XV. However, this word appears well before the reign of this king in 'Abdi Beyg,[51] in the declaration of the seven principles by Sadeqi and Qotb al-din and, as we have just seen, in Saleh.

-*Fassali*, which appears in the "seven principles" only in Qotb al-din is mentioned by Qazi Ahmad, not only in the passage borrowed from Qotb al-din about these seven principles, but also in the biography of Abu al-Ma'sum Mirza,[52] and in the *Resale-ye jeld-sazi*.[53] In two latter cases, it is clearly a book-binding term (see below). However, 'Abdi Beyg says:

"*ze fassali-ye hezaran fasl tasvir/nemude nuk-e kelk-e mamlekat-gir.*"[54]

"The nib of the pen which delights the kingdom/has shown the drawing of the *"fassali"* of thousands of seasons".

Fassali is difficult to translate here: on account of *tasvir*, the drawing, it could be felt that it relates to a technical term; but there is question also of *fasl* (season, division); the assonance is easy but is it significant? This word is replaced in Sadeqi's list by *nilufar* (convolvulus). Although mentioned by 'Abdi Beyg in his descriptions,[55] it cannot be said with certainty that it relates to a technical word.

-*Abr* is mentioned, in the context of the "seven principles", by Qotb al-din and Sadeqi. 'Abdi Beyg notes it several times, when referring to description,[56] without it being possible for us to know whether it relates truly to clouds or any particular decorative design. On the other hand, I have shown that in the case of *kaghaz-e abri*, this undoubtedly means marbled paper.[57] It remains to be decided whether *abri*, considered as marbled paper, is really one of the seven principles. Uncertainty hangs over, as for the binding term *fassali*.

-*Vaq* or *dagh*, mentioned by Qotb al-din and Sadeqi, do not appear anywhere else. Some art historians call *vaq-vaq* the tracery design showing heads of animals or of persons, which recalls the *Shahname* tree or the legendary island whose inhabitants grow, according to Qazvini, on trees. It seems curious that so literary a reference should have given rise to the name of a decorative design. At any rate, the design is an old one, and appears, in particular, on a ceramic tile from Kashan, dated 656/1259.[58]

Apart from these "seven principles", other technical expressions exist, which sometimes appear in texts and are still well known in our time. Some of these illumination terms indicate their position in the manuscript, like *dibace* ("preface"), *'onvan* ("title"), *sar-lowh* ("top of the page").

Dibace is mentioned by Mirza Haydar Dughlat concerning a frontispiece on which Mahmud Mozahheb worked for seven years.[59] This same word is used several times in the *'arze-dasht* of the workshop of Baysanqor, in relation to the illuminator Mowlana 'Ali and Mowlana Shahab.[60]

Sar-lowh is seen in this same document. The text also mentions the term *lowh* (literally "slab") probably to indicate the headings of secondary chapters. We find, for example:

> *"Mahmud az dah lowh-e divan-e Khvaju haft lowh be bum resanide baqi mashghul ast.*"[61]

"Mahmud has completed the background of seven of the ten *lowh* of the Khvaju (Kermani) divan and is in the process of completing the (three) other".

Sar-lowh is also mentioned by Qazi Ahmad when referring to 'Abd-allah Mozahheb.[62] In the *Mer'at al-estelah*, it is said that *sar-lowh* is the "painting of the leaf on which is found the *bismillah* ("In the name of God", therefore the first page[63]).

'Onvan ("title", but also "lintel of a door") is mentioned by Qazi Ahmad when describing an epigraphic frieze that the calligrapher Ebrahim Astarabadi designed for the tomb of Fatima in Qom.[64]

Toronj ("citron") is widely used to indicate the central medallion, often an oval one, of the binding (or of carpets). In doublet with *konj*, it indicates the central medallion with the four corner pieces.[65] The latter are also called *lacak*. The medallion may be topped with a *sar-toronj*. The oval is also called *badamak* ("almond shaped")

To indicate the round medallion of the frontispiece, *shamse* ("sun") is prefered. This is mentioned in the *'Umdat* among the decorations of bindings,[66] and by Qazi Ahmad.[67] In the *'arze-dasht* of the workshop of Baysanqor, it is said that Mowlana Shahab painted eight *shamse* in a *dibace*.[68] This kind of *dibace* with medallions, quite characteristic of Timurid manuscripts, often includes a "table of contents". (see pl. no. 2)

As we saw for the *jadval* or the *mastar*, these various technical terms are a delight to authors of the prefaces of albums. A common example, the medallion, *shamse* or *toronj*, is compared to the sun placed on the lapis-lazuli page of the sky.[69]

NOTES

1. Nezami, *Khosrow and Shirin.*
2. Fattahi, *Dastur al-'oshshaq.*
3. Nezami, *Sharaf-name,* Dastgerdi ed. p.287.
4. See on this subject P. Soucek, "Nizami on Painters and Painting", p.15 and our Part Two, Introduction.
5. Sadeqi, *Qanun,* lines 25-26.
6. *Id.* line 32.
7. *Id.* line 111; it should be noted that Dickson's translation (I, p.264) is not only a highly inventive one but is also fairly erroneous: "When there has already been a Mani and a Bihzad, how else (except through the direct observation of Nature) could one break free of the crushing weight of past perfection?"
8. "The City as an Artistic Center", p.112.
9. Quoted by Abu al-Fazl, *A'in,* I, 670; M. Brand gives another translation of this *beyt.* Bada'uni also quotes it *(Montakhab al-tavarikh,* transl. III, 271). He says about Peyrovi: "He is a skilfull painter and has attained by means of studying the outward form to hidden truths, and has written on outward form and hidden essence a poetical treatise which begins as follows..." M.Brand does not seem to have known of this passage. See also the transl. by Blochman I, 670 note 2, who points out that the poem entitled *Form and ideal* (probably *Surat va ma'ni*) whose text has been lost, started with these lines.
10. See also Part Two, Introduction.
11. *A'in,* I, p.102.
12. *Bayan,* p.348.
13. See for instance Anand Ram *Camanestan,* fol. 93a and 129a, about the painter Govardhan.
14. *Voyages,* V, p.203.
15. M.T. Danesh-Pazhuh adds that this Abu Nasr is the same as Abu Nasr Mansur b. 'Ali b. 'Eraq Gilani *Khvarazmi,* the master of Biruni, executed on order from Mahmud in 408/1017; see *Cahar-maqale,* ed. M.Qazvini, p.120; Danesh-Pazhuh, *"Moraqqa'",* pp.154-155.
16. *'Alam-ara,* p.176. A painting from the *Zafar-name* of Sharaf 'Ali Yazdi copied at Tabriz in 1529 shows some European ambassadors presenting the son of Sultan Murad I (fol. 520, Teheran, Golestan); reproduced in B.Gray, *Persian Painting,* p.132. It is however probably not the first time that Europeans are shown in Persian painting.
17. Ed. p.137, trans. p.181.
18. *'Alam-ara,* p.174.
19. Arnold, p.141, translates this passage as "The pictures in the royal palace and the *assembly hall* of Chahil Sutun..."; the word *majles* therefore loses here its technical meaning!
20. Ed. p.138, trans. p.182.
21. *Dowhat al-azhar,* p.94; see Danesh-Pazuh, *"Rang-sazi",* p.24.
22. *Dowhat al-azhar,* pp.78, 91, 93.

23. *'Alam-ara*, p.176.
24. Ed. p.201.
25. Fac-sim. in G.Lowry, *Timur*, p.160.
26. *'Alam-ara*, p.176.
27. *Qanun*, lines 113 to 125.
28. *Khamse* of Shah Tahmasp, British Library; Aqa Mirak is not to be confused with Khwaje Mirak, see article by A.S. Melikian-Chirvani on this subject.
29. Jahangir, *Tuzuk*, II, pp.108, 145, 157.
30. *Dowhat al-azhar*, p.67.
31. See for example F.Nasiri-Amini, p.13; Homayunfarrokh, p.145.
32. 'Afif, ed., p.374.
33. *Qanun*, lines 76-79.
34. See Danesh-Pazhuh, *"Rang-sazi"*, pp.20-23.
35. Ed., p.673; repeated by Qazi Ahmad, ed. p.132. trans. p.178; the *haft asl* mentioned by Minorsky are defective: *islimi, khita'i, firangi, fisali, abr, akrah, salami; salami* is an incorrect spelling of *eslami/eslimi;* see below for *akrah*; one "principle" is therefore missing from the list.
36. *Qanun*, lines 77-79.
37. Danesh-Pazhuh, p.20.
38. See earlier, "Composition".
39. Danesh-Pazhuh, *"Rang-sazi"*, pp.20-23.
40. Fac-sim., in G.Lowry, *Timur*, p.160; trans. Thackston, *id.*, p.364.
41. Ed., p.196.
42. Anand Ram, fol.11b.
43. Part Two, Introduction.
44. *Mer'at al-estelah*, fol. 11b.
45. *"Rang-sazi"*, p.21; correct in the text of his article: *va an-ra band-e rumi* (instead of *ruy*) *niz guyand."*
46. 'Ali b. Mahmud al-Kermani, ed. p.45.
47. Ed., p.202.
48. I do not know this word; it is however mentioned also by Nasiri Amini, pp.9 14; Homayunfarrokh, p.140 mentions *buturme* as being a decorative design; is it comparable to *katreme*?
49. Qazi Ahmad, trans., p.178 and his note 621.
50. *'Amal-e Saleh*, III, p.35.
51. *Dowhat al-azhar*, p.67.
52. *Golestan-e honar*, ed. 149, trans. 190.
53. pp.111-112.
54. *Dowhat al-azhar*, p.67.
55. *Id.* pp.86-87.
56. *Dowhat al-azhar*, pp.86, 87, 99.
57. Y.Porter, *"Kaqaz-e abri"*.
58. Y.Godard, fig.148.
59. Trans. *B.W.G.*, p.191; see also Sakisian, p.146.

60. Fac-sim, G.Lowry, *Timur*, p.160; trans. Thackston, *id.*, p.364; See our plate no. 9.
61. *'Arze-dasht*, fac-sim., *id.*
62. Ed. p.148, trans. p.190.
63. Anand Ram, fol.160a.
64. Ed. p.47. trans. p.89.
65. *Jeld-sazi*, p.125.
66. Trans. Levey, p.42.
67. Ed. 128 and 148; trans. 174, 190.
68. Fac-sim. G.Lowry, *Timur*, p.160; trans. Thackston, *id.*, p.364.
69. Preface to the album of Mirza Mo'ezz, Patna, ms. no.1098; see also Part Two, Introduction.

6

BINDING AND SPECIAL OPERATIONS

1. Bookbinding

Binding is the technique which makes it possible to give shape to the codex. It is, therefore, more than anything else, essential to the production of a book. Binding includes several operations. Between the moment when the calligrapher, the illuminator and the painter complete their work, and the moment the book is given to the person for whom it is intended, the loose sheets pass through several stages before receiving a cover.

After the pages are delivered, in the form of double sheets, generally arranged two by two (quaternion), they are collated with the help of the catchwords the calligrapher notes at the bottom of each page repeating the first word of the following page. They are put under a press and cut with a sharp blade (*seyfe*). Then each quire is stitched separately (*joz-bandi*). Once the quires are stitched, they are again pressed tightly and bound to each other by stitching on the spine (*piraze*). In some cases, the thread of the stitching meets that of the headband (*shiraze*), which is done at the top and the bottom of the spine, with coloured threads. Then comes the manuscript cover (*rukesh*): the pieces of cardboard, prepared according to the size of the work, are bound with leather or other suitable covering material.

Chardin describes binding in Persia:

> "The binders work badly also; and although it is difficult to believe, they cannot make the cover all in one piece. They make it in two pieces which they stick together at the back, which is always flat as they do not know how to make it round; and although they stick

these pieces very neatly, the gluing starts to show in time."[1]

W. Hoey makes similar observations about Lucknow, as late as 1880. It can be seen that despite the late date, the techniques and the means described in this text seem to be hardly more evolved than those of the Moghul period:

> "The work of the oriental bookbinder has not the durability or finish of English work. His appliances are rude, and consist of a wooden screw-press called *shikanja,* a long steel blade called *saifa* for cutting the edges, and a long, coarse needle, *suja,* for sewing. He usually makes pasteboard for his own use, from waste sheets, or buys them from *daftris* who make them up the same way. These countrymade boards sell at Rs.4 a maund. One sheepskin (country leather) will suffice for 12 octavo books half-bound, and for the same number of books one quire of marble paper (*abri*) is needed. The leather costs 5 annas, and the paper 5 ¼ annas. Boards for covers cost 4 annas. Thread and paste will be about 9 pies. Total cost 15 annas. For binding a book of this kind the *jildband* receives 2 annas. He has thus 9 annas on 12 books, and the time required for that number is 2 days. Clearly the *jildband* is not a case of taxation."[2]

It is essentially on the basis of one text, the *Resale-ye jeld sazi,* that we have some details about the different operations involved in binding. However, this Indo-Persian text is sometimes difficult to grasp: Indian words, and incomprehensible phrases either badly transcribed or too technical, mean that a translation of the entire text would have proved a far too arduous task, particularly since we are concerned with a study on painting. We have nevertheless tried to reproduce instead of an incomprehensible and literal translation, at least the basic information contained in this text. Further in-depth research in the field of book-binding will probably result later on in the undertaking of a complete translation of the work. Let us now examine these operations in detail.

Repairs and layout of the margins (vassali, fassali)

The binding of works of a great age, or the composition of albums, sometimes necessitate repairs or the rebinding of pages.

The first operation is called *vassali* (putting together). This operation consists in rearranging the pages on new paper, particularly silk paper, in such a way as to reconstruct the quires. The *Resale-ye jeld-sazi* describes these operations as follows:[3]

> "We first of all make a size out of starch mixed with lemon juice. We take the pages of old books which are to be reassembled, and silk paper of the same colour; the pages are placed on a marble slab *(takhte-ye sang, sang-e zir-e dast);* a thickener is spread on the damaged sheets and they are glued on to the silk paper, then beaten with a wooden polishing device *(mohre-ye cubin, moshte*). If there are some loose sheets, some double pages are remade; care must be taken not to make the repairs too voluminous, so that everything is uniform".

Several artists practising this technique are mentioned by Qazi Ahmad: the calligrapher 'Abd-allah Tabbakh and the painter-illuminators Mohammad Amin Jadvalkesh and Abu-al-Ma'sum Mirza.[4]

Fassali is the operation which consists in setting the margins. As we saw earlier, the term is found in the definition of the "seven principles". This operation is also described in the *Resale-ye jeld-sazi*:[5]

> "If a book does not have margins and only has a text, take some paper of the same colour and same texture, or of a different colour but the same texture; cut the middle out of this paper, according to the measurement of the text; make the margin you require but in such a fashion that it should induce one to say 'That's better!'. Some guiding marks have to be made, otherwise it becomes difficult to manage. Thereafter, the manner (of arranging) the pieces of calligraphy and the albums will hold no more secrets for you".

This term *fassali* is used by Qazi Ahmad when describing the numerous qualifications of the painter Abu al-Ma'sum Mirza.[6]

Stitching of the quires (joz-bandi) and headband

Here is what the *Resale-ye jeld-sazi* says about the stitching of the quires, in quite a confused way:

> "Gather the different quires together and align them. Make a mark in the middle of each, one on the right and one on the left. That should be done for the stitching of the quires, otherwise the headband will not be straight. Place the sheets side by side sideways, put them together and make a quire. Put the press and the quires on the stone slab, put the screws in the press, with the height, width and base absolutely equal, then tighten the press. There are two

kinds of *joz bandi* (stitching of quires); one is the stitching at one stroke *(yek-bandi)*, the other at two strokes *(do-bandi)*.
-*Yek-bandi*: make marks at two places on the spine of the quire; draw a line with a *jadval* (...*kesh*?); two lines will appear on the spine of the book,[7] one at the top and the other below. Pull some silk threads out of the *khart-e makhbat* (?); drive them in to mark the quires. Pull the threads in such a way that they remain on the inside. From the two quires left open, take (the thread) from the inside; make a knot on the back.
-*Do-bandi*: draw four lines on the spine, as before, join together two lines at the middle. Mark one part, then the other: a dot will appear on the spine. Push the needle in at this spot, but do not join the thread to the middle. Let it flow under each (of the threads) in such a way that they get woven together. Stitch each quire in this manner and join them together. For the lengthened format, use the two-stroke stitching; for the square format, one stroke is enough."

Once the quires have been stitched, they are tightened under the press. In the *Resale-ye jeld-sazi*, a band of leather is stuck on the spine of the quires at this moment. This may appear strange as the text then goes on to describe, after the preparation of the cardboard pieces, the stitching of the spine and the headband *(piraze va shiraze)*. It may however be that this leather band does not cover the top of the quire, but on the contrary, stops a little below it. The transversal stitching described below indicates that "a space of one or two fingers" should be left, perhaps because of this leather band.

Transversal stitching and headband

"Take the book by a corner, in the screw-press; make the *shiraze* and the *piraze:*
piraze: pass the needle through the place marked, leave a space of two fingers on the spine; if the book is small then one finger only. Pass (the needle) through for each quire, and pull the thread so that it comes from each cord; do not pull too hard so as not to tear (the paper). For each quire, one knot must be made; pull gently so that there are no folds".

This operation consists apparently in joining the various quires at the back, thanks to the threads left free during the stitching of the quires *(joz-bandi)*. However, this stitching is different in the East and the West; the difference lies in the fact that in the East, the rounded back being unknown in binding, the stitching is done without ribs. The ribs are thin straps of leather or of thread attached to boards which were originally made of wood; these boards were meant to protect the codex and make it easier to handle. In the Western manner, the stitching of the spine is done on these ribs.[8] *Piraze* is therefore like an intermediary headband, a sort of spine rib, formed by the transversal stitching of the quires. The "true" headband is called *shiraze*.[9]

Several types of headbands are described in the *Resale-ye jeld-sazi*: *band-e ney-shekar* ("sugar cane"), *dali* (the letter *dal*), *muce* (?).

> "Take two curved needles; in the hole of each, a different colour; make these two silk (threads) into a single one. Pass the needle through the first mark and pull as you did for the *piraze*: this is called *langar* (anchor). Take the two threads from below the *piraze*; with the two needles, pull out one of them. Then, in the same way, take again (the other) needle and the thread on the right and, with the two needles, proceed towards the other end (the left). When each needle is on the other, this is called *rast raftesh* (going straight?); then start again from left to right. If (the seam of the stitching) is absolutely straight, we call it *muce*. It can be recognised from the line which forms the design of a path. When the needles are crossed from below, this is called *cap* (left). If you weave all (the threads) on the left, you will obtain this same *muce*. If you alternate (one stitch) to the left and one to the right, you will make the *band-e ney-shekar* (in fact, the Jersey stitch). If you make four (stitches) to the left and four to the right, you will make the *dal* design. Both heads of the cords (of the *piraze* ?) should be covered, so as to make it very solid. When you pull the needle, do it towards yourself. Now that I have shown you how (the headband) is woven, make new designs. After which, take (the quires) in the cover".

In Western medieval bookbinding, originally the headband covered the thin straps connecting the two boards of a book. This was a thread of coloured flax or silk, stitched in large stitches within the folds of the quires. It was meant obviously to cover up the *piraze* or transversal stitching.

Cardboards and covers

The boards of the book are made of cardboard on which the cover is placed. Before paper was invented, these boards were generally made of wood. The first cardboard pieces were made of sheets of paper stuck to each other (*moqavva*). Sheets of old manuscripts were often used for this purpose. That moreover is how some pages of Rudaki have been preserved. Carboard pulp seems to have been invented later on. According to F.Nasiri Amini,[10] it was invented by Ghiyas al-din Naqqash, who had reportedly brought the secret of its manufacture from his journey to China. In the *Resale-ye jeld sazi*, although later, the technique described is that of sheets stuck to each other. A size is made out of gum, some peas *(mash)*, some starch, and some aloe, all of which is finely dissolved and cooked; the sheets of paper are glued to each other without making bubbles or folds.[11]

As we pointed out when discussing grounds, F.Nasiri Amini also notes the use of *laye-ye cini* or *batane*, the ground for lacquer, for making boards (see "Other grounds").

Covers

Several types of covers *(rukesh)* have been used in Iran. Leather is by far the most important; from the 12th century onwards it was decorated with some cold gilding created by the pressing of small wooden or iron moulds.

The different leathers used are moroco *(timaj)*, kid *(sabru)*, sheep *(misan)*, and chagreen *(saghari)*. Other leathers, of lesser quality such as cow or camel, make thick covers which do not require cardboard.

Apart from leather, cardboard may be painted with lacquer *(rang-o-rowghan)* and *rowghan-e kaman* varnish which gives light and solid bindings. Some types of cloth are also used, brocades *(zarrin-baf)*, printed calico *(qalamkar)*, *terme* from Yazd. Marbled paper or other coloured paper stuck on cardboard, have also been used (see "Marbled paper").

The *Resale-ye jeld-sazi* describes some dyes for leather, in red, yellow and black; then it explains how to cut the leather, on a stone slab *(sang-e zir-e dast)*, using a knife *(nashgarde)*.

Then there is one long passage about the *monabbat*. This word stands generally for the cutting of the cardboard or of the leather into a real lace pattern, used mostly for the lining *(astar)*. Here this term seems to indicate a sort of mould in cardboard used, like a gilding iron, to make hollowed out decorations on the leather:

> "Some lines are drawn on a cardboard piece, leaving a margin on the sides *(zanjire)*. Two lines (no doubt perpendicular ones) passing through the middle, mark the position of the *toronj* (medallion). The corner pieces *(konj)* are drawn at the four corners, and on the

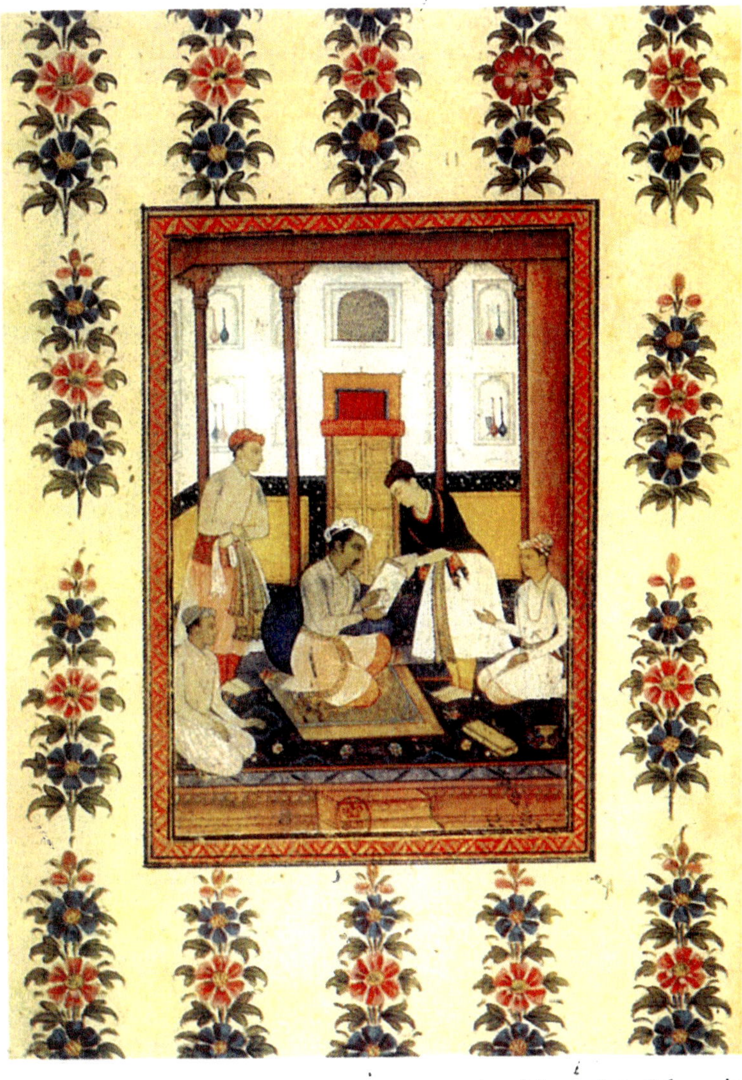

1. Abu al-Hasan Nāder al-Zamān presenting his work to Jahangir. Moghol school, ca. 1610.

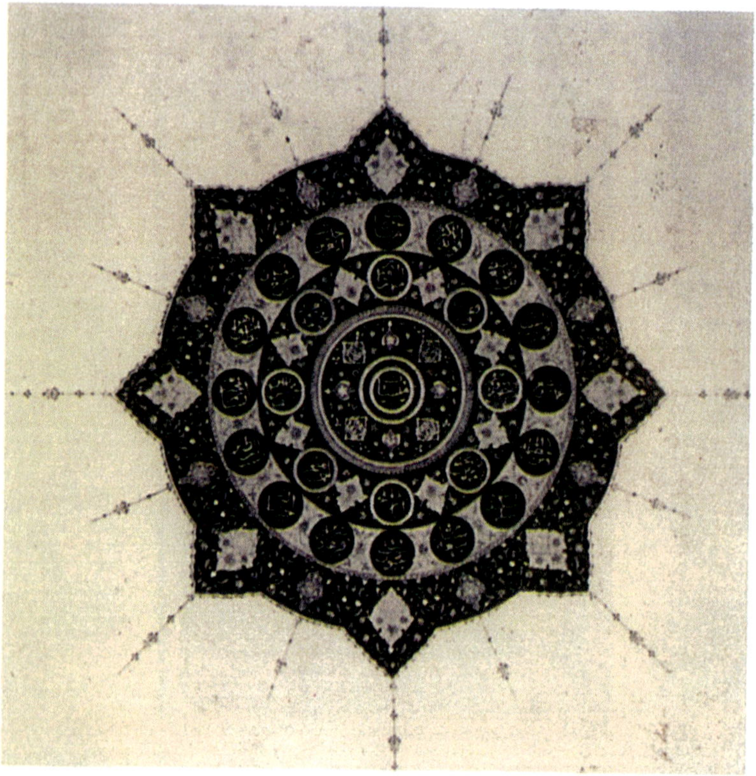

2. *Shamse*. Rosace on the frontispiece of a manuscript of the *Kolliyāt* of Mir ʻAli Shir Navāʼi copied in Herat ca. 1526 by ʻAli Hejrāni.

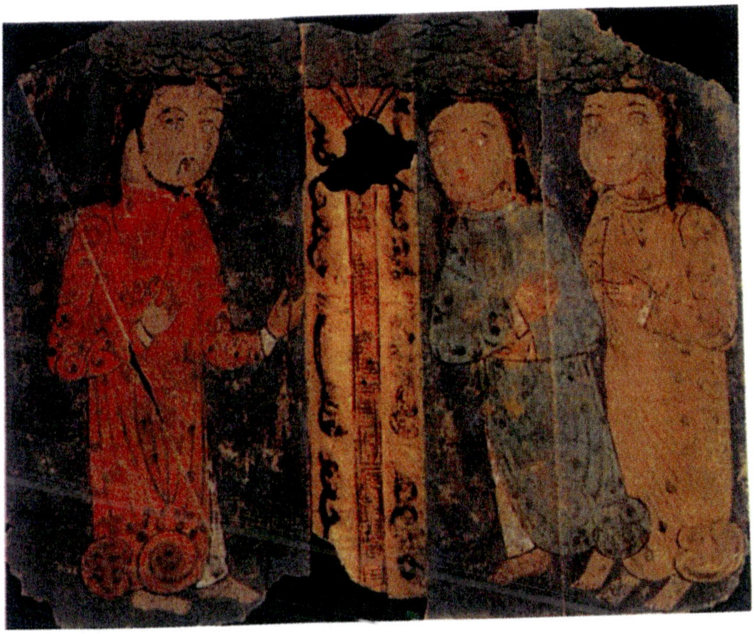

3. Three men under a tree. Irak, or oriental Iran (?), 9th century.

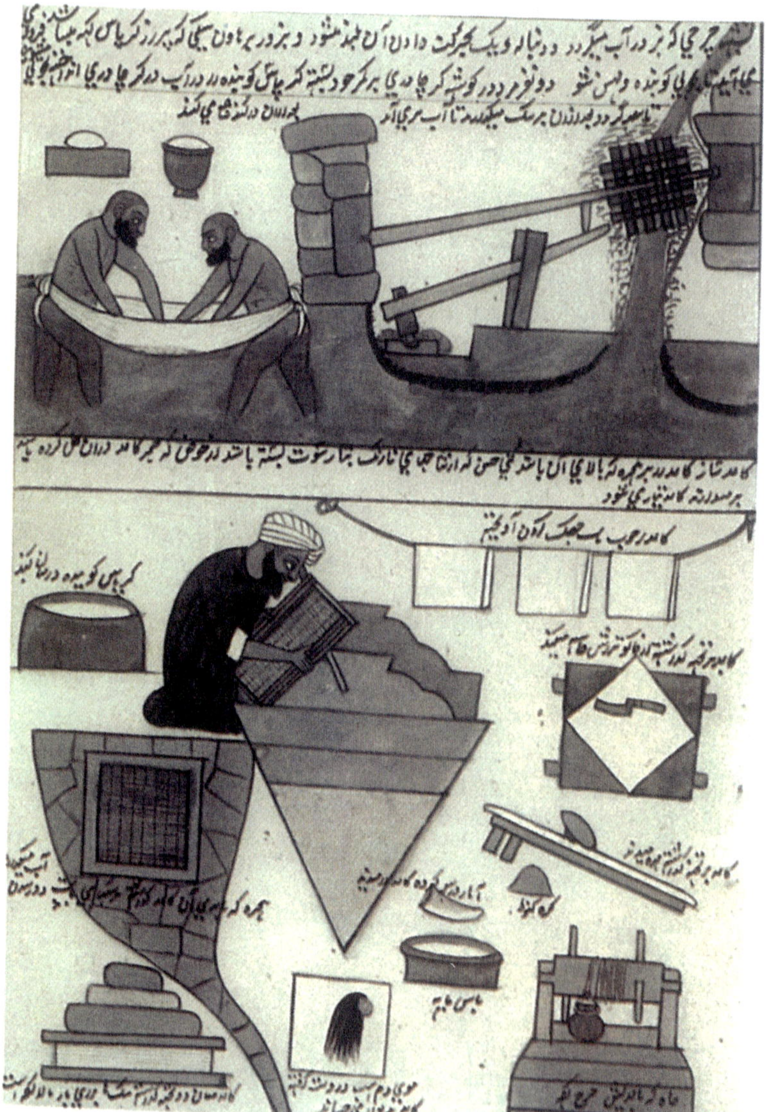

4. Makers of paper. Page from the *Album of the Crafts of Kashmir*. Srinagar(?), India, ca. 1850-1860.

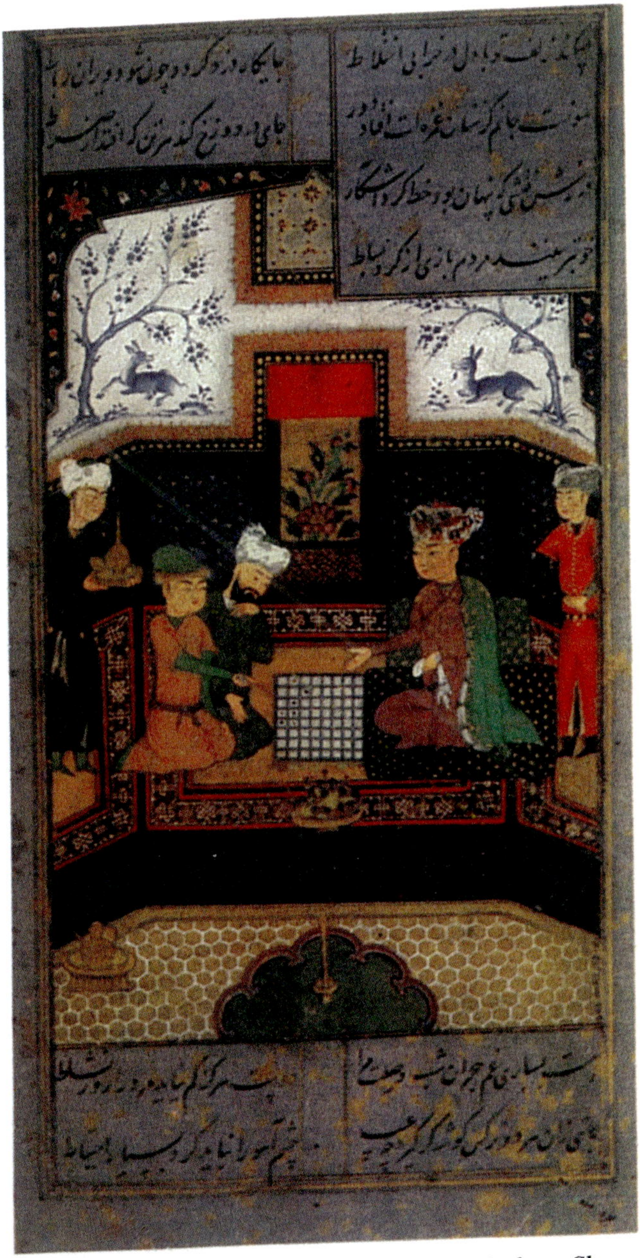

5. Chess players. Page copied from a poetical anthology. Shamakha, Shirvān, 1468.

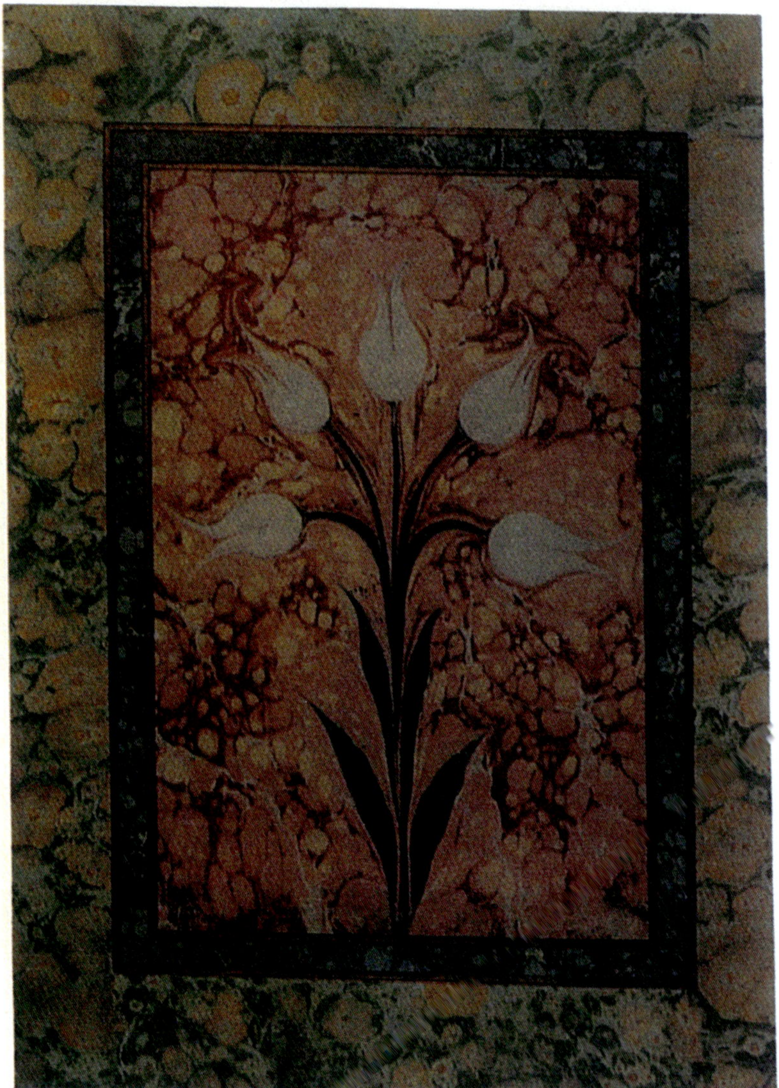

6. Marbled flowers in the technique of Necmeddin. Turkey, 20th century.

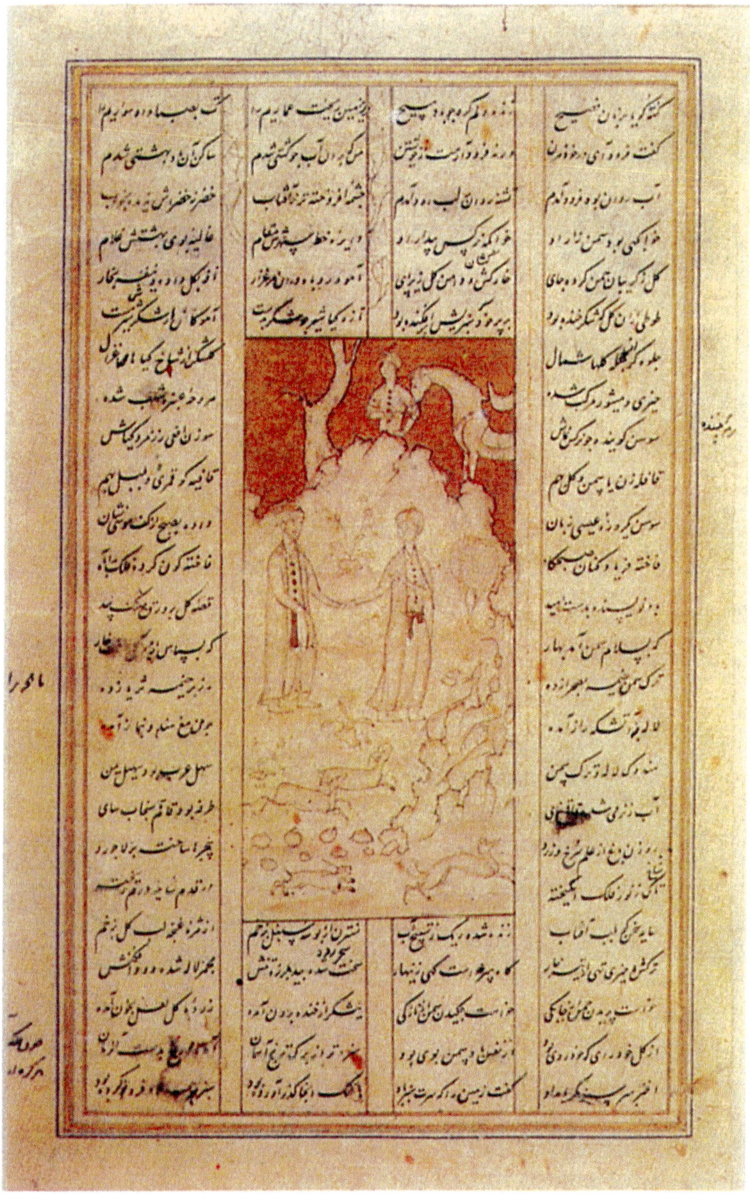

7. Three men in landscape with animals. Shiraz, end of 16th century.

8. Pounced drawing, showing a man riding a horse. Jodhpur, early 19th century.

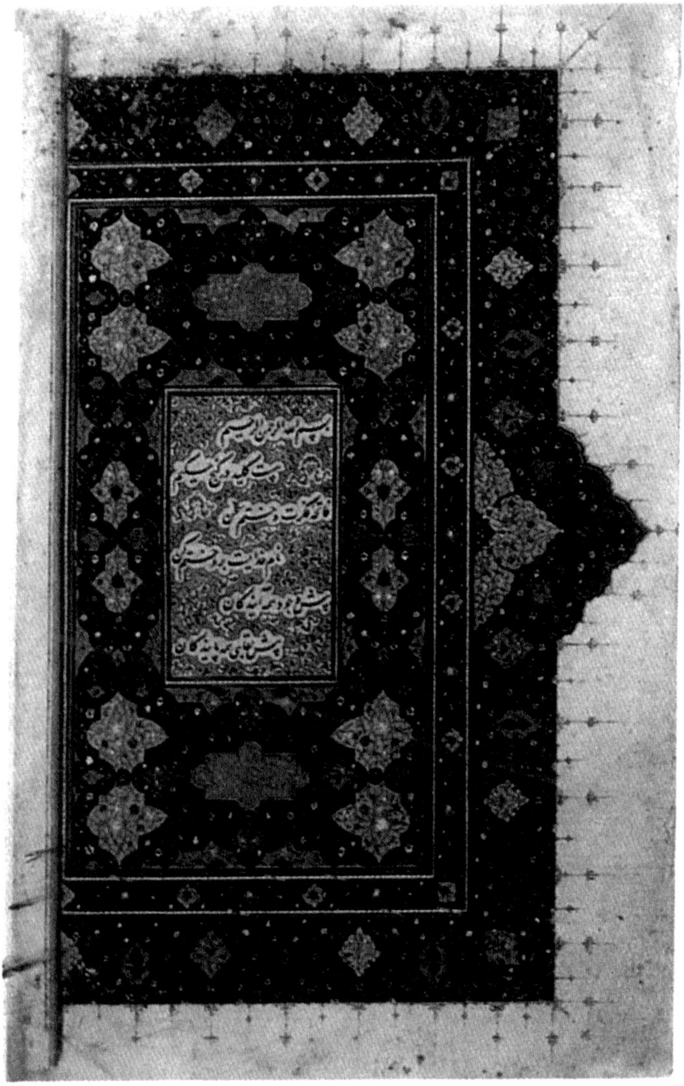

9. *Dibāce*, Frontispiece from a manuscript of the *Makhzan al-asrār* of Nezāmi copied in 1538.

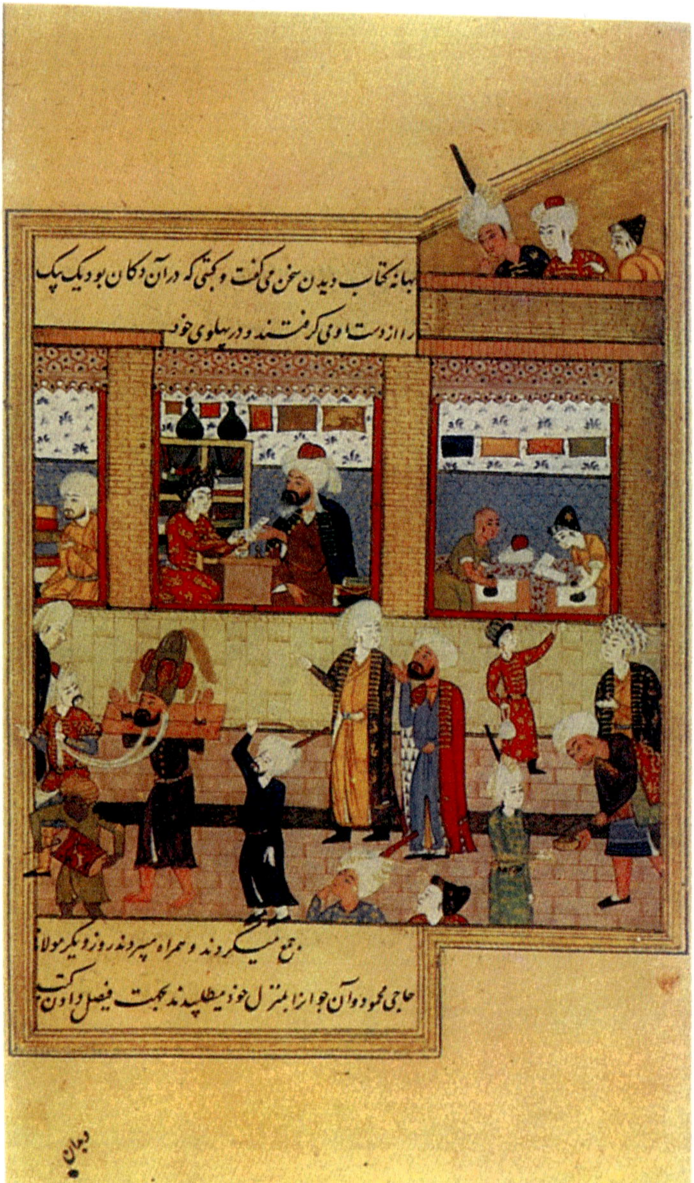

12. Scene from a bazar. Illustration from a *Majāles al-'oshshāq* probably copied at Shiraz by the end of the 16th century.

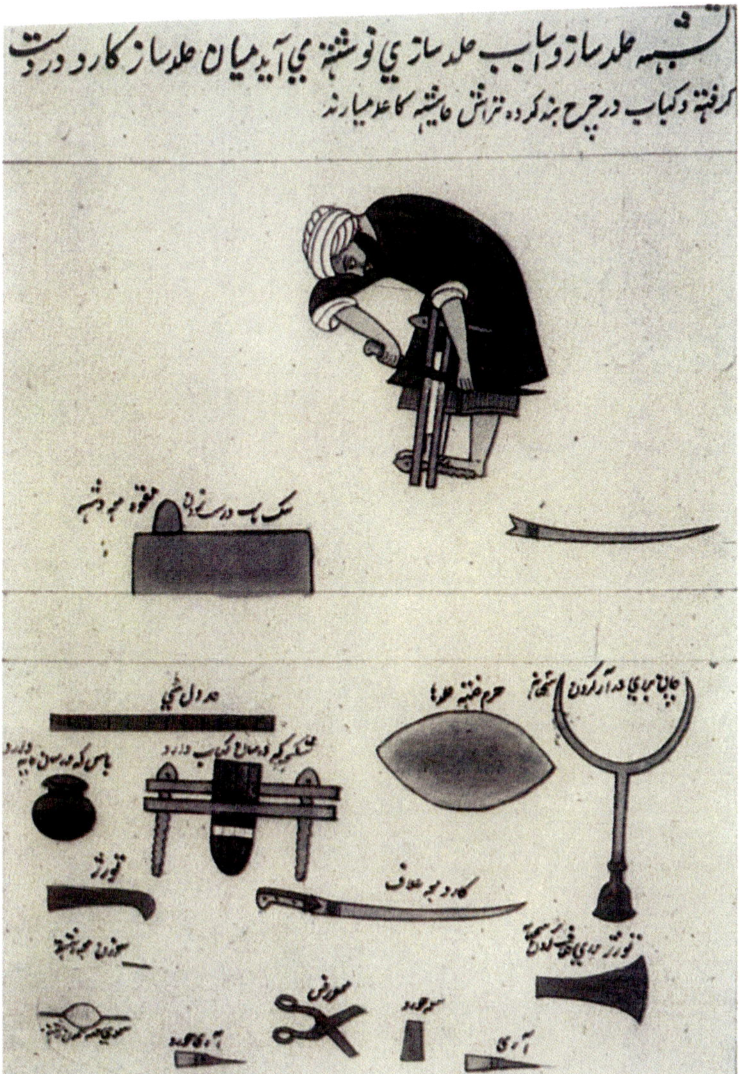

13. Bookbinder. Page from the *Album of the Crafts of Kashmir.* India, ca. 1850-1860.

sar-e barg (the top of the sheet). Then with the knife (*naqsh-bor*) the design is cut out according to the lines drawn. Once the cutting has been completed, the *monabbat* is placed on the humidified leather. The places meant to remain blank are polished with a ruler and a polishing device. Then, after a sheet of paper has been placed on the work, it is beaten with a hammer till the drawing gets printed on the leather. The work is then pressed between two boards on which some stones *(langar)* are placed. The leather lining is then stuck (on the inner side of the flat surface)."

The text specifies that it is possible to make the cover in one or two skins *(yek-pusti va do pusti)*. Some decorations are painted on the leather. An example of mixed covers is also given: some leather is put on the corners and the middle (spine), and some coloured paper is stuck on the rest of the cardboard.

A passage in the *'arze-dasht* of the Baysanqor workshop describes the decoration of the covers *(ruy-e jeld):*

"*Mowlana Qavvam al-din ruy-e jeld-e Shahname ra hashiye-ye eslimi mokamal karde va 'eysh-e tamasha-ye matn-e jeld ra be qalam gerefte va (?) do dang bum shode ast va posht-o sar-o gardan casbanide va tariq keshide shode ast.*"[12]

"Mowlana Qavvam al-din has completed the border of arabesques for the binding of the *Shah-name;* he has painted with a brush, a scene on the center of the cover; two-thirds of the background are complete; the front, the back and the spine have been stuck and the *tariq* (?) has been drawn".

2. Special operations

Jamali-ye Yazdi, in his *Farrokh-name* (580/1185) suggests several ways of removing stains, making invisible inks and other special tricks. These were borrowed by Teflisi, then subsequently by other compilers of recipes as in the *Majmu'at al-sanaye'*. One should however be on one's guard as some of the recipes, which are sometimes not very professional, are perhaps deliberately meant to be "amusing".

Removing marks and making corrections

Teflisi gives several recipes for erasing what has been written.[13] The simplest of these consists in just covering the writing with a layer of white tin solution in gum arabic. This method is also described in the *khateme* of the *Golestan-e honar*. Another recipe consists of alum, dried milk (*tarf*) and soda, mixed with the juice of bitter oranges. The mixture is allowed to dry and is then dissolved in vinegar. Another process consists of pouring melted wax on the area which is to be removed and then removing the wax; when this operation is repeated several times, the mark disappears.[14] Teflisi suggests also that chewing gum (*'alak*) be taken and rubbed on the paper, then hot ammonia gum be applied to it. Jamali-ye Yazdi suggests the use of mastic for this process.

Minor corrections can be made by scratching the paper with the tip of the reed pen sharpener. Simi recommends that this be done with the paper placed on a board, so as to prevent its being perforated. When making corrections, care should be taken to use the same reed pen and the same ink as before.[15] Soltan 'Ali Mashhadi, however, condemns the use of reed pen sharpener:

> "Do not use the reed pen sharpener (for corrections);
> What have calligraphers to do with the surgeons?"[16]

To remove grease stains on a piece of paper or a book, take some fresh plaster and grind it finely, place another sheet of paper on the stained one, then above it the crushed plaster, and on top of it all a stone slab; leave it like this till all the grease has disappeared.[17] Sadeqi uses sarcocolla to remove grease stains.[18]

"Tricks" and invisible inks

To protect paper from water, Teflisi suggests that alum be mixed with milk and the paper starched with this mixture; once dry, the paper should be polished; paper starched in this manner will not be harmed by water.

To protect paper from fire, mix some talc dissolved in alum from Yemen and some cotton seeds and coat the paper with this mixture; it does not burn if set on fire.[19]

To protect paper from insects, starch it with colocynth pulp; it keeps flies and mice away.[20]

To keep flies away from the inkpot, colocynth pulp and ox gall are mixed to the ink.[21]

There are numerous recipes for invisible inks, which become legible in the dark, or when in contact with water or with fire. However, since they are merely anecdotal in nature, we just refer our reader to the texts where they can be consulted.[22]

NOTES

1. *Voyages,* IV, p.149.
2. *A Monograph on Trade and Manufactures in Northern India,* p.122.
3. Ed. p.112.
4. Ed. pp.67, 148, 149; trans. pp.66, 189, 190.
5. p.112.
6. Ed. p.149, trans. p.190.
7. The *jadval-kesh* is a pen which can draw two or three lines at a time; see the *Jadval.*
8. See *Archéologie du livre médiéval,* pp.50-51.
9. See the photographs in G.Bosch *et al.,* pp.54-55.
10. Nasiri Amini, p.6.
11. pp.110-111.
12. Fac-sim. G.Lowry, *Timur,* p.160; trans. Thackston, *id.,* p.364.
13. *Bayan*, chap. 11; see also Jamali Yazdi, p.357.
14. See also Simi, fol.48a.
15. Simi, fol.48a.
16. Ed. p.76; trans. p.121.
17. *Majmu'at al-sanaye',* fol. 35a.
18. Lines 158-159.
19. Jamali Yazdi, p.200.
20. *Id.* p.356.
21. *Id.* p.355.
22. Jamali Yazdi, pp.358-9; Teflisi, chap. 11; *Majmu'at* fol. 37a-37b.

7

MURAL PAINTING AND CERAMICS: A PARALLEL

In the introduction, we mentioned the continuity in the history and the techniques of painting in the Iranian world. At first sight, the techniques and particularly the grounds of mural paintings and ceramics are very different from those of manuscript paintings. On the other hand, the pigments and the binding agents used in mural paintings and for manuscripts, are the same.[1] In addition, we will see further on, that some painters of manuscripts are also known to have executed mural paintings. The techniques of ceramics, however, are quite different, and apart from some rare examples, hardly any manuscript painters are renowned for their paintings on ceramics. However, this brief survey of mural paintings and ceramics aims at bringing out the continuity in the history of painting in the Iranian world; for this painting on different grounds has to be considered, as a unity.

1. Mural paintings

When we approach the subject of mural painting in the Iranian world, the first thing we note, if we treat this cultural area as a whole, is that it displays a remarkable continuity, which can be traced back from Parthian times to the Qajar era, without denying obvious differences in style between, for instance, the paintings of Doura Europos, with their Graeco-Roman influence, and the distinctly more oriental ones, such as those of Pendzhikent.

Some traces of painting prior to the Seleucid and the Parthian eras have been noted, in Assyrian palaces, in the *apadana* at Susa, or in the Persepolis Treasury, for example.[2] We could similarly consider the ceramic tiles of Susa as the precursors of mural paintings. These are in a better state of preservation than any Achaemenid frescoes, given the nature of the material itself. They show, at any rate, a great mastery of drawing and chromatism and of the use of mural space.

At the site of Kuh-e Khvaje (Sistan) discovered by A. Stein, who dated it between the 1st century B.C. and the 1st century A.D.,[3] several fragments of mural paintings still exist. These paintings are undoubtedly the oldest fragments found in Iran, and they represent one of the rare examples of painting from the Parthian age.

Practically no remains of any fresco from the Sasanid era have come down to us.[4] Ammianus Marcellinus mentions the mural paintings which embellished the Sasanid palaces.[5] Later, the Arab historian Yaqut[6] describes the castle of Dukkan, near Qarmisin (Kermanshah) and mentions a painting showing Khosrow I (531-579). Similarly, the poet al-Buhturi (d.897) describes, in his *divan*, the frescoes of Ctesiphon showing the siege of Antioch by Khosrow I in 538.[7] The taste of the Sasanid rulers for monumental displays of their glory (rock reliefs), or for more decorative designs (such as the mosaics of Bishapur[8]) would lead us to assume that mural painting also played a role during the Sasanid era.

Excavations at the Pendzhikent, Afrasiyab and Varakhsha sites, in Central Asia have brought to light some very important series of paintings.[9]

Pendzhikent is undoubtedly the site which has supplied, and continues to supply, the largest amount of material for the study of mural painting in this part of Central Asia. P.I. Kostrov has analysed the paintings found on the site and has defined three chronological phases between the 5th and the 8th centuries, each one characterised by a particular palette.[10] His observations appear to have been confirmed by the analyses carried out by the authors of the study on the Dilberdzhin paintings.[11]

The mural space of the Pendzhikent frescoes is divided into sections. Most likely an initial outline defined the main lines of the composition. The colours are applied in flat tints and juxtaposed. The contours of the figures and of the coloured areas are outlined with a dark colour, probably according to the initial design which may have been corrected. The figures are set against a monochrome background which suggests a neutral space. They occupy the entire height of their section which gives them a monumental aspect. These various features of the composition are found again in paintings on other grounds, such as the shield of Mount Mugh,[12] as well as in some of the oldest known Persian illustrated manuscripts.[13] Guity Azarpay writes:

> "The extent of the influence of this distinctive and secular tradition of painting, on the development of miniature painting in Muslim times, is still undetermined. However, the stylistic and iconographic links between the two suggest the existence of Sogdian antecedents for some of the artistic formulas found in the later miniature painting tradition."[14]

Moreover, there is a clear association between the iconography of Sogdiana and that of Ferdowsi's *Shah-name*. His description of the city of Siyavushgerd, for instance, is perhaps inspired by a Sogdian version, but there is no reason to believe that this description was not close to some contemporary reality:

"He painted in the palace numerous images
Of kings, battles and banquets.
He painted in one place Kavus, with his mace and his armlets,
Crowned on his throne, with Rostam, who is like the elephant,
And Zal, Godarz, and all his companions.
Elsewhere, he painted Afrasiyab and his army,
Piran and Garshivarz the avenger."[15]

These verses may well have been inspired by the paintings of the Ghaznavi palaces, as we shall see later.

Mural paintings of the Muslim period

T. Arnold, in his *Painting in Islam* notes that during the first centuries of Islam the Arabs do not appear to have been very interested in the plastic arts and in painting.[16] According to this author, it would seem that most of the paintings done for the Arabs in the first centuries of their rule, were the work of non-Arab artists. Indeed, the Qusayr 'Amra[17] or the Samarra paintings point to a non-Arab hand, and this fact is confirmed in some texts.

One of the most important series of Arab mural paintings of the first centuries of Islam which have come down to us, is that of Samarra, executed between 836 and 883.[18] This ensemble of frescoes gives an idea of what the decoration of the Caliphate palaces must have been like. Some faces, with calligraphic features, bring to mind those of Miran, in Xinjiang.[19] In Samarra, as in Qusayr 'Amra, T. Arnold perceives the hand of a Christian, not only because priests are represented but also on account of some signatures detected by E. Herzfeld.[20] This fact is confirmed by several Arab sources.[21]

T. Arnold adds that the painters of the manuscripts of the *Kalila wa Dimna* or the *Maqamat* of Hariri, and even the painted ceramics of Reyy from the 6th and 7th centuries of the Hegira (12th and 13th centuries) are probably the work of Christian artists.[22] In any case, our main objective is to show that these Arabic paintings perpetuate the pre-Islamic pictorial tradition, whether they be Christian or otherwise.

Mas'udi, in his *Muruj al-zahab*[23] relates that the Caliph Muhtadi (869-870) got the paintings in his palace removed. Maqrizi mentions a work he himself composed on the life of the Fatimid painters, which is unfortunately lost.[24] Other information about painting of Fatimid Egypt are known to us through the *Safar-name* by Naser-e Khosrow (442/1051).[25] This author also tells us that he painted the mosque of Falij, with cinnabar and lapis.[26]

Finally, the *Arabian Nights* abound in descriptions of marvellous palaces, often decorated with paintings of azure and gold. As has been noted earlier for Ferdowsi, these descriptions are probably based on actual observations.

Mural paintings of the Muslim Iranian world (9th to 18th centuries)

It has already been noted that our knowledge of Persian painting, up to almost the 14th century, is extremely fragmentary. This could lead us to believe, because of negative evidence, that since very few mural paintings from before the 12th century are found in the Iranian region, these never existed. Now, it appears from the discovery of some rare fragments, and from the few literary passages which make mention of paintings, that the pictorial tradition we have tried to trace back to the pre-Islamic period, survived the Muslim invasion and developed in the Iranian courts.

Some fragments of mural decorations, frescoes and stucco have been discovered in Nishapur and in Siraf,[27] dating from the 9th and 10th centuries. These fragments are therefore practically contemporary with the Samarra paintings. The posthumous publication of the works of Ch. Wilkinson on Nishapur[28] enables us to get an idea of what the mural decorations of Samanid homes must have been like. Several sites, showing the old quarters of the Samanid city have been brought to light, particularly at Tepe Madreseh, Vineyard Tepe, Sabz Pushan and Qanat Tepe. Some important fragments, one of them showing a horse rider,[29] have been preserved.

The Ghaznavid site of Lashkari Bazar constitutes undoubtedly one of the oldest almost intact group of Iranian frescoes from the Muslim era that have come down to us. When the French Archaeological Delegation discovered it in Afghanistan,[30] this series displayed 44 richly dressed figures. Unfortunately, the heads have not been preserved as they were situated at the same height as a wooden beam which caught fire, destroying the painting at this level. The figures are painted on a background decorated with flowers, birds and fruit trees. The technique used is very close to that of Pendzhikent: it is tempera on a dry plaster ground.[31] Some fragments have been detached and taken to the Kabul Museum where they have undergone restoration. Another small fragment of painting on a column, showing the head of a young man surrounded by a halo, with narrow eyes and a round face, enables us to establish a link with the iconograpby of contemporary ceramics and thus verify their similarity.

Some sources of the Ghaznavid period, or others which give information about this period, describe the frescoes of the palaces of Mahmud of Ghazni: Farid al-din 'Attar, in his *Tazkerat al-awlia*,[32] says that Abu al-Kheyr, the father of Abu Sa'id, reportedly painted the frescoes of Mahmud's palace. He then regretted this impious act and removed them. Similarly, Mahmud is supposed to have had a pavilion constructed in a garden whose walls were decorated with episodes from the *Shah-name*.[33] An anecdote, related by Beyhaqi,[34] tells us that the Prince Mas'ud got a tent or pavilion constructed for his private conversations, which was painted with erotic figures (*alfiye-shalfiye*).

Few traces of Seljuk mural paintings have come down to us. One example is the painting on the tomb of Kharraqan, of the Alp Arslan era (460/1067).[35]

Ebn Esfandiyar[36] describes a palace which Hosam al-Dowle Ardashir b. Hasan Bavandi (567/1172-602/1204) got constructed, and which was decorated with paintings in gold, relating the vengeance of Afrasiyab.[37]

B. Gray points out that the need to add colour to the buildings persists with the introduction of polychrome ceramics in the 14th century, but that there is no certainty that mural painting existed during this era.[38] He however mentions some fragments of paintings from Reyy dating from the 14th century, and preserved in American collections.[39] The paintings of the cupola of Torbat-e Sheykh Jam, which Lisa Golombek[40] has studied, are dated 1361-62. It would appear moreover that the paintings of the dome of the tomb of Oljaytu in Soltaniye replaced, in fact, a decoration done initially in ceramic.[41]

Shams-e Seraj 'Afif, author of the *Tarikh-e Firuz-Shahi*, mentions the law decreed by Firuz Shah (1351-88), the Sultan of Delhi, prohibiting the display of living beings "as is done normally in the decoration of royal apartments."[42] This fact shows that the Muslim courts of India also had a liking for mural decorations.

Sharaf al-din Yazdi[43] mentions the paintings executed for Timur in Samarkand. These paintings are also described by Ebn 'Arabshah.[44] They were reportedly painted by the artists from the Jalayerid workshops of Tabriz and Bagdad. This leads B. Gray to believe that these frescoes must have been done in accordance with the miniature tradition.[45]

Babur[46] points out that Timur had a pavilion constructed in the garden of Delgosha in Samarkand, decorated with paintings narrating his Indian campaigns.

'Abd al-Razzaq Samarqandi[47] refers to the paintings of one of Shahrokh's pawilions (1404-1447) at Herat. Babur, similarly, mentions the paintings in a room of Abu Sa'id's (1452-1467) palace at Herat, the Tarab-khane, showing the prince's[48] battles.

Among the remains of mural paintings of the 15th century, we can mention those of the Zarnegar-khane of Gazurgah,[49] dating from the end of that century, and those of the Masjed-e Shah of Mashhad, which are from 1451. Lisa Golombek is of the view that the decoration of the Zarnegar-khane, with its arabesques of azure and gold, probably owes its inspiration to textiles and to carpets rather than to illuminations. But does this not mean we are underestimating the role of the painter decorator *(naqqash)*, not only in mural painting, but also in the making of sketches for textiles and for carpets? We will return later to this question.

The Safavid frescoes are better known to us not only on account of the paintings themselves but also because of their fairly detailed descriptions, such as those given by 'Abdi Beyg Shirazi[50] or by Western travellers.[51]

The decoration of the palace of Nayin, which I.Luschey Schmeisser dates from the years 1550-60,[52] and particularly that of Isfahan with the 'Ali Qapu and Chehel Sotun groups enable us to fully appreciate the style as well as the technique of these paintings. The restoration and analyses which have been made, particularly on the Isfahan paintings, give us a good knowledge of the techniques used.[53] We know, moreover, that painters of manuscripts participated in the production of these paintings.[54] The link between mural painting and manuscript painting thus seems to be established, since both are done by the same artists. Certainly the purely decorative, non-figurative parts of the mural paintings, since the Timurid era, are often executed on a stucco and the painted design is accentuated by the relief. This technique is naturally foreign to manuscript art (but not to the painting on wood or leather). Here again, we should be able to specify what part the painter plays in the various types of mural decorations.

Finally, from the end of the 17th century, we begin to see the appearance of large oil paintings on canvas, which progressively replace mural paintings in the decoration of houses and palaces. Mural painting however survives till the Qajar era.

This survey has enabled us to show the continuity of the tradition of Iranian mural painting from ancient to modern times. The study of mural painting has been kept separate from that of manuscripts on account of the difference of ground. The difference however, is much less significant than would appear at first sight. Indeed, we have just seen that manuscript painters also distinguished themselves in mural painting. Similarly, the influence of the aesthetics of the pre-Islamic fresco, which we have noted on several occasions (monochrome background, monumental composition over horizontal areas, calligraphic outlining of the figures) are also definitely observed in the Persian manuscripts of the 13th and 14th centuries.[55] Conversely, the composition of the Safavid mural paintings owes a lot to manuscript paintings. B. Gray talks, on this matter, about "a period during which mural painting was predominant (till the Timurid era), followed by another during which it became subordinate to miniature painting."[56] This argument is based, in fact, on negative evidence: few pre-Timurid Iranian manuscripts are known. How can we then compare them to mural paintings of the same period? In fact, rather than one ground having supremacy over another, it is probable that painting on both grounds, wall and paper, followed a parallel evolution.

2. Ceramics

As A.S. Melikian-Chirvani[57] has shown, there are more examples of ceramics displaying decorated figures before the end of the 12th century than there are manuscript paintings. We already noted this with regard to the Achaemenid glazed decorations at Susa: ceramic resists the vagaries of weather better than painting. Indeed, some Iranian painted ceramic pieces are still extant. True, the techniques of paintings are different from those of ceramics. The ceramist painter has to cope with the technical constraints of the material he uses, which are unknown to the painter of manuscripts. These constraints vary according to the ceramic techniques used (slip, glaze,...). On account of these constraints, the very style of the paintings can be affected, as the technique conditions the style. These ceramics therefore display a certain variety of styles and illustrate the iconography of their time.

A.S. Melikian Chirvani has made use of the Seljuk ceramics to back up his belief that the three manuscripts he describes, are works which conform to an aesthetic similar to that of the painted ceramics of the same period.[58] Moreover, we know the names of some ceramist painters from the end of the 12th and 13th centuries, because they have signed their works. No signature is found of any manuscript painter during this period. For example at the end of the 12th century Abu Zeyd painted and signed a ceramic dish from Kashan.[59] He is undoubtedly the oldest Iranian painter whose signed work we possess. Moreover, it is not impossible that Abu Zeyd was also a manuscript painter.

Abu Rufaza, who was active around 1200, and Tahr al-din, who worked around 1263, specialized in the decoration of wall tiles in glazed ceramic.[60] An inscription on a *mehrab* in glazed ceramic at the shrine of Ja'far in Qom reads:

> "Made on the 10 Rabi II of the year 738 (6th November 1337) at Kashan, in the workshop of Seyyed Rokn al-din Mohammad b. Seyyed Zeyn al-din al-Qaza'eri, it is the work of the venerated and respected Jamal al-din Naqqash."[61]

Some authors have already noted the importance of mural painting, even non-figurative, as well as of ceramic tiles, in the history of painting. Thus, E. Gasparini has noted,[62] in addition to the paintings done in 827/1424 at the Yeshil Cami in Bursa by 'Ali b. Eliyas (an Iranian artist who came to Anatolia at the time of Timur), some ceramic tiles from Bursa, signed as being "works of the masters of Tabriz". He points out that there are hardly any manuscript paintings of this period in Turkey. Similarly, in his various studies on the Safavid wall tiles, I. Luschey-Schmeisser perceives a very close, if not direct, influence of some painters, such as Mo'in Mosavver.[63] Similar work has been done by R. Neumann in the field of textiles.[64]

It is still difficult to know what role the painter played in the making of decorated ceramics.[65] Did he work in collaboration with ceramists, only supplying the sketch? Or did he himself execute the painting on the ceramic ground? H. Wulff[66] gives the example of decorated tiles where the design is transferred by means of pounce. In his article on Mohammad Reza al-Emami, D. Pickett[67] seems to state that the work of this calligrapher was restricted to the sketch. We will return later to the specializations of artists; however, the link between painted ceramics and painting, whether mural or on paper, can already be noted. Both share common aesthetic and a common concept of images.

C. Adle has even gone further, since he has shown that the same composition module used for manuscripts is found again in a pair of ceramic tiles.[68] This therefore means that even if the painter does not directly take part in the technical aspects of ceramics, he proposes at any rate not only his imaginative repertoire but also the canons of composition.

NOTES

1. See Table at Annexe 1.
2. R. Ghirshman, p.182.
3. Stein, *Innermost Asia,* II,pp.913-921; reproduced in E.Herzfeld, *Iran and the Ancient East,* pl.ci-civ.
4. Apart from a fragment discovered by R.Ghirshman at Susa, see p.183, fig. 224. According to this author, it would appear that the palaces of Eyvan-e Kerke, during the time of Shapur II, were widely covered with paintings, *id.* p.181. R.Ghirshman also presents us with the drawing of a painting on the rock of Dokhtar-e Anushiravan, in the east of Khorasan p.318.
5. *Rerum gestarum,* XXIV.6.3.
6. *Mo'jam al-buldan,* IV. pp.330-331; Barbier De Meynard, p.438.
7. However, E.Herzfeld seems to say that these relate more probably to mosaics, see *Samarra,* p.6.
8. Ghirshman, *Iran, Parthes et Sassanides,* pp.141-147.
9. See particularly G.Azarpay and M.Bussagli.
10. *"Tekhnika zhivopisi..."* p.175; see also G.Azarpay, pp.159-169.
11. Zelninskaya, Z.M. *et al. "Analizy krasok..."*
12. Talbot Rice, fig.78.
13. Melikian, "Trois manuscrits".
14. "The development of the arts in Transoxiana", p.1131.
15. *Shah-name,* ed. Moscow, vol. III v. 1731-1734.
16. *Painting in Islam,* p.52.
17. See C.H.Becker.
18. Discovered and published by E.Herzfeld, *Der Wandschmuck der Bauten von Samarra.*
19. Stein, *Serindia,* I, pp.492-529. Concerning these frescoes of Miran, A.Stein

says moreover that when he discovered them, he felt as if he were in Syria rather than in Central Asia (Hopkirk, p.155). Some of these paintings from Miran carry a signature of the name Titus; see Stein, *Serindia*, I, pp.530-531.

20. Arnold, p.58; Herzfeld, *Samarra*, p.91.
21. Yaqut (vol.III, pp.173-178), says that some Christian painters worked on these paintings. Maqdisi *(Ahsan al-taqasim*, p.73), mentions the frescoes of the Arab houses, painted by Christians; further on (*id.* p.81), this author relates that the Caliph Walid (705-715) asked Justinian II to send him some artisans to reconstruct the mosque at Medina. Similarly, Ebn al-Faqih al-Hamadani *(Kitab al-buldan*, pp.136-137) speaks of the art of the Byzantium painters in very praiseworthy terms.
22. Arnold, p.60.
23. Transl. vol.VIII, p.19.
24. Arnold, p.22.
25. Trans. Scheffer, pp.157-158.
26. *Id.*, pp.221-222.
27. B. Gray, "The tradition of wall painting", p.314.
28. Ch. K. Wilkinson, *Nishapur, Some Early Islamic Buildings and their decorations.*
29. Preserved in the Iran Bastan Museum of Teheran; see Wilkinson, *op. cit.* pp.205-208.
30. D. Schlumberger.
31. *Id.* p.268.
32. Ed. Nicholson, II, 322-323.
33. See the *Divan* of Farrokhi, p.54; see also Danesh-Pazhuh, *"Moraqqa'"*, p.156.
34. *Tarikh-e Mas'udi,* pp.121-123.
35. See D. Stronach and G. Oney.
36. *Tarikh-e Tabarestan,* II, 122-123, Danesh-Pazhuh, *"Moraqqa',"* p.156.
37. We should point out here the recent article by A. S. Melikian Chirvani, "Le Livre des Rois, Miroir du Destin" which also quotes this passage by Ebn Esfandyar, as well as other details relating to the representation of the *Shah-name* in Iranian courts.
38. "Wall paintings", p.317.
39. *Id.;* the collections are not specified.
40. "The Chronology of Turbat-i Shaikh Jam".
41. B.Gray, "Wall-painting", p.317.
42. Ed. p.374.
43. *Zafar-name*, I, 802.
44. Stchoukine, *Manuscrits Timourides,* pp.3 and 6.
45. B.Gray, "Wall-painting", p.318.
46. Trans, Beveridge, p.78.
47. Arnold, p.27.
48. Trans. Beveridge, p.302.
49. Lisa Golombek, "The Timurid Shrine of Gazur Gah".
50. *Dowhat al-azhar, Rowzat al-safat;* see also E.Echraghi.
51. Della Valle, III, pp.380-381; Chardin, IV, p.117; V, pp.201-203.
52. "Der Wand-und Deckenschmuck...".

53. See H. Aqajani and G. Zander.
54. See our Part Two; also Gray, "Wall-painting", p.313.
55. Melikian, "Trois manuscrits", p.13.
56. Gray, "Wall paintings", p.328.
57. Melikian, "Trois manuscrits".
58. *Id.*
59. T. Falk, pp.230-231.
60. Wulff, p.149.
61. Quoted from Pope, p.1574.
62. *Le pitture murali della Muradiye d'Edirne.*
63. See for instance *The pictorial tile cycle of Hasht Behesht in Isfahan*, and "Ein safavidischer Drachen-Bogen in der Ermitage".
64. See *Persische Seiden.*
65. See W.B.Denny.
66. Wulff, p.164.
67. Pickett, "Inscriptions..."
68. "Recherches sur le module, 2".

PART II

THE PAINTER, THE WORKSHOP, THE LIBRARY

After analysing the techniques of painting and the arts of the book, we must now turn to the main instruments of this production, that is to say the artists and the material resources at their disposal. This is therefore, in a way, a repetition of the previous chapters, seen from the viewpoint of those who use the techniques described earlier. Rather than make an exhaustive study of the subject, we shall put forward a few questions about the status of the painter and about the function of the workshops and the libraries. Indeed, as already pointed out, a manuscript with paintings is the result of a collective effort, carried out, on royal command, in the workshops. We saw earlier how the preparation of a module governed the execution of the manuscript as a whole. In this part, we will examine the social organization which makes this work possible.

The painter and literature

Before approaching the purely biographical aspects of the painter such as are described in the *Tazkere* (biographical collections), and in historical works, it is important to see how the painter is described in literature. In fact, we shall see that there exists a whole repertoire of literary images, commonly used in biographies, but originating probably in Koranic literature and then in poetry. This is a very vast subject of analysis and is worthy of study in the field of literary criticism. We will however restrict ourselves to a few examples which appear significant to us.

The image of the painter has been widely used in poetry. For one thing, we find in some great epics, personalities who are gifted painters, such as Shapur in Nezami's *Khosrow va Shirin*,[1] or Khiyal in Fattahi's *Hosn-o del.*

Moreover, we often find the image of the Creator compared to a painter, the craftsman par excellence as he is referred to in the Koran:

"He formed you, and formed you well."[2]

This image also occurs in poetry.[3] In biographical works, the comparison is made all the more frequently as it operates on two levels, that of God the Creator, and that of his human counterpart, the painters:

"When the divine brush has sketched some figures,
Favour and merit are the lot of humankind."[4]

The poetic metaphors describing the painter and his work derive from Koranic inspiration. Progressively however, the image developed to designate creators of a more human nature.

Two references, particularly used to describe the magic quality of the painter, Mani and the Chinese, were added to the image of the painter/creator. In fact, the excellent reputation of these "painters" is probably due more to the element of the marvellous and the exotic in them than to a real knowledge or admiration of their art. Let us see how they are described in literature.

Mani

We find, in the *Shah-name* of Ferdowṣi[5] a passage which relates a discussion between Mani and the high priest *(mowbed)*. This discussion, during which there is a confrontation between the representatives of the two doctrines, leads to Mani's execution. P.Soucek notes the importance of the use of the image in the discussion between Mani and the priest. She points out, particularly, that the importance given to the image in this confrontation, complies probably with a Muslim interpretation of the phenomenon. This interpretation of the anecdote aims at portraying Mani as being doubly heretical in the eyes of Muslim readers, not only because of his doctrine, but also as a painter.

Mani appears among other works, in the *Sharaf-name* by Nezami,[7] in the *Golestan* by Sa'di,[8] as well as in the *History of the Sasanids* by Mirkhvond.[9] While, as we have seen earlier, it would appear that a copy of Mani's *Arzhang* was available in the library of Mahmud of Ghazni, it is however improbable that all the poets who talk about this book with its mythical paintings, had the opportunity to see it.

The Chinese

The Chinese are often presented as painters with a magic touch, and extraordinary prowess. Thus, in the *Shah-name,* Mani himself is Chinese (see note 5). The architect Farhad and the painter Shapur, who are the artists in the poem *Khosrow and Shirin,* had learnt their science in China.[10] In poetry, references to the art of the Chinese are a customary stereotype.[11]

One of the most famous episodes concerning the art of the Chinese is the anecdote relating the rivalry between the painters of Rum and of Chin. This anecdote has been used by Ghazzali,[12] then by Nezami, in his *Sharaf-name,*[13] by Mowlavi[14] also, and by many others.[15] Over and above the simple description of an artistic rivalry between two cultures, what has undoubtedly to be understood both in Ghazzali and Mowlavi as well as in Nezami, is a reflection of a much deeper kind. For these authors, the anecdote only serves as a pretext for illustrating the idea of the superiority of the mystical experience over acquired knowledge. However, P.Soucek[16] is of the view that the object of this anecdote, in Nezami, is to show that the active production of images, like their passive reception, are two aspects of artistic and scientific activity. She lays stress on the fact that Nezami is preoccupied with linking painting to the scientific disciplines (in this case, to optics). In fact, this example of "optical science" is comparable to that of the cup of Jamshid related by 'Attar: when Key Khosrow looks into the cup, he sees the entire world, but one thing escapes his sight: the cup itself.[17]

Iranians probably had an early knowledge of Chinese art, both directly, notably through porcelain and textiles, as well as indirectly, through the tales of travellers.[18] However, in literature and particularly in poetry, the main thing is to describe an object of reference not according to a realistic observation, but in terms of the eventual repercussion in the world of the imagination (*khiyal*).[19] In this case, by comparing the painter to what is most fantastic, i.e. the Chinese painter, they pay a compliment to the wondrous nature of the painter.

A phenomenon similar to that of the reference to the Chinese made by Iranians, is found in India, where the painters of Khorasan are described as being excellent. The 14th century historian Esami says:

> "During the reign of Soltan Mohammad b. Tughluq (1325-51), many artists and painters from China and from Khorasan came to Delhi."[20]

Similarly, in the chronicle about the Khalji kings of Malwa, the

Ma'aser-e Mahmudshahi by 'Ali b. Mahmud al-Kermani[21], it is related that:

"In 845/1441, the artists who had come from Khorasan or from Hindustan, got together in the capital (Mandu) and set about working".

Further on, the text reads:

"In 844/1440, the artists of India and of Khorasan, decorated the 'golden pavilion' *(kushk-e zarrin)*".

Beyond the geographical reference which may be correct, I think we should perceive in the supposed origin of the artists, a symbol of what is considered best in painting.

From the 16th century onwards, we see, together with the legendary references, some comparisons with real painters. Behzad is the paragon of these comparisons. He is often found quoted along with Mani, in several descriptions of paintings in Safavid Iran, but we see him even in the India of Shah Jahan. Here is an example taken from the description of the Red Fort of Shahjahanabad (Delhi), given by Mohammad Saleh:

"On the attractive wall of the *hamam*, such "meaningful figures" *(negaresh-e ma'ni)* had been drawn for purposes of decoration that, if Mani had seen them, he would have been petrified like the images on the wall. The magic painters of *'Eraq* had made decorations of ornamental foliages on the ceilings of the *hamam* with such great refinement that if Behzad had intended to imitate them, the brush would have fallen from his hands and he would have been obliged to recognise in his students (his successors) his own masters".[22]

These marvellous comparisons are found above all in the biographies of artists such as those by Qazi Ahmad, Eskandar Beyg or Khvandamir, and in the prefaces of albums and descriptive poems. Among the latter, those of the palaces of Qazvin, composed by 'Abdi Beyg Shirazi[23] are worthy of note as they have undoubtedly influenced later texts.[24] One "purple passage" in this style, is the *Preface* to an album offered to Behzad, written by Khvandamir,[25] which brings together a large quantity of images and clichés about the excellence of the painter.

M. T. Danesh-Pazhuh has not only shown the similarity of these texts but also what they have borrowed from each other.[26] We thus know that whole passages of the *Golestan-e honar* of Qazi Ahmad are in fact copied from the treatise by Qotb al-din Qesse Khvan, who took them from the poet 'Abdi Beyg Shirazi. The episode of the painters of Rum and of Chin that we mentioned earlier, is also found in 'Abdi Beyg[27] where, no doubt, it is devoid of any mystic content, being reduced to the marvellous anecdote which pays compliments to the qualities of the painters and to the enlightened mind of Alexander.

This literary imagery, often diverted from its initial objective (from mystical reflection, for instance) becomes, admittedly, quite annoying when we have to retrieve the technical aspects from these texts. Within the *estelahati*[28] and redundant style of the chroniclers, we have to detect the words that matter. P.Soucek notes: "an obstacle to the full use of the information contained in these texts is, however, the style in which most of them are written."[29] The Persian language, as we know, loves doublets; the literature of the chronicles makes entensive use of them. That is why, when reading the biographies of painters, we have undoubtedly to be careful not to attach too much importance to each word, but rather to the general meaning that arises from them. Otherwise, we may easily get lost in the literary flow.

An example of this kind of writing is the *Royal Warrant* appointing Behzad as the head of the royal library. It was drawn up by Khvandamir, probably on behalf of Shah Esma'il:[30]

> "Like the will of the Painter of the studio of creation and invention, and in accordance with the good wishes of the designer of the picture gallery of sky and earth, who, according to his Word "He formed you, and formed you well,"[31] has drawn, with the force of his reed pen, the living beings descended from Noah, in the most beautiful shapes on the pages of the possible, and the image of the superiority of humans over the other creatures of the Lord, according to his words "We have placed them well above many of those that We have created";[32] he has signed with the hand of his wisdom the decree "We have made you a vicar on earth"[33] on the page of the Sun's solution of colours, with the pen of Mercury, in our auspicious name, and he has ordered that the sheets of the lapis sky be painted and embellished so as to write on them the account of our victorious works, with the silver spangles of the stars and the cinnabar borders of the dusk; it is fitting therefore that the tablet of the divinely inspired spirit of the king, who is the shining repository of divine lights and the place in which the astonishing forms of his benevolence become manifest, be decorated in such a way that all the important matters relating to the royal workshops be entrusted to scholarly, capable and skilful persons who, through the drawing of their sharpened mind and the harmonious mixture of the colours of their beautiful nature, will deploy on the tablet of existence, the drawing of the most varied subtleties and the image of the invention of skills of

all kinds and will raise the veil from the desired face.
Therefore, he who is today the marvel of this period, the example to set before painters, the paragon of illuminators, the master Kamal al-din Behzad, who with his brush-which-unveils-faces, puts the soul of Mani to shame, and who with his pen-which-decorates-faces, has rendered useless the pages of the *Artang,* he who, like the reed-pen, places his head on the line of the *firman* which must be obeyed, and who has made of his foot a compass in the circle of obedience at the threshold of the shrine of the caliphate, has been showered with royal favours and with the kindness of the sovereign.
We order that the management and the stewardship of those who are a part of the royal library, calligraphers, painters, illuminators, those who trace borders, the colour makers, the gold beaters, the lapis washers and other persons working in the above-mentioned service, in our entire well-kept kingdom, be commended to him and entrusted to his care.
All the enlightened princes and the ministers beyond compare, the assistants to the court, refuge of the world, the envoys of our celestial court, the administrators of the affair of the kingdom, the agents of our ministers in general, and in particular all those persons deputed to the royal library and the above-mentioned groups of workers, must recognise the above-mentioned Master as the director in charge of the administration; they must submit for his inspection and his administration all matter relating to the library and must yield to all that he will have examined and to which he will have put his signature and his seal; they must not disobey his advice and his orders on all matters concerning the royal library. All that concerns these matters must be considered as his own prerogative. He, for his part, must display the countenance of confidence and the face of honesty on the writing tablet of his soul and on the page of his rectitude, by abstaining from arousing envy and from practicing favoritism, and must not move away from the path of truth and of uprightness. When this royal decree will carry the august signature of his sublime majesty, all must obey it and put their trust in it. Written on 27th 1st Jumada of the year 928 (24 April 1522)."

As we noted earlier, a particular characteristic of this literature is the figurative use, of a number of technical words that are specific to illumination and manuscript art. A.-M. Schimmel, in her excellent work on Islamic calligraphy,[34] has analysed the relationships between calligraphy and poetry, and she has particularly noted the large number of poetical metaphors having their origin in the vocabulary of the arts of the book. The affected and *estelahati* style of Persian poetry, particularly of the *sabk-e hendi* or Indian style, means that works such as the *Mer'at al-estelah* by Anand Ram Mokhles[35] whose only object is to clarify the meanings of the technical and laboured phrases used in poetry, are particularly necessary.

Let us now study the vocabulary used to describe the painter. Eskandar Beyg says of the painter Mir Zeyn al-'Abedin: *"naqqash-e khub, majles-saz va mosavver-e bi-qarine pakize-kar cehre-pardaz bud".*
"He was a good painter who painted scènes de genre and figures incomparably and without blemish, and he was a portrait painter also".

Naqqash is sometimes set in opposition to *mosavver* to distinguish non-figurative painting *(naqqashi)* from figurative painting *(suratgari)*; here, it would seem that *naqqash* is quite redundant, considering what follows, *majles-saz*, painter of scènes de genre, *cehre-pardaz*, portrait painter.

Qazi Ahmad says of the painter Abu al-Ma'sum Mirza: *"dar naqqashi va naqqari, va vassali va fassali, va afshangari va sahhafi, va moqavva' sazi va hakkaki, va khan tarashi va qashoq tarashi, va lajvard shu'i va sandarus tarashi, va sayer-e khorde kari va digar sanaye', 'adil va nazir nadarad."*[37] "He has no peer in painting and engraving, in the assembling of sheets and the mounting of pages, in gold flecking and in binding, in cardboard and in the polishing of stones, in shaping tables and spoons, in washing lapis and in crushing realgar, as well as in other small jobs and techniques".

It may be observed that the numerous abilities of this artist have been listed in doublets, giving importance to the assonance of the words; but does each word taken separately have the same effect?

Among the names of the function or specialization of artists, the following can be noted:
-*naqqash*, the painter, originally the engraver, subsequently sometimes the decorator or "designer" (see below).
-*mosavver,* "he who fashions", often the portrait painter.
-*tarrah*, the sketch-maker, who makes the initial outline *(tarh).*
-*mozahheb,* the illuminator, who works with gold.

These four terms, we have seen, may indicate a particular function in the workshop, or on the contrary they may be various terms for the same person.

Some functions at times more precise, made up of compound nouns, are also common:

-*Cehre-goshay, cehre-pardaz, surat-pardaz, yeke-surat,* portrait painter.

-*majles-saz*, painter of scenes de genre.

-*naqsh-band,* "binder of designs", foliage painter (see "Subjects of Painting, *band).*

-*kuh-pardaz,* landscape painter (mountains).

-*rang-amiz, gune-saz,* colour-maker, colourist.

Terms qualifying the painter in poetry approach the supernatural:

-the painter is a magician *(sehr negar)*; he has the power to bring life into what he creates;[38] he creates marvels and idols *(badaye' negar, cehre-goshay-e peykar).*

-he is complimented on his qualities of bringing out resemblances which compete with life itself.[39]

-the fineness of his work and its accuracy *(pakize-kar, daqiqe-kar, rize-kar)* are praised.

-the painter is extraordinary and none can rival him *(bi-badal, bi-qarine).*

-his work is a kind of miracle; he spends seven years on one frontispiece,[40] he paints on a grain of rice or on a narcissus petal,[41] he paints with a strand of hair that has been split.[42]

A. Sakisian has even noted some notions of art criticism, notably in Mirza Haydar Dughlat.[43] However, it should be noted that criticism is quite rare in biographical texts and that Persian authors prefer to be panegyrical.

NOTES

1. See article by Mrs. P. Soucek; we have taken several references from this remarkable article which we recommend; see also, above, our "Portrait" p.104.
2. *Qoran,* XL 66.
3. Dehkhoda, art. *naqqash,* gives numerous examples of this; see, among others, *naqqash-e azal* and *naqqash-e son'.*
4. Khvandamir, Preface to the *moraqqa'* of Behzad; trans. Bouvat and Qazvini, p.1.
5. Moscow ed. vol. VII, pp.251-252.
6. See note 1.
7. Vahid-e Dastgerdi ed., pp.404-405.
8. *Kolliyat,* Eqbal ed., p.8.
9. (Paris, 1843) pp.188-190.
10. Dastgerdi ed., pp.216-217.
11. See again Dehkhoda, art. *naqqash.*

12. *Ehya' 'olum al-din*, III (Cairo, 1962), p.22.
13. Dastgerdi ed. pp.401-404.
14. *Masnavi*, Nicholson ed., I, pp.213-215.
15. Sho'a'i, pp.206-208 mentions Anvari Abivardi *(Divan)* and 'Abdi Beyg Shirazi *(A'in-e Eskandari)*; see below.
16. See note 1.
17. *Elahi-name*, trans., pp.235-237.
18. See the embassy of Ghiyas al-din Naqqash in China in the *Majma' al-tavarikh* of Hafez-e Abru and the "*khata'i*" in our chapter "Subjects of painting".
19. *Khiyal* is also the name of the painter of the *Hosn-o del* of Fattahi; see also P.Soucek, op. cit., pp.11-12 about the definition of *khiyal* given by Nezami 'Aruzi.
20. Esami, pp.114-115.
21. Ed. pp.45 and 58.
22. *'Amal-e Saleh*, III, 35.
23. See for instance *Rowzat al-safa* and *Dowhat al-azhar;* see our chapter "Mural painting", Safavid period.
24. See M.T. Danesh-Pazhuh "*Rang-sazi*".
25. Ed. and trans. Bouvat and Qazvini, "Deux documents relatifs à Behzad".
26. See "*Rang-sazi*".
27. *A'in-e Eskandari;* see Danesh-Pazhuh, "*Rang-sazi*", pp.27-29.
28. "Which uses technical expressions in poetic contexts"; see for ex. Bombaci, *Litterature Turque*, p.207.
29. Soucek, p.9.
30. Bouvat and Qazvini, trans. pp. 152-154; text, pp. 159-161; the translation suggested by these authors does not take sufficient account of the double meaning of the technical words used; therefore we give a new translation here.
31. *Qoran*, XL, 66.
32. *Qoran*, XVII, 72.
33. *Qoran*, XXXVIII, 25
34. *Calligraphy and Islamic Culture.*
35. See Bibliography.
36. Ed. p.174
37. Ed. p.149; trans. p.190.
38. See the anecdote about "Jesus's birds", Qazi Ahmad, ed. p.134, trans. p.180; see also the *Shah-name* on the subject of Mani, *loc. cit.*
39. See our chapter "Subjects of painting", Portrait.
40. Mirza Haydar Dughlat, about Mahmud Mozahheb, *BWG*, p.191.
41. Anand Ram, *Camanestan*, fol. 93a and 129a.
42. Sadeqi, *Qanun*, verse 22.
43. "Esthétique et terminologie".

8

THE ARTIST

1. His origin

As opposed to Hindu India in which painters belong to a particular caste, the social or geographic origin of the artist does not follow any rule in the Iranian world, and in Islamic countries in general. That is why we will give only a few examples here, each case being unique. Indeed, some artists belong to reputed families of a city or a region: Aqa Mirak is a Seyyed from Isfahan [1] Sadeqi belongs to the Afshar tribe.[2] Others, on the contrary, are of humble origin: Siyavush Beyg is a Georgian slave;[3] Daswanth, Akbar's painter, is the son of a palanquin bearer;[4] the calligrapher Bulbul is a black slave.[5]

Some artists are descendants of families of painters or of calligraphers and have, so to speak, been born in the workshop. Among these are Mir Seyyed 'Ali, son of Mir Mosavver,[6] Mirza 'Ali, son of Soltan Mohammad,[7] or Mozaffar 'Ali, nephew of the calligrapher Rostam 'Ali, and probably belonging to the family of Behzad.[8]

2. His training

Little information concerning the training of the artist, is found in texts. Generally, the treatises recommend practice,[9] the search for a master who has good pupils,[10] the careful execution of work,[11] all of which are obviously good pieces of advice.

Moti Chandra[12] describes the relationship between the artist and the student in very poetic terms:

"In the days of the Mughals, the pupils were admitted by the master artist when they were children, after they had worshipped him with flowers, etc., and presented him with eatables. They began their lessons in drawings by practising circles and spirals on a wooden panel seared with the bole. When they had thoroughly mastered the designs they began to practise in drawing lotus flowers, fish, peacocks, deer..."

No doubt, in many cases, things did not happen in this way. For example, Daswanth was discovered one day by Akbar and put under the care of 'Abd al-Samad. In a little while, he surpassed all the other painters. Abu al-Fazl says moreover that all the students of 'Abd al-Samad became masters.[13] M. Chandra notes also: "Even the present day Mughal artist (!) has no respect for an amateur who is called *atai,* or an artist who has not learnt the art methodically under an accomplished teacher."[14]

In the case of artists born in the workshop, it can be imagined that their training was guaranteed. Chardin moreover, when talking about apprenticeship, says:

"There is no commitment point for apprenticeship and nothing is given for learning the skill. On the contrary, the boys who train under a master receive wages from the very first day."[15]

3. His career

While in fact training does not seem to be an insuperable obstacle, a career, on the other hand, is secure only from the moment the artist is noticed by a patron. Whether he be a prince or a workshop patron, the artist's existence depends on him and he sometimes contributes towards his training. He ensures his survival by giving him work regularly, and enables him to use costly material which he would have found it difficult to procure by his own means. It is therefore under these conditions that the artist abides by the social order. Once the artist has proved his worth, he becomes a part of the royal house and has the status of an official *(sarkar)* in it. A painter or a calligrapher can become a general or a governor. He can be the object of an "exchange" between princes, or fall from grace, depending on princely favour. His physical entity no longer belongs to him. His functions are attributed to him more often according to the needs of the court than in conformity with his artistic talents. Here again, one can only mention some specific cases, such as the following:

-Exchanges. Mir Mosavver is the object of Homayun's desire and the latter offers Shah Tahmasp a thousand *tomans* in exchange for the artist.[16]

When Mir 'Emad was assassinated in 1027/1618 by order of Shah 'Abbas, Jahangir said: "If Shah 'Abbas had given him to me instead of putting him to death, I would have rewarded him with his weight in pearls."[17]

Habib-allah of Saveh worked under Navvab Hoseyn Khan Shamlu, governor of Qom, who later took him to Herat. 'Abbas I took him away from the governor and put him in his own service as a painter.[18]

-Irresistible rise. 'Abd al-Samad, originally from Shiraz, comes to India with Homayun who gives him the title of *Shirin-qalam*. Under Akbar, he first of all looks after the painting workshops and particularly supervises the production of the 1400 paintings of the *Hamze-name*.[19] Then, in 1577, he manages the mint at Fatehpur-Sikri.[20] In 1582, he is put in charge of the trade of leather objects and gets the profits from their sale.[21] The following year, he is put in charge of the house of Prince Murad.[22] In 1586, he is appointed *divan* of Multan.[23] His son, an intimate friend of Jahangir, becomes Amir al-omara in 1605.[24]

-Rise and fall. The painter Khvaje 'Abd al-'Aziz, son of the painter 'Abd al-Vahhab, taught painting to Shah Tahmasp with whom he struck a close friendship. Having committed forgery with the royal seal, he lost his nose and ears.[25]

'Abd-allah Mozahheb worked for twenty years with the prince Ebrahim Mirza. When the latter was executed, in 1577, under orders of Esma'il II, the artist left the court and became a *farrash* at the shrine of Mashhad.[26]

Mir Seyyed Ahmad, calligrapher of Shah Tahmasp, was the object of envy and intrigue. Shah Tahmasp asked him to return the salaries he had received. He was restored to favour by Esma'il II.[27]

-Change of direction. At the time of the second editing of the *Golestan-e honar*, Aqa Reza, in the service of Shah 'Abbas, preferred wrestling to attending to his paint-brushes[28].

Siyavush Beyg, after he came to the notice of Shah Tahmasp who attended to the completion of his training, worked for several years in the royal library. In 1606, he was living in Shiraz where he was carrying out various functions (*yaraq*), which were perhaps very remote from the field of the arts.[29]

These few examples show the mobility of the artists within the royal workshops, and the ease with which their careers succeeded or failed according to their being in or out of favour.

There were undoubtedly other artists who were more independent, or who lived practically as hermits in a *madrasa* or attached to a shrine. Qazi Ahmad describes the illuminator and paper cutter Nazar 'Ali Qate' as coming from Badakhshan to Mashhad, dressed in felt, like a *dervish* and says that he lived quietly.[30]

Eskandar Beyg says that Mir Zeyn al-Abedin's students had a workshop but that he himself only worked for princes.[31] He says that 'Abd al-Jabbar Astarabadi also had a workshop, but as he himself was not very interested in painting, it was his students who looked after the workshop.[32]

It is obvious that the larger part of the information that we have about artists and the way the workshops functioned, concerns royal or princely establishments which are the only ones that had chroniclers, from whom we derive our information. In fact, we know almost nothing about the "ordinary" painter. However, M. Chandra makes this charming remark:

"In the age of the Great Mughals, mediocre and third grade painters were not in demand.[33]"

That is understandable since there is no reason why the Mughal sovereigns, who were in a position to avail of the best would have wanted the worst! That does not mean that a great number of lesser painters whom we know nothing about, did not exist; the little we do know about them is from manuscripts of very average aesthetic quality, which authors of catalogues consider as being of "provincial style". Only these manuscripts testify to an undoubtedly commercial production, executed by second rate artists.

Therefore, while we do have some more or less important information about known and respected artists, about their various origins, their training, and their fortunes, it is not really possible to draw conclusions of a general nature about the status of the painter, from the court artist to the local illuminator, on the basis of the available data.

NOTES

1. Qazi Ahmad, trans., p.185.
2. *Id.*, p.191.
3. *Id.*, p.191.
4. *A'in*, I, p.108.
5. Qazi Ahmad, trans., pp.82-83.
6. *Id.*, p.185.
7. *Id.*, p.186.
8. *Id.*, Eskandar Beyg, p.174.
9. Seyrafi Sha'er, ed. p.33, line 46.
10. Sadeqi, Qanun, line 52.
11. Simi, see Y. Porter, "Un traité..." p.191.
12. *Techniques of Mughal Painting*, p.74.
13. *A'in*, I, p.107.
14. M. Chandra, p.74. It should be noted that this word *('ata'i)* was originally not used at all in a disparaging manner, since it meant "gifted". In India, of late, it has taken on a negative connotation, particularly in musical circles, as it is now used for an artist who has been trained without a *guru*.
15. *Voyages*, IV, p.94.
16. Qazi Ahmad, trans., p.185.
17. Quoted by C.Huart, p.242, without indicating the source; this passage is not, at any rate, found in the *Memoirs* of Jahangir.
18. Qazi Ahmad, trans., p.191.
19. Abu al-Fazl, *A'in*, I, p.107.
20. Abu al-Fazl, *Akbar-name*, III, p.321.
21. *Id.*, p.585.
22. *Id.*, p.598.
23. *Id.*, p.779.
24. *Tuzuk*, I, p.14.
25. Qazi Ahmad, trans., p.186.
26. *Id.*, p 190.
27. *Id.*, p.140.
28. *Id.*, p.193; see also Y. Porter, *"Notes sur le Golestan..."*.
29. *Id.*, p.191; Eskandar Beyg, p.176.
30. Qazi Ahmad, trans., p.193.
31. Eskandar Beyg, pp.174-175.
32. *Id.*, p.175.
33. M. Chandra, p.76.

9

THE WORKSHOP, ITS OPERATION AND DIVISION OF WORK

1. The place of work

Restricting our description of workshops to those belonging to princes is undoubtedly a constraint imposed by our limited knowledge. But it is obvious that, apart from the princely commissions, there was also a general production of illuminated manuscripts, and therefore that there existed workshops other than royal ones. An example is the workshop of Mir Zeyn al-'Abedin's students which we have just mentioned.

What does a painter or a calligrapher need in order to work? His tools, naturally, whose degree of sophistication will depend on the means at his disposal, and a little corner where he can squat. In short, the "basic" workshop can be set up anywhere.

Mir 'Ali Heravi, in his treatise *Medad al-khotut*[1] describes the place of work *(dar makan-ė ketabat)* as follows:

> "Doors open on the four sides, in the morning one sits facing the east, at noon, the south and at the end of the day, the west; however, in summer, it is better to remain till evening in the breeze which comes from the pool pavilion."

Here is Chardin's description of Persian craftsmen:

> "The observation that I want to make next about the methods of the craftsmen of the East is that they need few tools to work. The ease with which these people settle down to work is really incredible in comparison to our countries. Most of them have neither shops nor work-benches. They go to work wherever they are summoned. They settle down in the corner of a room on the bare ground, or

on a ragged carpet, and in an instant their work place is ready. Seated on his haunches, the worker starts on his task, holding his piece of work with his feet and working on it with his hands."[2]

I had myself the opportunity of seeing a gold beater at work in Jaipur; he came to the house with his material to prepare a gold solution. His work-tools fitted into a tiny bag.

It is of course a different matter in the royal workshops. The structure in these workshops is meant for a prestigious production which requires, within the administration of the palace, a certain organization of the distribution of space and work.

Little information has come down to us about the way the workshops functioned, before the Timurid period. One exception is the *Vaqf-name* by Rashid al-din: in his testament, he makes provision for the setting up of a studio for copying. This is probably one of the rare detailed references to a non-princely studio. It is also one of the oldest: "The book house is located near the *satvi* (winter) mosque."[3] Two calligrapher-copyists are employed in the "book house."[4] Everything, right down to the oil lamps, the bread for the employees and their salaries, is provided for in the instructions left by Rashid al-din. We also find reference to a paper mill *(kaghaz-khane[5])*. Only illumination and not painting is expressly mentioned. However, it could be surmised that the illustrated copies of the *Jame' al-tavarikh* from the early part of the 14th century, which are known to us, or at least some copies which resemble them, may have been produced in this workshop.

The workshops for painting and manuscript production form a part of the various *karkhane* or *boyutat* of the royal house. This organisation of intendancy in the various workshops is undoubtedly a very old one and is widespread in the Muslim courts. Thus the organisation of the house of Firuz Shah of Delhi into thirty-six workshops is certainly borrowed from an Iranian model.[6] These workshops are divided into *ratebi* (those which collect a salary) and *gheyr-e ratebi* (those which do not). Unfortunately, out of the thirty-six studios, 'Afif only names seventeen, and the painting workshop is not among these. Another mention, later on,[7] enables us to note however that Firuz Shah possessed some painting workshops.

This arrangement of the royal house divided into various workshops is adopted also by the Safavids and the Mughals. Most courts maintain workshops. In a Mughal treatise on household, some details are given about what is required for the workshop and the library.[8] Shrines and *madrasas* also contain workshops, if not for painting, at least for manuscripts and for illumination.

In the palace, the artists' workshops are found in the area of the *boyutat,* which includes the stables as well as shops and repair workshops. In the *'arze-dasht* which is attributed to the court of Baysanqor,[9] it is noted that a building meant for the painters and the calligraphers, has just been completed. However, the royal workshops should probably not be seen as being heavy and immobile structures: in the *A'in-e Akbari,*[10] the description of Akbar's workshops shows their arrangement during military operations, which would imply that they travelled with the court. At Fatehpur-Sikri, Akbar had a big square building constructed, surrounded with domed galleries, in the manner of caravanserais, which must have housed the mint and the workshops.[11] This was active from 1571 till 1585, the time when Fatehpur-Sikri was abandoned for Agra, then for Gujerat and Panjab, where military operations were taking place.

Chardin describes the workshops of Isfahan as follows:

> "These studios are called *carcane* or work-houses; they are thirty-two in number, all in different places. The recruitment to these studios takes place in the following manner: the worker presents himself to the head of the group to which he desires to belong (...) along with a piece of his work, and a request. If the head of the studio approves of him, he takes him to the *nazir,* who is the superintendent of the royal house (...); he takes him before the king with the work he has done, or he simply shows the work to the king; and, depending on whether the king is pleased with them, he decides the wages and the maintenance of the worker (...) All these studios are called *sercaar (sarkar).*"[12]

Mohammad Saleh writes that as the Mughal capitals of Agra and Lahore had become too small and crowded, Shah Jahan decided to construct a new capital, Shahjahanabad.[13] This author says, among other things, that the workshops of Agra and Lahore were within the fort, near the door, and that they were crowded and not spacious enough. During the construction of the new capital, the workshops also must have been inside the fort, along the Lahore gate side (west): "From the north gate to the south gate, two rows of domed archways were raised, to serve as stables and workshops."[14] In fact, it would seem that this part of the fort, which no longer exists today, was never completed. According to later descriptions, this was the part where the craftsmen, the stable boys and soldiers lived. It was built of rather precarious material and it caught fire several times.[15]

In the *Tazkerat al-moluk* by Rafi' al-din Shirazi, the library of 'Ali 'Adelshah II of Bijapur is described in the following terms:

> "Around sixty men, calligraphers, illuminators, binders and painters are busy at work in this library."[16]

There is a common confusion, both in Persian texts as well as in contemporary works, between the painting workshop and the library. In fact the former is *a priori* the place where books with paintings are produced, and the latter is the place where these are stored. This is a difference that is often difficult to grasp. Thus, the *Tazkerat al-moluk*[17] differentiates between the two, *ketab-khane* and *naqqash-khane*. Was the latter possibly a sub-division of the first?

It should be noted, finally, that the workshops are sometimes forced to shift. Like the library, the workshop also arouses envy. Thus, Baysanqor's workshop in Herat which, on his death, went to 'Ala' al-Dowle, was shifted to Samarkand by Ulugh Beyg, with its entire staff.[18] Earlier, Baysanqor had already sent for artists from Tabriz for his studio.[19] Similarly, when 'Obeyd Khan Uzbek took Herat, he brought back some artists to Bukhara, among these being Mir 'Ali.[20]

2. Division of the work

Some texts give us information about the organisation of painting workshops. The *'arze-dasht* of the court of Baysanqor, is perhaps the oldest of these texts;[21] There are also the Royal Warrant of Behzad,[22] a passage from the *Tazkerat al-moluk*,[23] and another one from the *Mohit al-tavarikh*[24] on workshops. Several functions are specified in these texts, which keep the different professional groups occupied.

Royal Warrant of Behzad	*Tazkerat al-moluk*
-kalantari-ye ketabkhane (intendant of the library)	*-saheb-e jam-e ketabkhane*
-kateban (calligraphers)	
-naqqashan (painters)	
-mozahheban (illuminators)	*-mozahheb*

Royal Warrant of Behzad	*Tazkerat al-moluk*
(jadval-keshan (those who draw the *jadval*) *-hall-karan* (colour makers) *-zar-kuban* (gold beaters) *-lajvard-shuyan* (washers of lapis) -others	 *-zar-kub* *-basmeci* ("printer") *-kaghaz-gar* (paper maker) *-qayceci* (scissor maker) *-gerek-yaraq* (intendent)

Before examining these functions one by one, it should be noted that very often these were versatile artists who, in addition to their main function, were also able to distinguish themselves in other fields.

The Calligrapher

It is impossible to conceive of the existence of manuscript workshop without calligraphy. Indeed, as we have seen earlier, while this subject oversteps the bounds of our study on painting, it is nevertheless indispensable to the very concept of an illustrated manuscript. From the very first centuries after the advent of Islam, the calligrapher enjoyed immense prestige. The lives and works of the calligraphers from the 8th to the 12th centuries are known to us much more than those of the painters of the same period. A single glance at the text of Qazi Ahmad makes us aware of this.

One must undoubtedly make a distinction between various categories, between the master calligrapher who is sometimes the director of the library, and the second rank scribe. Here are a few categories:
-khoshnevis, khattat (calligrapher)
-kateb (copyist)
-monshi, dabir (secretary)
vaqaye'-nevis (secretary)
-farman-nevis (calligrapher of *farmans*)

Calligraphers, like other artists attached to the court, receive salaries and allowances according to the quality of their work. Like other artists, they are "officials" *(sarkar-e homayuni)* and sometimes they execute tasks that are quite remote from their artistic qualifications. They are very often attached to the Chancery *(Dar al-ensha')*, where they participate in the calligraphy of the *farmans* as well as in administration work.

Among the calligraphers who have been in charge of libraries, mention may be made of Moheb 'Ali, son of Rostam 'Ali, from the library of Ebrahim Mirza;[25] Mohammad Amin 'Aqili, from the library of Ismi Khan Shamlu;[26] 'Enayat-allah, from Akbar's library.[27]

Among calligraphers attached to the *Dar al-ensha'* (Chancery), are most of those mentioned by Qazi Ahmad in his second chapter ("Masters of the *ta'liq"*): Khvaje Jan Toghra'i, reputed for his *toghra*,[28] Sheykh Mohammad Tamimi, Mowlana Idris, Hajji 'Ali Astarabadi,[29] Darvish 'Abd-allah,[30] Khvaje 'Atiq Monshi, secretary to Shah Esma'il, who made his *toghra*.[31]

Other calligraphers carried out administrative or religious functions: Mir Ne'mat-allah, who became *qazi* of Isfahan,[32] Mir Nezam al-din Ashraf, who became *sadr* of Abarquh.[33]

In fact, we find in the Chancery not only secretaries, calligraphers of *farman* and subordinate scribes, but also illuminators, in charge of the decoration of *farmans*,[34] as well as calligraphers specialized in the engraving of stones for making seals.

- *Epigraphist calligraphers*

Numerous calligraphers also made a name for themselves in monument epigraphy, among them being: 'Abd-allah Tabbakh,[35] Adham Yazdi,[36] Mahmud Zarrin-qalam,[37] Malek Daylami,[38] Salim Kateb,[39] Mohammad Hosein. The latter was specifically entrusted by Esma'il II with making inscriptions for official monuments.[40]

- *Copyists*

Chardin gives the following information about copyists:

"There are a large number of copyists in Persia, particularly in the big cities; but they can hardly make a living in this profession; they normally earn just fifteen sols a day, for writing from morning till evening. The most that one can write when one is very expert at the task, and works without a break, is from 500 to 600 couplets a day."[41]

Chardin is obviously describing copyists who have set up business on their own. Moreover, it is understandable that Simi's contemporaries should be astonished when Dowlatshah reports that this calligrapher composed and wrote two thousand lines in twenty-four hours.[42] Besides, the price for a single line by a master calligrapher would undoubtedly have paid for several days work of a copyist!

The painter and the illuminator

The painter is generally called *naqqash*. We have seen that this word has various meanings and does not necessarily indicate a particular specialization. In fact, most painters have many strings to their bow, as is apparent from their biographies. Some painters are known for their specialization, such as 'Abd-allah Mozahheb[43] or Mohammad Amin Jadvalkesh whose *laqab* (nicknames) indicate their particular field of work. Others, on the contrary, are gifted in a number of different techniques, as Abu al-Ma'sum Mirza.[44]

The main specialisations are: *tarrahi* (drawing), *naqqashi* (painting in general), *surat-gari* (portrait painting), *tazhib* (illumination), *jadval-keshi* (border design), *rang-o-rowghan* (lacquered "oil" painting).

The division of work, not only within a manuscript, but even on a single painting is known to us, thanks to notes in the margins of Mughal manuscripts. There are numerous examples though with little variation in the wordings. The most common notes, as we have seen, are *tarh, 'amal, rang-amizi, cehre-gosha'i* or *surat*.[45] By way of example, we could quote this in an illustration of an *Akbar-name*:[46] *"tarh-e La'l, 'amal-e Dhanu, cehre-gosha'i-ye Khemkaran"* (drawing by La'l, "work" by Dhanu, faces by Khemkaran). La'l and Khemkaran are mentioned by Abu al-Fazl.[47]

Such examples are particularly numerous at the time of Akbar, due to the keen interest that this sovereign took in manuscript art whose large production necessitated a real team work. Jahangir even went as far as saying that he could recognize the different painters who had contributed to a single work.[48]

Less is known about the paintings of Safavid manuscripts. However, a manuscript of the *Makhzan al-asrar* by Nezami, copied at Bukhara in 1540, contains a painting with the note *'amal-e Mahmud Mozahheb, cehre-ye Mohsen, raqam e Mohammad*.[49] The habit of writing these notes in the margin may therefore have been born in the Iranian world. Any discovery of more notes of this kind would enable us to re-examine the idea prevalent nowadays in circles close to the art market, according to which each painting should be attributed to a single painter.

Workshop production is certainly the main reason why the paintings are rarely signed or attributed to a painter during his lifetime. True, there are some known exceptions, such as the famous painting of the court of Kayumars executed by Soltan Mohammad, in the *Shah-name* of Shah Tahmasp, described by Dust Mohammad as causing much admiration;[50] It is believed that he executed it alone. The same applies to the frontispiece of Mahmud Mozahheb mentioned by Mirza Haydar Dughlat.[51] The illustration of Shah Tahmasp's *Khamse* of Nezami[52] showing Majnun in the desert, bears the note *'amal-e* (work of) *Aqa Mirak* clearly written in the middle of the page. In Iranian manuscripts that have found their way into India, some attribution have been added in the margins. These are often incorrect.[53] Other "signatures" are "disguised", hidden within the composition or the figurative inscriptions in the background of the paintings. An example of this is given by A.S. Melikian-Chirvani, concerning the painter Khvaje Mirak.[54]

Abu al-Fazl or Qazi Ahmad recognise, in their books, the personal value of artists. They talk of their talent, while judging their works. This does not necessarily contradict a collective conception of the work. This idea is not alien to the Western world either, where the master leaves the larger part of the work to his students, as was the case with Rubens. In the same way, the concept of a completed work is apparently not universally recognized. Indeed, an old painting may be completely repainted according to the fashion of the day, or abusively restored, as was the case with Timurid manuscripts "restored" by the Mughals. Some manuscripts, such as the *Khamse* of Nezami, executed for Shah Tahmasp, were "completed" almost a century after the first phase, by the addition of new paintings.[55]

Some painters have their specialization. Among the artists of the Mughal court, Mansur for instance won renown for his execution of plants, flowers and animals. Every time Jahangir wanted a bird or a flower to be drawn, he sent for Mansur. We thus find in his *Memoirs* mention of a falcon, of the hundred flowers of Kashmir, and of the *saj* bird, that Mansur painted for him.[56]

Similarly for the portrait, Jahangir has his specialists such as Abu al-Hasan Nader al-zaman, who painted the portrait of the king on the day he was enthroned, to serve as a frontispiece to the *Jahangir-nama*.[57] One day, when one of his courtiers asked him for his portrait, Jahangir sent for this particular painter, to make it.[58] When his courtier 'Enayat Khan was dying, Jahangir found the physiognomy of the sick man so striking that he ordered his painters to paint his portrait.[59]

Among the portrait painters of the Safavid period, Qazi Ahmad mentions Mir Mosavver, Qadimi, who was the official portrait painter of Shah Tahmasp's library, Zeyn al-'Abedin Tabrizi and Sheykh Mohammad.[60]

The illuminators are also often painters or calligraphers, like Simi Nishapuri,[61] Mohammad Amin Mashhadi.[62]

Illuminator-painters include: Mozaffar 'Ali (p.186), Zeyn al-'Abedin (p.187), Sheykh Mohammad (p.187).

Illuminators (called *mozahheb*): Mahmud Mozahheb,[63] Hasan Mozahheb Baghdadi (he also made some mural decorations; p.189[64]), Mirak Mozahheb,[65] Ghiyas al-din Mohammad Mozahheb (p.189), 'Abd-allah Mozahheb (he also made "lacquer" paintings; pp.189-190), Yari Mozahheb (p.188), 'Abd-allah Shirazi,[66] Qavvam al-din Mas'ud, son of Mirạk Mozahheb,[67] Kamal al-din 'Abd al-Vahhab.[68] Mohammad Amin Jadvalkesh (p.189) is mentioned as a *jadval-kesh*.

Lacquer painters include Mozaffar 'Ali (p.186), 'Abd-allah Mozahheb (pp.189-190), Sadeqi.[69] None of them does only lacquer-painting.

- *Mural painting*

We pointed out in a preceding chapter that manuscript painters also participated in mural paintings. Among these are Hasan Mozahheb Baghdadi (see above), Aqa Hasan Naqqash,[70] Mozaffar 'Ali,[71] Sheykh Mohammad Sabzevari.[72] Unfortunately, the technical details concerning the manner in which these artist worked, are missing. Did they themselves make the drawings on the walls and did they paint the backgrounds, or did they have the larger part of the work done by their apprentice painters? Did they work with sketches and patterns traced with pounce, or did they draw their lines directly on the walls? It is important to note, on the other hand, that figurative painters as well as illuminators and calligraphers (see above) have worked on mural paintings.

- *Naqqash/"Designer"*

The collaboration of manuscript artists was probably not limited to mural decoration. We have already noted that it is highly probable that painters took an interest in other grounds, such as ceramics or cloth or may be even gardens and carpets. One important text on this subject is the *'arze-dasht* of the court of Baysanqor.[73] It specifies for example, that Khvaje 'Abd-al-Rahim is busy making drawings *(toruh)* for binders, illuminators, tent embroiders *(kheyme-duzan)* and mosaicists *(kashi-tarashan)*. Further on, the author reports that Khvaje Mir Hasan copied the drawing of a saddle made by Mir Dowlatyar, and that Mir

Shams al-din and Ostad Dowlatkhvaje are reproducing it in mother of pearl. Several painters tried their hand at ceramics, such as Hajji Mohammad Naqqash,[74] Mani Mashhadi[75] and Esma'il 'Aref Kermani.[76] However, as a general rule, we lack information to specify whether it is the painter who decides to make a drawing or a sketch, for a wall hanging, for example, or if it is another craftsman who adapts the drawing of the painter, for his own use. There is a hanging conserved in Los Angeles[77] which has a striking resemblance to a drawing of Aqa Reza Jahangiri[78] and which shows a young man with a cup in his hand. The hanging is dated *circa* 1570 and the drawing *circa* 1600 (would it not have been more logical for the drawing to be dated earlier than the hanging?). This is no coincidence: the drawing of Aqa Reza Jahangiri was perhaps meant for the weaving studios?

When discussing the grounds for painting, we mentioned the role that the painter may have played as a sketch maker for textiles. In the Istanbul albums, some pages of line drawings really seem to be sketches for embroidery or illumination, meant undoubtedly to be reproduced on other grounds.[79] Gathered together later in albums, these pages were quite possibly circulated among the workshops.

What we do know for certain is that the painting workshop was part of a group of creative workshops and that there was a certain amount of contact and exchange between them. We have seen how 'Abd al-Samad, who was in charge of Akbar's painting workshop, was transferred and made responsible for the mint. While this may have been the result of a promotion within the hierarchy of the *sarkar,* the artistic aspect was probably not absent either. By putting a painter-calligrapher at the head of his mint, it is possible that Akbar hoped for coins of a better artistic quality (however, to confirm this hypothesis, it would be necessary to look for numismatic proof). But this is not a general rule; it has also been seen that the artistic worth of the *sarkar* is not always taken into consideration.

Here again, we are talking of the painters of the royal workshops, but there were many other *naqqash*. One interesting case, which gained some renown, is that of the designers of shawls in Kashmir. Some interesting samples of their art were noted by W.Moorcroft during the 1830s;[80] some copies were also made in France, in the form of an album called *Le Cachemirien*.[81] In the India Office *Album of the Crafts of Kashmir*, there is a plate showing these *naqqash* at work.[82]

Binders

Binding work, as we have seen, is quite diversified and it includes, not only the work in leather or lacquer for the cover, but also the layout of the margins, the manufacture of cardboard and of decorated paper and the creation of albums (see plate no.13).

Here are a few binders names: Abu al-Ma'sum Mirza,[83] Qasem Beyg Tabrizi,[84] Mohsen Mojalled,[85] Fonuni Esfahani,[86] 'Eshrati Qalandar,[87] Fekri Astarabadi, Zati Lari, Ramazan Astarabadi, Mir Shokri Shirazi.

Afshan-gar (makers of gold-flecked paper): Mozaffar Ali,[88] Ghiyas al-din Mozahheb,[89] 'Abd al-Samad Mashhadi.[90]

Vassal (repairs and margin lay-out): Mohammad Amin Jadvalkesh,[91] Abu al-Ma'sum Mirza,[92] Yahya Qazvini,[93] 'Abd-allah Tabbakh (calligrapher).[94]

Abri-saz (marblers): Mohammad Amin Jadvalkesh,[95] Yahya Qazvini,[96] Mir Mohammad Taher.[97]

'Aks-saz (stencil makers): Mohammad Amin,[98] Mowlana Kepek.[99]

Qat'e saz (paper cutters): Nazar 'Ali Qate'.[100]

Colour-makers and lower staff

These are obviously the lower ranks of craftsmen working in the workshops, whose names have not come down to us. The texts tell us that some painters were gifted at *rang-amizi*, but does that really refer to the "mixing of colours", or is it a term in art criticism, suggesting the painter is a good colourist? The following are described as such: Sheykh Mohammad,[101] 'Ali Asghar Kashani,[102] Sadeqi,[103] Simi Nishapuri.[104]

The Royal Warrant of Behzad drawn up by Khvandamir (see above), mentions: *halkaran* (those who grind and dilute colours), *zar kuban* (gold beaters), *lajvard-shuyan* (lapis washers). Sam Mirza tells us that Mir Shokri of Shiraz and Nabati of Tabriz were excellent washers of lapis.[105] This is again one of the techniques practiced by the endlessly resourceful Abu al-Ma'sum Mirza.[106]

In the *Tazkerat al-moluk*[107] we find mention of:

-basmeci: Minorsky translates as "printer"; this "printer" is not a printer in the modern sense of the word, but an iron gilder, or printer of tampons on leather as well as on cloth or on paper.

-kaghaz-gar: paper-dealer or paper-maker (see plate no.12); it would seem in fact that in some cases the product is made in the workshop, as in the Rashid al-din foundation (see earlier) and in others it is bought

from outside. In the *Dastur al-moluk*,[108] it is specified that the *majles-nevis* receives thirty reams of paper from Dowlatabad, in other words imported paper (see above, Paper). Zeynati and 'Abdal-e Kashani are two paper merchants mentioned by Sam Mirza.[109]
-*qayceci*: according to Minorsky, this would be the scissor maker; he perhaps makes other tools also.

The *Matla' al-'olum*[110] describes, among others, the professions of *zengar-saz* (verdigris maker) and of *rang-saz* (oil colours; see above).

3. Management and administration work

Commissioning of the work

While discussing composition, we saw how a manuscript was brought into shape, particularly by means of the *mastar*. On the other hand, little is known about the situations which give rise to the creation of a work. The simplest example is that of the "ordinary" copy. Another case is the religious institutions or foundations such as Rashid al-din: in the chapter on "Business of the book house",[111] it is specified that every year, the following must be produced:
-a large sized Koran in thirty volumes, in beautiful handwriting, decorated with illuminations, and with a leather or morocco binding,
-a collection of *hadis* in four volumes or more, in beautiful handwriting, on beautiful paper, so that it should be expensive, with beautiful ink, and with illuminations on the pages; the gilding of the binding and of the encasing should be in gold.

Further on,[112] it is requested that two copies of all the works of Rashid al-din be produced each year, one in Persian and the other in Arabic, on fine paper, in beautiful handwriting, bound in morocco leather and copied from the original manuscripts kept in the library of the Rashidi foundation.

In the case of royal studios, the commission comes probably from the prince himself. The example of the album of Baysanqor, copied from that of Ahmad Jalayer, shows how, in deference to the desire of the prince, various artists (Seyyed Ahmad Naqqash, Khvaje 'Ali Mosavver, the calligrapher Farid al-din Ja'far and the binder Qavvam al-din) are brought together and put to work.[113]

It seems that among the Safavids, and certainly even before that, there was a desire that each reign be marked by the production of a *Shah-name*. Certainly the most beautiful of all Safavid manuscripts, the *Shah-name* of Shah Tahmasp -which, alas, is now in several parts and places-, along with those of Esma'il II from 1576-77[114] and 'Abbas I from 1587-97,[115] seem to be commissioned works meant to mark a special occasion.

In other cases, such as the *Memoirs* of Jahangir, the manuscript was published immediately after it had been dictated:

> "When the events of the first twelve years of the *Jahangir-name* were recorded, I ordered the copyists of my private library to make a volume of these twelve years, and to prepare copies of the same so that I could offer them as gifts to my close friends. As soon as the first copy was ready, I gave it to my son Shah Jahan.[116]"

The workshops of the Moghul sovereigns, particularly from Akbar's time, produced an enormous number of manuscripts which were greatly illustrated. Perhaps the most monumental example of a work commissioned by Akbar is the *Dastan-e Amir Hamza,* a story that this sovereign apparently was particularly fond of. It appears that 'Abd al-Samad was in charge of the production of this gigantic work, in twelve volumes and containing 1400 paintings.[117] A production of this magnitude undoubtedly makes the collaboration of a large number of artists indispensable.

Supply of material and salaries

The head of the workshop receives money for purchasing the material *(masaleh-e naqqashi)* along with his salary.[118] The *gerek-yarak* is the person who supplies the material to the workshop. He acts somewhat as superintendent of the workshop and he probably assists the master. Aqa Mirak held this position under Shah Tahmasp.[119]

As we saw earlier, some goods are produced in the workshop, others are supplied to it, such as the paper given to the *majles nevis.* Baysanqor sent paper to the calligrapher Ma'ruf of Baghdad so that he should copy out the *Khamse* of Nezami for him (which, finally, he never did).[120]

According to the *Tazkerat al-moluk*[121] and the *Dastur al-moluk,*[122] the master of the library *(saheb-e jam'-e ketabkhane* or *ketabdar-bashi)* receives 50 tomans and the master of the painting workshop *(saheb-e jam'-e naqqash-khane* or *naqqash-bashi),* 30 tomans per year. The *Dastur al-moluk* specifies that the *naqqash-bashi* receives an allowance of 30 tabrizi tomans per year for his work as superintendent, and it is understood that he receives nothing else by way of payment.[123]

The A'in-e Akbari says only that the artists of the workshop are paid, like other officials of the court, according to the system of *mansab*, granted with relation to military rank. Abu al-Fazl specifies that the pay of the soldiers belonging to the infantry ranges from 600 to 1200 *dam*. The higher the artist rises in the hierarchy, the more his *mansab* increases. Thus, we know, thanks to the *Memoirs* of Jahangir, that Maktub Khan, manager of the library, received a *mansab* of 1500 *zat*, which constitutes a very respectable salary.[124]

Qazi Ahmad occasionally specifies the salary status of artists:[125]

-Mowlana 'Ali Asghar Mosavver, of Soltan Ebrahim Mirza's library, is a "courtier" *(molazem)* and he receives a salary (p.188).

-Mir Zeyn al-'Abedin Tabrizi worked all his life in the royal workshops and received a salary and gifts (p.187).

-Sheykh Mohammad worked at Mashhad, in the library of Soltan Ebrahim; he was a courtier and received a salary (p.188).

-'Abd-allah Mozahheb was employed for twenty years in the library of Soltan Ebrahim; he was courtier and received a salary (p.190).

-Shams al-din Mohammad Kateb worked in the library of Shah 'Abbas; he received a salary and a *tiyul* (ground rent, p.170).

Apart from salaries, some artists whose work was admired, also received gifts. Thus, Bishan Das, sent by Jahangir to Shah 'Abbas, whose portrait he was asked to paint, received an elephant, on his return.[126] Similarly, on the occasion of Shah Jahan's marriage, Jahangir gave two thousand rupees to the painter Farrokh Beyg.[127]

The *Matla' al-'olum*[128] specifies the salaries of some craftsmen: *zengar-sazan*, 3 or 4 rupees a month; *rang-sazan*, 3 to 5 *ana* per day.

In some cases, the artists are paid by a Trust: "The salary of the calligrapher will be paid out of the income of the Rashidi Foundation."[129]

O. Akimushkin also examines the problem of the salaries of calligraphers.[130]

NOTES

1. Ed. p.117.
2. *Voyages*, IV, pp.91-92.
3. Ed. p.43.
4. *Id.*, p.193.
5. *Id.*, p.204.
6. 'Afif, p.337.
7. *Id.*, p.374; we have also mentioned this in Part One, when talking about the ban on the representation of images in the apartments.

8. *Bayaz-e khoshbu'i*, chap.12. *Dar asbab-e ketabkhane az qalamdan va gheyre* (objects for the library, pen-stands and others).
9. Istanbul, Topkapi, H 2155, f.98a; Dated *circa* 1427-28; see trans. by W.Thackston in G. Lowry, *Timur and the Princely Vision*, pp.364-365.
10. Vol.I, p.50 and pl.IV.
11. Rizvi, pp.19-20; see our plate no.11.
12. *Voyages*, IV, pp.499-500.
13. *'Amal-e Saleh*, III, p.27.
14. *Id.*, p.43.
15. See H.C. Fanshawe's plan p.1 and that of the presumed reconstruction, Frykenberg, ed., pp.168-169.
16. Ms. fol. 106b.
17. Manual of Safavid administration (not to be confused with the earlier one), trans. Minorsky, p.100.
18. Dust Mohammad, p.199.
19. *Id.*, 198.
20. Qazi Ahmad, trans., p.130.
21. See note 9.
22. See the introduction to this section.
23. Trans. Minorsky, p.100.
24. Mohammad Amin, trans. pp.127-138.
25. Qazi Ahmad, trans., p.147.
26. *Id.*, pp.170-171.
27. Bada'uni trans. vol.III, p.391.
28. See the heading *toghra* in the *Mer'at al-estelah* fol. 196b-197b; Qazi Ahmad, trans., p.85.
29. *Id.*, p.85.
30. *Id.*, p.86.
31. *Id.*, pp.87-88.
32. *Id.*, p.79.
33. *Id.*
34. See "Illuminators" and *Mer'at al-estelah, "toghra"*.
35. Qazi Ahmad, trans. p.66.
36. *Id.*, p.133.
37. *Id.*, p.138.
38. *Id.*, pp.142-144.
39. *Id.*, p.152.
40. *Id.*, p.165.
41. *Voyages*, IV, pp.281-282.
42. *Tazkerat al-sho'ara*, p.412.
43. Qazi Ahmad, trans. pp.189-190.
44. *Id.* pp.190-191.
45. See the study by John Seyller, "Scribal notes on Mughal manuscript illustration".

46. Around 1590-95; Jaipur, City Palace, no.AG 1148; there are many other examples (see for instance, W.Staude, "Les artistes de la cour d'Akbar").
47. *A'in,* I, p.108.
48. *Tuzuk,* trans. II, pp.20-21
49. B.N. Suppl. Pers. no.983, fol. 34; indicated by Francis Richard.
50. p.201.
51. Trans. *BWG,* p.191.
52. British Museum.
53. See for instance in I.Stchoukine, *Manuscrits Timourides,* pl. LXXXVI, which bears the names of both Mirak and Behzad; this second attribution, made perhaps by Jahangir, is definitely incorrect.
54. "Khwaje Mirak Naqqash", *J.A.,* 1988, pp.97-145; see his fig 3.
55. In this ms. (British Museum Or. 2265) some painting have been added, such as those of Mohammad Zaman (fol. 203b).
56. *Tuzuk,* trans., II, pp.108, 145, 157.
57. *Id.,* II, p.20.
58. *Id.,* II, p.36; other example, II, p.90.
59. *Id.,* II, pp.43-44.
60. Qazi Ahmad, trans., pp.185, 186, 187.
61. *Id.,* p.125; most of the artists are quoted from Qazi Ahmad; we are giving here the page numbers relating to the trans., only the references to other texts will be given as notes.
62. Abd al-Baqi Nahavandi, III, p.1688.
63. Mirza Haydar Dughlat, *BWG,* p.191.
64. Also Eskandar Beyg, p.177.
65. Dust Mohammad p.202.
66. Eskandar Beyg, p.177.
67. Dust Mohammad, p.202.
68. *Id.*
69. See his *Qanun.*
70. Qazi Ahmad, trans., pp.186-187.
71. Eskandar Beyg, p.174.
72. *Id.,* p.176.
73. See trans. W.Thackston in G.Lowry, *Timur...* p.364, and the fac-sim of the text, *id.,* p.160.
74. Khvandamir, *Habib al-siyyar* (Teheran), IV, p.348.
75. Nava'i, *(Majales al-nafayes),* pp.67 and 240.
76. *Tazkere-ye Mohammad Taher,* p.382.
77. Country Museum of Art, M73.5.702.
78. Harvard University Art Museum 1921.33; these two works are reproduced in *Fatehpur-Sikri,* ed. M.Brand, pp.116-117.
79. See for example Ipsiroglu, *Saray-alben,* pl. XXXV and B.Gray, *The arts of the book,* fig. 56 to 59.
80. Some of these drawings are reproduced by F.Ames, p.85 and pp.91-93.

81. Ames, pp.163-166.
82. Ms. no. Add.Or. 1666-1745, fol.45.
83. Qazi Ahmad, trans. p.190.
84. *Id.*, pp.193-194.
85. Dust Mohammad, pp.202-203.
86. Sam Mirza, p.243.
87. *Id.*
88. Qazi Ahmad, trans., p.186.
89. *Id.*, p.189.
90. *Id.*
91. *Id.*
92. *Id.* p.190.
93. *Id.* p.194.
94. *Id.* p.66.
95. *Id.* p.189; see also his namesake in 'Abd al-Baqi Nahavandi, III, p.1688.
96. *Id.*, p.194.
97. Danesh-Pazhuh, "*Rang-sazi*", mentions his correspondence on this subject, pp.21-22.
98. 'Abd al-Baqi Nahavandi, III, p.1688.
99. Qazi Ahmad, trans., p.195.
100. *Id.*
101. Eskandar Beyg, p.176.
102. *Id.*
103. Qazi Ahmad, trans., p.191.
104. *Id.*, p.125.
105. Sam Mirza, p.242.
106. Qazi Ahmad, trans. p.190.
107. Trans., p.100
108. Mirza Rafi'a, ed., p.93.
109. Trans., p.243; see also the article by I.Afshar, "*Sahhafi az negah-e farhang va tarikh*", pp.77-80, who mentions several bookbinders who were also *varraq*, paper merchants.
110. Fol. 297b and 309a-310a.
111. Rashid al-Din, *Vaqf-name*, ed. p.133.
112. *Id.*, pp.257-258.
113. Dust Mohammad, p.198.
114. A.Welch, *Artists for the Shah*, pp.206-214; see also Robinson, "Isma'il II's copy of the *Shahnama*".
115. A.Welch, pp.106-125; D.James, The Chester Beatty *Shahnamah*.
116. *Tuzuk*, trans. II, pp.26-27.
117. *A'in*, I, p.108.
118. *Tazkerat al-moluk*, p.100.
119. *Id.*, p.178; Qazi Ahmad, trans., p.185.
120. Qazi Ahmad, trans., p.66.

121. Trans. p.100.
122. Mirza Rafi'a, p.435.
123. *Id.*, p.436.
124. *Tuzuk*, II, p.22.
125. All references, Qazi Ahmad, trans.
126. *Tuzuk*, II, pp.116-117.
127. *Id.*, I, p.159.
128. Fol. 297a and 310a.
129. Rashid al-Din, ed., p.237.
130. "Persidskaja rukopisnaja Kniga", pp.388-396.

10

THE LIBRARY

1. The place

The library is basically the place where the books are stored, but it also serves as a *scriptorium.* It is found in shrines, in *khaneqah* and in palaces. It is a centre for culture and for exchange. It is also the place where the translators work.[1] Abu al-Fazl describes Akbar's library:

> "The library of His Majesty is divided into several parts; some books are kept in the *harem* and others outside. Each part of the library is divided according to the value of the books and the esteem in which the science dealt with is held. Prose, poetry, Hindi, Persian, Greek, Kashmiri and Arabic are kept separately. They are regularly inspected."[2]

The library is one of the treasures of the palace. Like the workshops, it follows the movements of the court, and it is jealously guarded. The houses of the nobles also had libraries: the *Bayaz e khoshbu'i* gives a list of the 52 titles of collections *(jozv-gir)* meant to include the "selected pieces" and *qat'e*, essential to a library of any standing.[3] The poet Faizi, brother of Abu al-Fazl, who himself was a man of letters, had, on his death in 1004/1595, 4600 manuscripts in his library.[4] Books produced in the palace, books bought or offered as gifts, are priceless objects, which one likes to exhibit on certain occasions. Thus, during the festivities celebrating Homayun's accession to the throne, some manuscripts, some albums and some valuable pen-cases were displayed in a room *(khane-ye sa'adat,* house of good fortune[5]).

Moreover, the library is often a coveted place where looting takes place in times of war. Thus Babur says: "When I entered the library of Ghazi Khan in Melwat, I found some precious objects which I gave to Homayun and to Kamran. There were many scholarly books."[6]

It was common practice to carry the treasure along, whenever the court moved. That was how Homayun lost many books from his library, at Cambay, during an attack by bandits.[7]

Similarly, in a description of one of Akbar's campaigns, Abu al-Fazl reports as follows:

> "At this moment of good fortune, two camels loaded with boxes, and left unguarded, were seen on the battlefield. His Majesty said: "Every one is busy collecting his share, allow me to take these two camels". He went there himself, ordered that they be made to sit down and that the boxes be opened: it was discovered that the books of the royal library, which had been lost during the battle of Qibcaq, were in these boxes."[8]

2. The librarian

The librarian is sometimes an artist, sometimes an "administrator". If he is an artist, he will look after both the artistic management of the production of the workshops and the management and maintenance of the books. The library of 'Abd al-Rahim Khan-e Khanan included a *nazim* or *mo'tamad* (director) and a manager *(darogha)* under his order, and about 95 people working on the various tasks of producing and preserving the manuscripts.[9] Although the number of manuscripts kept in his library is not mentioned in the *Ma'aser-e Rahimi* by Nahavandi, there must have been several thousands. A large number of these manuscripts survive in Indian collections, in Patna, Rampur, Hyderabad and Calcutta.[10]

It sometimes happened that the librarians appropriated the treasures kept in their custody. We saw in our first chapter how the references to *vaqf* had been erased from the books taken out of the *madrasas*. Jahangir relates how Sadeqi, the librarian of Shah 'Abbas, had stolen and sold a painting showing a battle fought by Timur, with 240 figures. This painting was retrieved by Khan 'Alam, Jahangir's emissary to the King of Persia, and was brought back to India with his permission.[11] As we have just seen, Abu al-Fazl points out that the books are inspected regularly, and it is not rare to find on the manuscripts notes written by the librarian, or even by the king himself.

3. Provisioning

We have little information about the supply of books to the libraries. Apart from those produced in the workshop, books were received as gifts.

The calligrapher 'Omar Aqta' copied a very large sized Koran, decorated and bound it, and gave it to Timur as a gift.[12]

Jahangir says that the Khan-e Khanan gave him a copy of *Yusuf-o-Zoleykha* written by Mir 'Ali, with paintings and a beautiful gilded binding, which must have cost at least a thousand *mohrs*.[13] He also says: "Yadegar Khvaje Samarqandi came from Balkh and gave me an album *(moraqqa')* as a gift. A robe of honour was given to him."[14]

As far as the price of books and their trade in the Indo-Iranian world is concerned, we know practically nothing. Most of what has been said till now on the subject is based on some stylistic criteria (manuscripts for "export"). Qazi Ahmad, however, gives us an interesting piece of information:

"Some copies of Korans made by Mirza Hasan Beyg are carried by some merchants to the four corners of the earth to be sold at high prices.[15]"

Taher Nasrabadi (d. *ca.* 1100/1689) relates the poet Qoruri's anecdote about the painter Sadeqi Beyg Afshar (1533-1610): "After a moment he (Sadeqi Beyg) returned with five tomans enveloped in a handkerchief and ten sheets of paper on which he himself had made some ink drawing. He gave (them) to me and said: - For each of my drawings the merchants pay me three *tomans* to take them to India. Take care not to sell them for less than that."[16]

The colophons or the marginal notes on manuscripts sometimes give information about the cost price of the books. Some examples are given by I. Afshar,[17] but no systematic survey has yet been made of these notes. Such a study would help us estimate the price of books during given periods and for different regions.

Bodaq-e Qazvini[18] (984/1576) provides some interesting information about the cost of both manuscripts and *qat'e* made by renowned calligraphers. Thus, a thousand *beyt* calligraphed by Mohammad Hoseyn Bakhar (who died after 976/1568-69) were sold in Qazvin for 5000 dinars. Each *qat'e* by Mir Seyyed Ahmad was sold for "5 *shahi*, which is the standard price". "The *qalam* of the two Soltan Mohammads (Nur and Khandan) is highly prized; when put up for sale, a thousand *beyt* of either of them are valued at three *toman*, each beyt therefore being worth thirty dinars. As for their *qat'e*, they are sold for a thousand dinars a piece."[19]

Chardin tells us about the price of books:

> "Books are quite common in Persia; and although they appear to be expensive, in comparison with our printed books, they are not expensive, considering that they are manuscripts. Those by ancient authors are the rarest; and often they have to be ordered. When one wants to have a book transcribed, it is necessary to supply the paper and bargain over the writing. The price is fixed for every thousand lines; fifty letters make a couplet; and thus a thousand lines make 50,000 letters of the alphabet. The most beautiful writing is done at the cost of four *abbassis* for a thousand lines. Ordinary writing is done for six *chaiets* for a thousand lines. When second-hand books are being bought, what is to be considered is the beauty of the characters, the lines of the margins, the ornamental borders and the miniatures, which are very costly.[20]"

We know very little about booksellers in the Indo-Iranian world because, as Chardin points out, it was not difficult to get a book copied; this was reason enough to justify the absence of "ready-made" books. The book trade therefore probably dealt only in old works. The bookseller no doubt also practised other professions: I.Afshar shows in his study on binding[21] that the binder or the *varraq* were often simultaneously binders, menders, dealers in old paper and occasionally booksellers. These occasional booksellers were found grouped together in the *bazar-e sahhafan;* this is so even today, as can be seen in the *sahhaflar-carshisi* in Istanbul, for instance.

NOTES

1. Bada'uni, trans. vol.II, p.356.
2. *A'in,* I, p.103.
3. Ms. chap. 12, fol.137b-139a.
4. C.R.Naik, p.269.
5. Golbadan Begum, trans., p.124.
6. Babur, trans., p.460.
7. Abu al-Fazl, *Akbar-name,* trans., I, p.309.
8. *Id.* I, p.571.
9. Naik, p.273.
10. *Id.* pp.276-279.
11. *Tuzuk,* II, p.116.
12. Qazi Ahmad, trans., p.64.

13. *Tuzuk*, I, p.168.
14. *Id.*, p.164.
15. Qa'zi Ahmad, trans., p.82. Akimushkin, "Persidskaja rukopisnaja kniga", pp.401-402, also gives references on this subject.
16. *Tazkere-ye Nasr-abadi*, ed. 1937, pp.39-40.
17. *Seyr-e ketab dar Iran*, pp.15-16.
18. *Javaher al-akhbar*, fol. 109b-110b Ms. Dorn 288, quoted by Akimuskhin, "Perskidskaja rukopisnaja kniga", p.397.
19. Akimushkin, *id.*, , pp.396-402 mentions yet other examples taken from authors such as 'Ali Efendi, Olearius, Mirkhvand.
20. *Voyages*, IV, p.280.
21. *"Sahhafi az negah-e farhang va tarikh"*, pp.77-94.

CONCLUSION

A systematic research into sources, started several years ago, and regularly enriched by new finds, has enabled us to discover some texts that are particularly significant to the history of techniques. Painting and the arts of the book are moreover, just one example of the analyses that can be carried out on the basis of these texts.

This method of analysis, based on the study of techniques, aims at providing criteria for description and appreciation, in the study of objects of art. There is a particular need for devising a technical vocabulary adapted to the description of the objects, for acquiring knowledge about the materials and the means of production, as well as about the prevailing conditions and about the authors of these creations. While, as we have said, this analysis is insufficient for describing an object if it is not accompanied by stylistic research, it could perhaps enable us to approach, some day, some wider questions, such as those of aesthetics and of taste. Indeed, these questions are as dependent on the subjective changes of "fashions" as on the constraints of techniques, which have to be adapted and assimilated. While the arrival of paper in the Iranian world brought about a revolution in the art of the book, this also was the case for other later inventions such as printing and photography, which have not only modified traditional perception but have also thereby changed prevailing aesthetics, creating a new taste. Naturally, the technical aspects are not enough in themselves to analyse the reasons for a change of taste, but it is important that we take them into account.

Familiarization with a technical vocabulary has brought about the identification of numerous elements, the clarification of expressions and the establishment of an important lexical corpus, which should be of interest to linguists as well as to art historians. Indeed, this corpus includes a large quantity of words and expressions that are uncommon in other fields, or which have meanings that are specific to manuscript art; their use in the lyrical poetry of the *estelahati* style or in descriptive poems is, as we have seen, abundant. Once this corpus has been enlarged and perfected, it should lead to a better understanding of these texts.

Texts do not suffice for teaching or for reproducing painting. Not only, as we have seen, do they lack conciseness in the instructions that they give, but it has been also noted that there are, in painting, a large number of gestures, tricks of the trade and more than anything else, basic know-how which can only be communicated by word of mouth; hence the need for a master and for a studio. Nevertheless, our research has proved that there are other important aspects worth developing.

Knowledge of the materials

The paper

In the almost total absence of watermarks or other identification marks to establish the origin of the paper, it was necessary to trace from the sources the main centres of paper production. A large amount of work, particularly in description and cataloguing, still remains to be done, to connect the various names mentioned in the texts with the paper used in the manuscripts.

Pigments

We have already noted that the techniques evolved very little with time, between the 12th and the 18th centuries, and that they are very similar also from one region to the other. Moreover, stylistic criteria often lead to a much more precise identification as regards dating and situating a painting. While in some cases the use of one or another pigment may be significant, in the *jadval* for example as seen above, in painting it is often the style which expresses more than the colours. True, there is a lot of difference between the range used in the Indian and the Persian miniatures; there is very little lapis in Rajasthan; *peori*, orange and green earth are much more frequent in India than in Iran, but this is, most of the time, noted only once the origin of the painting has been established.

On the other hand, the compilation and analysis of colour recipes is useful for getting to know the different methods of preparation of each pigment, and can lead to the invention of new pigments; these could be used for restoration, for instance, but also contribute towards a better understanding of the characteristics of the materials (particularly for the microscopic observation of samples).

Apart from this, the study of the origin and of the quality of the materials used, gives us a good deal of information about the conditions of production and the cost price of the works, and therefore about the economic organisation of the workshops.

Means of production

By means of operations described in the different texts, we have tried to reconstruct the different stages of work in the creation of an illustrated manuscript. An essential element has been identified in this study: the preparation of the module. Considering the immense production of manuscripts in the Indo-Iranian world, it is certain that all these manuscripts were not of modular composition. A very large part of these were "ordinary" manuscripts, copied for utilitarian purposes. Though they are less spectacular than the royal manuscripts, it has yet to be seen, however, whether some kind of modular system was not involved in their ruling. In the case of large painted manuscript, commissioned by princes, the preparation of the module is crucial since, as we have seen, it defines the structure of the manuscript as a whole. Therefore, in this respect the paintings are inseparable from the rest of the book and cannot be treated out of their context.

Devising a module for the composition of a manuscript involves collective work. The different stages in the preparation of a manuscript of this kind correspond to the hierarchical structure of the work done in the studio. The manuscript takes shape through a close collaboration between the various artists of the workshop, the calligraphers, colour-makers and gold beaters, the painters, the illuminators and the binders. A powerful economic organisation and the collaboration of the various craftsmen, maintained by princely patrons, permits the use of costly materials and of the diverse abilities of the artist.

In order to understand the place of the artist in society, an attempt can be made to bring out the social implications of the painters within the studio; this can be done on the basis of the biographical information available, as well as the notebooks concerning administration.

The state of "miniature" painting

Having examined the development of painting and Indo-Iranian arts of the book practically from its origins to recent times, what remains to be seen now is the state they are in today. It is curious to note that in very late Persian works, such as the *Matla' al-'olum*, while painting continues to be denigrated as being contrary to the *shari'a*, printing which had so much difficulty in penetrating into the Muslim countries, is praised in the most laudatory terms.[1] This invention obviously influenced the future of the manuscript. After the very limited success achieved by the first efforts in typography in Iran and in India, lithography made its appearance; unlike the former it was unanimously accepted. Indeed, this process enabled the manuscript aspect of the book to be maintained, since the reed pen was used for printing on stones, and line illuminations could be executed on them at little cost. The cost, which was derisory compared to that of the manuscript, led to a rapid development of this technique. The development of printing increased with the birth of the press and succeeded in creating a growing demand for written material. It goes without saying that the development of the printed book sounded the death knell for manuscript art. Some later works, such as the colossal *Arabian Nights*, commissioned by Naser al-din Shah, are the last testimonies to the splendour of this art. Painting took another path, separating itself from the book particularly in the form of canvases. The "miniature" also made its way out of books and albums, and onto walls. Today this genre is unfortunately almost confined to the rank of souvenirs for tourists, and contemporary production almost entirely ignores traditional techniques.

NOTES

1. Vajed Ali, *Fasl* 16 of the 2nd *daftar*, "The printing press" (fol.282a-284a), and *fasl* 18, "On Painting" (fol.285a).

ANNEXE 1
PIGMENTS USED IN PRE-ISLAMIC TIMES

Colours used at Pendzhikent (according to Kostrov)

The first phase made use mostly of pure colours:
-ferruginous earths: - yellow, orange, red, brown, violet-purple
-cinnabar. - vermillion
-gypsum: - white/grey
-animal charcoal: - black

The second phase introduces some shades:
-lapis-lazuli: - ultramarine
-kaolin: - white
-orpiment: - lemon yellow
-realgar: - bright orange
-plant soot: - dark brown

The third phase adds the following colours:
-indigo: - dark blue
-indigo and orpiment: - green
-other mixtures: - bright red; brownish pink

Colours used at Dilberdzhin (according to Zelninskaya)

Name of colour	Method of analysis	
	Infra-red spectroscopy	Thermal analysis acid, alkali, sulphur
Red pigments	iron oxides	colcothar cinnabar realgar

...

../...

Name of colour	Method of analysis	
	Infra-red spectroscopy	Thermal analysis acid, alkali, sulphur
pink	iron ox. + gypsum	
yellow	iron ox.	ferric yellow orpiment
orange	iron ox.	minium
black	organic mineral	
blue	lapis-lazuli	lapis-lazuli
white	gypsum, earths calcium carbonates	
green	chrysocolla (copper silicate)	

Comparative Table of Colours

Colours	pigments	Penzhikent Dilberzhin	Pliny Vitruve	Silpa	after 12th c.	India 20th c.
White	earths sea-shells ceruse	gypsum kaolin	*paraetonium* *melinum* ceruse	*sitamrd* *sarikha*	 *sefidab*	*karya* *safida*
Yellow	earths orpiment	+ +	ocre +	*dhatun pita* *haritala*	+ *zarnikh*	+ *harital*
Orange	minium realgar	Dilber. +	+ sandarac	*sindura*	*soranj* *zarnikh*	*sindur*
Red	cinnabar earths	+ +	minium sinope *syricum* *sandyx*	*hingula* *gairika*	*shangarf* -	*inglu* *geru*
Brown	laquers ocres Ormuz mud	- +	*cinnabaris* *rubrica*	*laksa* -	*lak* - *hormozi*	*lakha* + *hiraunji*
Violet	madder		*purpurissum*	-	-	
Blue	azurite indigo lapis	- + +	*armenium* *indicum*	*syamu* *nila* *rajavarta*	- *nil* *lajvard*	- *nila* *rajvart*
Green	chrisocolla earths verdigris malachite	Dilber. - - Shahrestan	+ + + -	- - - -	- *zengar* -	- *harabhata* *jingar* *danafarang*
Black	vegetal animal mineral	+ + +	*atramentum* +	*kajjala* -	*siyahi* - -	*kajal* -

We have tried, on the basis of the analyses carried out on the pigments of Pendzhikent and Dilberdzhin, to compare them with ancient sources, Latin on the one hand[1] and Sanskrit on the other,[2] in order to discover whether there was some relationship between the pigments used in the West (the Graeco-Roman world) and in the East (India) of the Iranian world. It should be noted however that while the Latin texts mentioned have been properly dated (1st century A.D.), the *Silpa-Saṣtra,* on the other hand, are diversely and inaccurately dated; this means that they have to be used with great care.[3] We therefore mention them mostly by way of comparison.

Reds

Cinnabar

Cinnabar is present in Pendzhikent and in Dilberdzhin from phase I. However, analyses do not clarify whether this cinnabar is natural or whether it has been chemically formulated. According to Vitruvius, cinnabar/*minium* was found first of all in the land of the Cilbians, near Ephesus, and it used to be prepared there also. This Latin author describes it in the following manner:

> "Pounded in iron mortars, the mineral is calcinated and washed several times; but the pigment obtained is fragile, sensitive to light and it becomes dark."

This description could relate as much to the preparation of minium as to cinnabar; and nothing indicates that it refers to the preparation of mercury sulphide; it seems rather to explain the purification of the mineral.

Minium

While it is not found in Pendzhikent, it does however make an appearance in Dilberdzhin. Theophrastus[4] says that the discovery of minium was made by Callias, 90 years before the archonship of Praxiboles, that is to say in 405 B.C.

Realgar

It is found in Pendzhikent from phase II, and in Dilberdzhin.

Earths

Red chalk originates in places as diverse as Lemnos, Egypt, North Africa and the Balearic islands. Red chalk is obtained by the popular calcination of ochre, as Dioscorides reported.[5] It was particularly popular in Rome before cinnabar was discovered in Spain. Other red earths are mentioned by Roman authors, for instance sinope, named after the city of the same name.[6] The *Silpa* mention a red earth called *gairika* (*geru* in Hindi). These ferruginous earths are found in Pendzhikent as well as in Dilberdzhin.

Mixed with other colours, these earths give a variety of shades, such as:

-*syricum*: sinope and sandyx[7]
-*sandyx*: realgar and red chalk
-*usta*: minium and red chalk[8]
-in Dilberdzhin we find a pink colour, made of a mixture of red earth and gypsum.

Violets and purples

Violets and purples are obtained from dyes such as madder (purpurissum[9]) or murex purple.[10] According to Plutarch, when Susa was captured, a large quantity of jars of purple dye were found in the workshops of the palace. Although one cannot testify to its use in painting in Central Asia, purple was already known to the Babylonians who used it as a dye.[11] Some kinds of lac, red exudations of several Indian trees, are mentioned in the Silpa.[12] We mentioned earlier Pliny's confusion concerning *cinnabaris* = dragon's blood; however, the use of these pigments does not seem to have been very widespread in painting in ancient times; no lac has been detected in the paintings in Pendzhikent or in Dilberdzhin.

Lapis substitutes

During the excavation of the Chaour palace in Susa,[13] a bright blue trapezoidal bar was found, having the appearance of lapis-lazuli; at the time of publication, its analysis was still being carried out; a similar bar has also been discovered in the excavation of the Sargon palace in Khorsabad; according to R.J. Forbes,[14] the usual pigment for the frescoes was either based on azurite or on an imitation lapis made of silica, malachite (natural copper carbonate) and calcium carbonate. R.J. Forbes specifies that the making of this imitation lapis of Egyptian frit dates back to the 4th dynasty, and that fritting furnaces have been discovered in El-Amarna.[15] Vitruvius[16] gives a recipe for blue *(coeruleum)* based on silica, aluminate of copper (natron) and copper filings, all ground together and heated in a furnace. This formula is very similar to that of frit, mentioned by R.J. Forbes.[17]

Blacks

All the blacks used in painting are a form of charcoal of plant, animal or mineral origin. In phase I in Pendzhikent, we find an animal black; from phase II, lamp black or plant soot is used. It is the only black mentioned in the *Silpa (kajjala*[18]). In Dilberdzhin, we find some mineral black (coal).

Ground and binding materials

According to Kostrov, the painting technique used in Pendzhikent is that of the *fresco secco*: the colours are applied on a dry gypseous coating; they are mixed with a medium which, in this case, is very definitely a plant gum.[19] With this technique, the colour hardly penetrates the ground; it is therefore very similar to tempera on paper, used for manuscripts.

The *Silpa*[20] describe a similar technique, and suggest a large variety of binding materials, among these being:

-resins: *Azadirachta indica, Mimusops elengi, Feronia elephantum*

-plant gums: *Griselia tomentosa, Ficus religiosa*

-floury matter such as rice paste and plant decoctions

-animal gums made of buffalo or goat skins

Initial outline and composition

It appears that in some cases, such as in the Tuen Hang frescoes[21] drawings were traced with pounce, probably in order to reproduce the same design several times, or simply to transfer a sketch. In Pendzhikent, as well as at other sites in Sogdiana, the paintings have a very vibrant and extremely unrepetitive composition; this could lead us to believe that paintings were executed directly on the wall, without the help of a pounced drawing.

NOTES

1. Pliny, *Natural History*, books 33 and 35; Vitruvius, *The 10 Books of Architecture*, book 7.
2. The *Silpa*, see following note.
3. Among these are, in particular, the *Visnudharmottara* (4th-7th c.), the *Abhilasitarthacintamani* (12th c.?) and the *Silpa-ratna (16th c.); see* Gunasinghe, p.1.
4. See Forbes, p.209.
5. See Forbes, p.208.
6. Pliny, book 35, 13.
7. *Id.*

8. Vitruvius, p.245.
9. Pliny, book 35, 26.
10. Vitruvius, p.249-250.
11. Forbes, p.214.
12. Gunasinghe, p.44.
13. Labrousse and Boucharlat, p.91.
14. Forbes, p.214.
15. *Id.*, p.216.
16. p.248.
17. See also article by C.Kiefer and Allibert, "Les céramiques bleues pharaoniques".
18. Gunasinghe, p.46.
19. Kostrov, p.161.
20. Gunasinghe, p.53.
21. Andrews F.H., *Ancient Shrines*, pl.I.

ANNEXE 2
PERSIAN TEXTS

1. Simi Nishâpuri's *Jowhar-e Simi*

This edition is based mainly on the manuscript Or. 7565 from the British Library. Indeed, this is the most complete version from this text known to this day. The interruptions in this text are shown by the passages between square brackets. These interruptions are additions and variations, on the one hand, concerning colours and dyes, from the two "anonymous" versions of the manuscripts *Majles* no. 2459 and 6150 (see Bibliography for the editions of these two texts). A fragment on the dyeing techniques only appears in the Hamadan version and is perhaps a later addition. On the other hand, the London manuscript being incomplete, our edition finishes with the manuscript from Oxford (Bodleian, *Ouseley* Add. 69). A complete study of this text, with a table of the variations, has been published in *Studia Iranica, 14, 2 (1985).*

NOTES

1. Beğinning of ms. Bodleian *Ouseley* Add. 69.
2. Majles, *in fine.*
3. Bodleian.
4. Majles
5. Not in B.L.
6. Ms. B.L.; not in Majles.
7. Ms. B.L.; not in Majles.
8. *Incipit* of ms. Majles.
9. Not in B.L.
10. Not in B.L.
11. Not in B.L.

12. Not in B.L.
13. Not in Majles.
14. Not in B.L.
15. Not in Majles; Bodleian fol. 345a.
16. Bodleian fol. 345b.; unreadeble in B.L.
17. Koranic letters.
18. *Jabril.*
19. *Mikâ'il.*
20. *Khezr.*
21. End of ms. B.L.; continues with Bodleian fol. 346a.
22. End of ms. Malek.

جوهر سیمی

حمد بی حد وقیاس و سپاس بی عد و احصا توجه سرادقات بارقات جمال و (جلال) بی شبیه ومثال صانعی که روضات محاسن کلام. . .

و سیمرغ قاف قرب رحمن چون کبوتران تیزپر ومژده آور حضرت او بود و نامهای اعمال و اقوام و احوال و افعال امت را تا قیام نانوشته برخوانده و ناخوانده بشنوده هرگز یك نفس چون زبان دربند کام خود نبود و یکدم بکام خود زبان نکشود.

شعر : امین وحی وصاحب سرمعراج — سربر عرش را تعلین تاج
حمید وحامد و محمود و احمد — سزای حمد ابو القاسم محمد

علیه من الصلوات ازکاها و من التحیات انماها و ذرات محرکات مهر آثار و مطالع و مشارق اقطار و امصار هر دیار و مزار تحفه روح و هدیه اشباح اولاد عظام واحفاد کرام و اصحاب و احباب بااکرام او که لسان صدق قرآن مجید و فرقان حمید بصدق لسان ایشان گویاست که و ینصرون امه ورسوله اولئك هم الصادقون.

فائده : بدانکه قسم استناد وانشأ و فن استدعا و استیفا طرزی شریف وطوری لطیفست و مقیمان هر مقام راالز خواص وعوام دانستن و بکاربستن و بقول و فعل در آوردن لازم و جازم است علی الخصُوص درین دور که طور تقاضای آن می کند کلام و سلام انام ایام مصنوع ومطبوع از حیز طبع سلیم ممکن فهن مستقیم بحد قوت ترتیب وقدرت ترکیب آید اما رابطهای بسیار وضابطهای بی شمار از بدایت تا نهایت رعایت باید کرد و در کل ابواب از حشو اطناب احتراز و اجتناب واجب باید شمرد چنانك از برای نمودار اظهار آن اسرار یکی از هزار و اندکی از راه تذکار و روی تکرار بمسامح مجامع طالبان حقایق صنایع و راغبان دقایق بدایع می رسد و این انتخاب از کتاب حاصل الحیوة و جواهر الصفاتست از تصنیف نحیف المحتاج الی العفو الغفوری سیمی النیشابوری غفر اله ذنوبه وستر عیوبه مبنی بر قواعد فواید مترسلان ومنشیان تا مبتدیان راالز مطالعه عبارت آن شروعی تمام و منتهیان را از ملاحظه استعارات آن شعوری مالا کلام به حصول موصول گردد ومجموع مسموع را در صورت احسن تحریر وکسوت ایمن تقریر در ناظر ناظران منظر ابداع و حضور حاضران محتضر اختراع جلوه می دهد و امید واثق و وثوق صادق و صدق کامل و کمال حاصل دارد که مبتلان درگاه و مبتلان آگاه راپسندیده آید وچون ازین زمان و اوان مدتی برآید ومهلتی بعید بگذرد وقواعد رسوم وعادات وآداب واصطلاحات اصحاب ازین سیاق ومذاق بگردد و طرح و طرزی عجیب و اسمی و رسمی غریب روی نماید این شرح و بیان و تبیان را که اکنون مطلوب و مرغوب و محبوب قلوبست ودبیران و مشیران دواوین و مقرران و محرران قوانین را مستحسن افتاده و از صنایع وبدایع آنچه

مستعمل وشایع است در سلك كلام نظام داده به عیب و ریب خط خطا بر ناصیه صافیه این ابکار افکار نکشید و بهمان تأویل و مستأویل [؟] اکنون امثله مختلف اسلاف اطراف را از روی انصاف و راه اعطاف عذر مسموع از زبان مجموع می خواهد که هر آئینه در آن زمان و اوان و محل و مکان که از مصنفات و مؤلفات از مصادر ظاهر شده پسندیده اشراف و صدور و حمیده اعراف و به دور بوده و همه کس بطوع و طبع گفته و شنوده حالا که از اختلاف ادوار و انصراف اطوار مصطلحات قدیمه و مؤتلفات مستقیمة تعبیر وتنکیری معاینه می توان کرد بر مصنّف ومؤلف آن هیچ غرامت و ملالت نیست بلك هر حرفی از حروف آن ظرفیست از ظروف ظرایف و هر رمزی از رموز آن کنزیست از کنوز لطایف و هر فصلی از آن اصلیست که در آن روزگار چندان هزار اثمار آبدار از ازهار شاخسار با برگ و باران بکام جان شیرین لبان جهان رسانیده و چون از طراوت و نضارت خود بیفتاده و برگها بیکبار بر باد داده هنوز از فصول آن ابواب می توان ساخت و از رسوم آن آداب می توان پرداخت و اگر آن نبودی این نبودی و اگر آن بودی این ننمودی الحق هرکس که در رشته نوشته می فروشد حسب المقدور و المیسور در اظهار آثار آب و تاب می کوشد باری بنده را نقد عمر عزیز و جوهر عقل و تمییز دربهای آن،در منظوم منضود و لولوی منثور معقود مصروف و معطوف گشته و از طریق فریق تکلیف و تسلف در کذشته و این مجموعه مطبوعه را که به جوهر سیمی مسمی شده و از چهار کتاب آداب مرکب و مرتب و منتخب است به چهار باب مبوب گردیده و الله اعلم بالصواب :

باب اول در تعلیم و تفهیم ضوابط و روابط که درین طرز و طور معتبر است.

باب دوم در انواع محاسبات و مراسلات آن و انواع و اصناف مجابات.

باب سیم در عرض عریضهای مصنوعه که بمشاهیر هر شهر نوشته شده.

باب چهارم در حج(؟) و . . . کان(؟) شرعیه وعرفیه . . . و محاسبات(؟)

یابم زبیوفایی ایام چون وفات	باشد حیوه حاصلم از حاصل الحیوة
سی روز با ضمیر پریشان چهل صباح	کردم صفات جمع درین مجمع الصفات
تاریخ سال هشتصد و سی و هفت بود	کین روزنامه یافت رقم در شب برات
دستم نمیرسد بملکی بغیر از کلك	پیدا نبود هم ادواتی به از دوات
آوردم از سواد سلامی دل سلیم	درکام جان بریختم از نی شکر نبات
تسلیم کرد بهر سلامی دل تسلیم	جانها درین رساله که هست ازمسلمات
از کیمیا (ی) فقر میا سیمیا بتنگ	هذا الرفیق منه طریق الی النجات

[1]فایده : بدانکه منشی باید که اگر در جمیع علوم و رسوم ماهر و متخبر نباشد باری از لغات مشهوره و نکات مأثوره و مقدمات نحو و صرف و معانی و بیان واقف و مطلع باشد

تـا درزمان تـركيب مفردات و اوان تـركيب مركبـات سوق و شـوق عبارات و كـلامات و اشارات او مخلوط بخلل و مسبوط بزلل نگـردد تا اصحاب این صنعت و ارباب این بدعت را بر الحاظ الفاظ و مبانی معانی او ایرادی وارد نیاید و اعتراضی عارض نشود.

فایده : منشی باید که مرتبه شناس و صاحب قیاس باشد تا مناسب منـاصب اصحاب انساب و ارباب ادات مناقب و محامد القاب بنویسد و از کمال کیاست و فرط فراست حکایت بسیار و شکایت بیشمار در اندکی عبارتی و کمتر اشارتی عیان و بیا کند تا خواننده مستمع و داننده مجتمع را ملالت نکیرد وکلالت نیفزاید وبر قوت و قدرت کاتب وخاطب تحسین وآفرین کند

فایده : منشی باید که درزمان هوای کتابت و اوان ادای عبارت دل بر تربیب معانی حاضر دارد و دیده بر ترکیب الفاظ ناظر تا حکایتی حشو و مهمل و روایتی سهو و نامستعمل بر کران زبان یا در میان بیان نگذارند و مع هذا هنوز اعتماد نکند وکسالت نورزد و چون مکتوب از افتتاح تا اختتام و از آغاز تا انجام رساند از ابتدا تا انتها ملاحظه ومطالعه کند تا اگـر در جائی خطائی نادر صادر شده باشد بصلاح کند یا بحك نیك گـرداند.

فایده : منشی باید که چون استحقاق انشاء و استعداد املاء پیدا کرد و ادوات و مصالح و آلات و حوائج کتابت بدست آورد تا صورت و معانی بهم موافق و مرافق آید اول قلم واسطی را و اسطه گـردد و تا زود بدست آیـد و از هربنـدی عقده از کـاربگـشایـد[۲] و علامت و امارت قلم خوب مرغوب آنست که رنك پوستش شفاف وسـرخ باشـد، وکـران وزن باشد، و بلند قامت و راست هیأت و رنکـه اندرون او، بغایت سفید وچون برجائی زندش آواز دلگشایی از صدغ او بسمع جمع رسد اما آنـچه از معایب اوست آنست که هر قلم که پوستش زرد و یا سیاه باشد، و خام و سبك وزن، و میانه او تیره و بی مغز، و کوتاه قد و کـژ بود، وآوازش گران بگوش رسد بروی اعتماد نشاید کرد، و خط از وی بر حسب ارادت کاتب واقع نشود.

فایده : منشی باید که چون قلم پسندیده یافت قلم تراشی لایق بدست آرد چنانکه تیغ او جوهر بی دریغ داشته باشد وآب او زیادت از عادت نداده باشنـد چنانکـه دایم روی افروخته شود و پـی آب تیز نباید که زود زود از حدت خود بیفتد و باید که باریك و کوتاه خانه و دراز دسته باشد و هرکس که قلم تراشی بدوستی بهدیه فرستد شرط ادب آنست که سوزنی بآن ملحق باشد بسبب آنك آن آلت قطع است واین آلت وصل تا نحوست آن بسعادت این مبدل گـردد و بحسب خواص اشیاء اثری تمام دارد.

فایده: منشی باید که چون قلم و قلم تراشی نیك بدست آرد ابتدای تراشیدن از طرف باریکی قلم کند و بند بر قلم نگذارد و تراشه قلم در زیر دست و پای نریزد که در این باب از کتاب و حساب منع کلی و نهی اصلی واقع است و هرچند ضرورت شود قلم را از هر دو سر نتراشد که کاتبان و محاسبان تجربه و امتحان کرده اند که بالضروره چیـزی از

صاحب آن ضایع و کم شود و کم گردد و قلم تراشیده به رسم تحفه و اسم هدیه به کسی ندهد و نستاند و نفروشد و نخرد که از روی امتحان قطع محبت و دفع مودت می کند و چون در میان کتابت و زمان عبارت چیزی از خاطر محو شود یا درحسابی عاجز فروماند و ضبط و نسق آن بر ذهن دراك و عقل چالاك او بغایت مشکل نماید علاج آنست که قلم را ساعتی در بالای گوش راست بنهد تا آن فراموش گشته باز آید و آن مشکل فی الحال حل شود و قلم را بر قلم دیگر و برانگشتری و ناخن و سنگ وآهن وچیزها که صلب باشد و محکم قط نزند و به تجربه مقرر شده که بر استخوان بهتر است و بر نی نیز نیکست و در وقت زدن باید که چنان به یك ضرب قطع کند که لفظ قط از صوت آن به گوش رسد و آن رشته های باریك [که ازمیان قلم][۳] بیرون می آید آنرا نال می گویند بعضی اصحاب دراین خواص گفته اند که شیره نال را به شیرینی بیامیزند در اصلاح ذهن کند فواید بسیار است و به ناشتا تناول کند و انواع خطوط که کاملان خلف و فاضلان سلف وضع کرده اند و قواعد و ضوابط آنرا به برهان و دلیل نظیر و تمثیل به اجمال و تفضیل معین و مقرر و مبین فرموده اند هر طرز خط را طور قلم باید تراشید تا مفردات و مرکبات آن به نهجی که معمول و رسمی که منقولست و در مواضع واقع شود و شرح کیفیت آن بسطی و عرض کمیت آن طولی دارد و در رساله علم الخط و رسم الحروف ذکر آن مرموز مذکور است اما اینجا آنچه محتاج الیه و موقوف علیه خط تعلیق دیوانی است که احکام حکام و مکاتبات و مخاطبات و مکالمات انام ایام بدان طریقه سمت اعتبار می یابد که خانه قلم را طولانی گیرد و زبان قلم را بسیار تنگ نگیرد و محرفی قط نزند تا خطوط و سطور مزبوط وپیچیده و روان و صاف آید و مدات و شمرات را به اسهل وجوه در غایت حرکت توان نوشت.

فایده: منشی باید که چون خواص و معایب و محاسن قلم را بدانست آنگاه ترتیب وترکیب[٤] مرکب کند ومداد سیاه روان و براق پیدا سازند، و [زیادت از عادت بدان مهم پردازند]، خود ساختن اولی می نماید. و متقدمان در باب آداب مرکب، نسخهای منتخب و مجرب، مرتب کرده اند. وآنچه از همه بهتر وآسانتر بود، اینست : باید که اول قدری روغن کتان خالص بستاند و از پنبه نو، فتیله سطبر بتابد، و اندك نم کند و در چراغ نهد و روغن پر سازد و در گوشه بنهد، که باد در او تصرف نکند، و روشن کند و سبویی آب نارسیده را، پاره (یی) ازطرف سربشکند، و بر سر آن چراغ بیاویزد، تا آنگاه که دوده جمع شود. آن دوده را از سفال به پر مرغ فراهم آرد، و درمیان کاغذ کند و محکم بپیچد، و درمیان خمیر گیرد، ودر تنوری که به هیزم در سنه تافته باشد در زیر خاکستر کند تا آنگاه که مثل نان پخته شود. پس چون از آن چربی، که اصل طبیعت

دوده ودیعت است، بشدت حرارت بسوزد؛ از تنور بیرون آرد، و مقدار ده درم برکشد و بنهد و صمغ عربی سفید پاك ـ که اگر یك حبه دردهن گیرد، در دم آب شود و هیچ جرم نماند ـ مقدار بیست درم بستاند، و سه شانروز در آب جوشیده کند، که سرد شده باشد، تا نیك حل گردد. آنگاه بکرباسی محکم بیالاید. پس دوده را در هاون کند، و بدان آب صمغ خمیر کند وبسیار بکوبد، تا هردو مضمحل شوند. بعد از آن، مازوی رسیده بی سوراخ را نرم کند، مثل جو و گندم، پانزده درم و پنج روز در آب کند و در آفتاب نهد، تا شیره وی تمام بیرون آید. آنرا نیز برکویی سطبر بیالاید و آب آنرا در دیگ سنگین کند وآت نرم کند تا وقتی که چنان بقوام آید که ار بر کاغذ نویسد نشو نکند. [و ازین آب مازو، اندك اندك در آن دوده می ریزد و صلایه می کند، تا تمام آن آب مازو را در وی صرف کند]. آنگاه پنج درم زاگ ترکی را برروی صفحه آهن یا مس نهد، و بر سر آتش دارد، تا آن گوگردی که در ذات زاگ ودیعت و طبیعت است، پاك بسوزد. پس نرم بساید، واندك اندك درسیاهی می ریزد؛ و چند روز بانجام بر دوام صلایه می کند، تا اجزاء مجموع بهم ضم شود. پس قدری آب حنا و آب برگ مرود وآب وسمه و قدری گلاب و عرق نسترن و آب زعفران و کف دریا و صبر سوده [و نمك فسانی و اندکی مروارید و مرجان سوده ومشگ و عبیر اشهب و زر و نقره و مس و برنج حل و شنجرف و لاجورد با آن سیاهی بیامیزد]، که ازینها هریك خاصیتی دیگر دارند، وفائده [یی] دیگر. و این ترکیب عجیب، هرگز بسبب آب و هوا تبدیل و تغییر نپذیرد؛ و سالهای بسیار وقرنهای بیشمار بر صفحات روزگار ناهموار، پایدار و برقراربماند. و این را کاتبان مداد کامل طاوسی میخوانند. ودیر غلیظ میشود. واگر بسبب مرور و کرور شهور و اعوام و حرارت و یبوست هوای صبح و شام، اندك غلظتی دروی مشاهده کند و ناروان شود، چاره آنست که، اندك کف دریا و صمغ و سندروس سوده در دوات کند. تا غلیظ تر شود. پس اندکی گلاب در وی ریزد. تا باز بحال اصل آید. واگرکسی قوت و قدرت آن نباشد، که از عهده تکلیف این مصالح و ادوات بیرون آید، نوع دیگر آسانتر آنست، که یکی از فضلا نظم کرده است؛ تا زودتر یاد گیرند. و ان رباعی اینست که برای مثال، نظم :

بستان دو درم دود چراغ بی نم صمغ عربی درو فکن چار درم
مازو سه درم و نیم درم ترکی زاگ ازبهر مرکبش بفرسای بهم

ـ نوع دیکر [از فواید، مولانا صدر الشریعه اختصار کرده است. نظم][۵] :

همسنگه دوده زاگ است، همسنگ هردومازو همسنک هرسه صمغست آنگاه زوربازو.

[٦] نوعی دیگر : یکی از شاگردان ملك الکتاب جمال الدین یاقوت رحمه الله علیه ترکیب کرده و بغایت پسندیده است. بیت :

دوده شش کن هر یك از صبر و نبات و صمغ زعفران دو، نیل دو، زنگار دو، نیکو بسای

وانگهی این جمله حل کن با گلاب و آب مورد   گر همی خواهی مرکب ساختن اینست رای
- نوع دیگر، و از این آسانتر آنست که قدری نشاسته را در تابه، آهنین کند و بر سر آتش بدارد. تا وقتی که آتش در وی اثر کند وپاك بسوزد آنگاه به آب گلاب حل کند و بدان کتابت کند. مدادی براق و روان باشد.
- نوع دیگر، قدری مازو را خرد کند، و سه روز در، آب بگذارد. پس آن آب صاف را در پرکارهٔ سنگین کند، وآتش نرم نرم کند، تا چنان با قوام آید، که چون بر کاغذ نویسد نشو نکند. آنگاه زاگ، پاك بی گوگرد و خاك با وی بیامیزد و بیالاید، مدادی نیکوست. اماازنم نگاه باید داشت که، نشو نکند و اوراق بر یکدیگر [نـ] چسبد.
(۷) [فایدهٔ : منشی باید که چون کیفیت و کمیت آداب سیاهی کماهی دانست کاغذهای نیکو پیداکند و کاغذهای جمیع بلاد را تجربه گرده اند، آنـچه پسندیده تر از همه اینست کاغذ سلطانی بغدادی و وزیری و دمشقی و مختاری آملی و حریری و بنگالهٔ و اشخواری سمرقند که برآن اعتمادست و کاغذهای جایهای دیگر اکثر شکننده و نشوکننده و ناپایدار است. و کاغذ سفید را اندك گونه دهند بهتر باشد بواسطه آنکه بیاض مغرق نور بصر است چنانك کسی دربرف نگاه کند بسیار چشم او خیره و تیره شود تا غایتی که خطوط و دروج استادان بر کاغذهای ملون مطالعه افتاده].
(۸) الوان مختلفه بسیار است. بعضی مفرد مجرد، چون : زرد و سرخ و آل و کبود و زنگاری و خودرنگ و گاهی. وآنـچه مرکب است ؛ بعضی دیگر، چون : عودی و سبز و گلگون و فریسه و نارنجی.
پس طریق هریك به نمودار بیان و عیان کرده می شود :
زنگ زرد، قدری زعفران بی غش را که نیك تلخ باشد، و زردرنگ بود، ریشه ریشه از یکدیگر جداکند و در شیشه اندازد. و هریك مثقال زعفران را پنج سیر آب پاك بیامیزد، و سرشیشه محکم کند، و در آفتاب نهد سه روز، تا تمامت شیره آن بیرون آید و جرم او چون کاه بماند. آنگاه آنرا به رکویی پاك [و] نازك بیالاید، و درقدح جینی بگذارد، تا نیك صاف شود. پس درطبقی پاك [و] بزرگ ریزد، و پهن [کند] وکاغذ را در آن بیالاید وچندان توقف کند، که رنگ در مجموع اجزاء کاغذ اثر کند. آنگاه پاره کرباس پاك را برطنابی اندازد، و کاغذ را بر بالای آن کرباس افکند، و در سایه خشك کند ؛ بعد از آن مهره زند.
رنگ سرخ به آب بقم جوشیده کنند، و به آب گل بستان افروز کنند، که جوشیده بود. و به آب شاه توت. اما این رنگها را بقایی نیست، و زرد و متغیّر می شوند، و کاغذ را درشت و شکننده میکنند. اما اگر از رنگ لاك کنند، بغایت خوب و بی عیب است. و هر پنج سیر رنگ لاك را، که در دیگ سنگین با یك من آب و نیم سیر لتر بجوشانند، تا با ده سیر آید ؛ صاف کند و کاغذ رارنگ کند، و برهمان منوال خشك کند.
رنگ آل، قدری گل معصفر را بررکویی افکند پاك. و اندك اندك آب بر وی میریزند، تا

هرزردابی که دارد، مجموع از آنجا بـچکد. هریك من گل معصفر را دوسیر اشخوار سوده بر وی افکند، و یك ساعت دست بر وی مالد. بعد از آن اندك اندك آب گـرم بر وی افشاند، تا رنگ از وی بیرون آید. آنگـاه پاره یی آب کشته ترش، یا آب نارنج یا لیمویا آب انار ترش یا آب غوره یا سرکـه کهنه، در آن رنگ کند ؛ تا صاف شود. بعد از آن، کاغذ را دررنگ نهد، و یك روز یا یك شب بگـذارد. بعد از آن بیرون آورد، و برهمان قانون خشك سازد. و احتیاط تمام باید کرد. و این رنگ مشکلترین الوانست.

رنگ کبود، به نیل سرابی صاف کرده کنند. و به آب گـلهای کبود. اما آن نیز پسندیده نیست. بهتر از همه آنست، که در فصل تـابستان، قـدری تخم علف آفتاب گـردش بگـیرد، و رکویی پاك را بشیره آن بیالاید، و در سایه خشك کند ؛ بازبیالاید، تا سه بار. بعداز آن، پاره [یی] خاك را به آب نوشادر نمکین کند. و آن رکوی رنگـین یك ساعت در زیر آن خاك نمناك کند، تا رنگ لا جورد گـیرد و خشك کند. هرگـاه که خواهد، قدری از آنکبودك در آب سرد بیفشارد و صاف سازد، وکاغذ بدان رنگ کند. اما این نیز پایدار نباشد، و از رنگ اصل بگـردد و بنفش شود.

رنگ زنگـاری خوب را که از ورق مس و سرکـه کهنه حاصل شده باشد، در کاسه چینی بسرکه صلایه کنند تا هیچ جرم در وی نماند. پس هر یك سیر زنگـار را ده سیر آب بیامیزد ؛ و یکشبانروز پنهد و سر بـپوشد، تا گـرد و خاك بروی نرسد. بعد از آن صافی آنرا بگـیرد و کاغذ بدان رنگ کند.

(۹) [رنگ خودرنگ قدری برگ حنا[ی] پاك بی غبار و خاك را، [که] ناکوفته بود، در آب گـرم کند ؛ و یکروز یا یکشب بگـذارد. بعد ازآن بیالاید، و صاف سازد، و کاغذ بدان رنگ کند. و هریك سیر حنا را، ده سیر آب باید. و اگـر آب زیاده کند، رنگ مله شود. و اکثر این رنگ اختیارکرده اند].

رنگ کاهی، قدری از آن زردآب، که از گـل معصفر گـرفته باشند، نیك صافی سازند ؛ و کاغذ بدان رنگ کنند ؛ و در آفتاب خشك گـردانند.

اما آنـچه مرکبست، هردو رنگ را بیامیزند ؛ رنگ دیگـر حاصل شود :

[رنگ عودی، قدری رنگ لاك و رنگ کبودك را باهم ضم کنند، و کاغـذ را رنگ کنند. و آمیزش الوان، تعلق به ارادت کاتب دارد. از هرکدام زیادت کند، تغییر درلون ظاهر شود ؛ تا هرکسی چه اختیار کند.

رنگ سبز قدری کبودی و اندکی زردآب باهم بیامیزد، و صاف سازد، و کاغذ بدان رنگ کند، و خشك سازد ؛ و باز رنگ کند.

رنگ گلگون قدری رنگ لاك و زعفران با یکدیگر بیامیزد، و کاغذ بدان رنگ کند، و اگر زعفران زیادت کند، بهترآید.
رنگ فریسه، قدری آب مازو و کبودك باهم بیامیزد، و یکروز بگذارد؛ تا صاف شود، کاغذ بدان رنگ کنند.][۱۰]
رنگ نارنجی، قدری زعفران و شاه آب گل معصفر باهم بیامیزند، و کاغذ را آل کند، پس از آن زعفران بر آرد، بهتربود.
[زردلعلی. بستاند به وزن تبریز نیمن گل کاجره اصفهان، و نرم بکوبد؛ و بپزد، و درکیسه کرباس محکم کند. و سرش ببندد، و کیسه را با گل در میان تغار نهد، و سه مشربه یا چهارمشربه آب بریزد، وکیسه را با گل درمیان تغار نهد، و سه مشربه یا چهارمشربه آب بریزد، وکیسه را با گل درمیان تغار نهد، و سردست چندان بمالد که آب زرد شود، و به سرخی زند، و آب که در تغار باشد زعفرانی شود. بعداز آن یك صاف کرده رنگ کند، و باز این کیسه گل را درمیان تغار نهد، و دو مشربه آب برىالای آن ریزد، و چندان دست بمالد که آب زرد را تمام بگذارد، و به سرخی آید. اگریك نوبت چنین نشود، دگر باره همجنس کند، تا به سرخی بزند. بعد از آن کیسه را بدوکس سخت بیفشارد چنانچه هیچ آب با گل در کیسه نماند. و بعد از آن سر کیسه را باز کند، وآن گل در جای پاك ریزد، و چندان بمالد که آن کیسه پاك کند، و در تغار نهد، و چندان بدست بمالد که آن کیسه لعلی شود. آبی که از آن حاصل شده باشد، یك دم بگذارد تا قرار گیرد، و هرقدر کاغذ که خواهد بیاض سازد و سرکه ترش صافی با آن ریواس صافی یا آب انار ترش صافی مقدر بیست درم در میان لعلی که در تغار است بریزد، و بهم برآرد، و یك عدد بیاض نهد، و یك لحظه صبر کند، و بعد از آن بیرون آرد، لعلی شده و باید که در تغار بزرگ باشد.
ـ رنگ چینی و لاله و سوسنی. ده مثقال آب زرد صافی بر سر آب کبود بیندازد، و اول حکم چینی کند، و دوم حکم لاله، و سیم سوسن. باید که مراعات بجای آورد، یعنی رنگ سوسن بردهد. و دو رنگ دیگر صبر کند.
ـ رنگ سبز. بستان چهاردرم اشخار، و آن را نرم بکوبد و بپزد، تا نرم شود به طریق سرمه. و دو مثقال در آن سر آب زرد کبودباش (؟) تا به همه جا برسد، هر قدر که بخواهی سبز سازد.
ـ رنگ بنفش خشکی. بیاض لعلی که خشك شده باشد درمیان آن کبودتر کند، خشکی بنفش سازد].[۱۱]
و چند نوع و گونه اختراع کرده اند، که خط بر وی خوب آید :

- قدری حنا و زعفران و کبودك باهم بیامیزد و کاغذ بدان رنگ کند.
دیگر، اندکی سیاهی و زعفران وآب غوره مختلط کنند، و کاغذ بدان گونه دهند.
دیگر، تخمی خطمی، شبانروزی در آب کند و بیالاید و کاغذ بدان گونه دهد. و این بغایت مختار وپسندیده است. و کاغذ را نرم سازد. و خط بر وی خوب آید.
دیگر، قدری نشاسته، آهار تنك پزند و بیالایند، و کاغذ را به آهار برهم میتوان چسبانید ؛ چنانکه هر دو یکی شود، مهره زند و بنویسد، که خط بر وی بغایب خوانایی و زیبایی بنهایت می آید. و با کاغذ سلطانی برابر آید.
دیگر، قدری سریشم ماهی سفید را، سه شبانروز در آب پاك کند. و بعد از آن به آتش، نرم گرم کند : درحال شود بیالاید، وکاغذ بدان برآرد و باحتیاط خشك کند و مهر زند و بنویسد.
فایده : و کاغذی که بسیار تنك و پرزناك بود و قلم کاتب را بوقت سرعت کتابت مانع باشد تدبیر آنست که به آب خربزه شیرین یا آب نبات مصری یا آب تخم مورد یا لعاب اسبغول یا حلیم برنج بی روغن و به چند چیز دیگر که مجموع مقوی کاغذ است کاغذ تنك را قوی توان ساخت تا پرزها که بر وی باشد و قلم کاتب را مانع و دافع سرعت حرکت شود بصلاح آرد :
- لعاب اسبغول را نیك صاف سازد و کاغذ را یك زمان در وی بگذارد بعد از آن خشك کند.
- آب خربزه شیرین و آب تخم خیارین و شیره انگور بی دانه و حلیم برنج بی روغن و آب صمغ عربی و آنچه بدینها ماند مقوی کاغذست وچون مهره زده شود مثل آئینه نماید پس هر کدام اختیار کند مجموع مجربست.
وشرح الوان از آن کرده شد و از آن فایده دهد که در این روزگار لطافت و طراوت بر طبایع مستولی شده و رقاعی که به بقاع نویسند از تکلف و تلطف حالی، خالی نباشد[وبعضی کاغذ را الوان و میده و افشان کنند]. اما هر چه از زبان سلطان زمان به اطراف و اکناف نویسند یا از اشراف و اعراف به خواقین و سلطان نویسند ادب آن است که بر قاعده سفید باشد. بلکه اگر مهر نیز نزنند اولیترست و لیکن کاغذی که تفرقا به ظرفا و یاران به یاران نویسند هر تکلف که کنند عیبی نباشد.
فایده : منشی باید که چنانکه در ترکیب عبارت و ترتیب استعارت سعی موفور و جهد ماثور به ظهور می رساند در حسن کتابت و زینت اشارت نیز اهتمامَ تمام نماید و اجتهاد مالا کلام جایز و جازم باید شمرد و این معنی جز به انواع الوان صورت نبندد و مثل زر ونقره و برنج و مس و قلع حل و لازورد و شنجرف و زنگار و طلق حَل و زرنیخ و گل بحری و اسفیداج و عروسك و هریك ازاین در موضعی بکار آید که آن محل را بحلل بیاراید چنانچه زر و لاجورد احکام حکام ایام و وقف نامهای امرای عظام و توقیعات وزرای انام بکار باید داشت وآیات قران و احادیث خاتم پیغمبران و اسامی و القاب انبیاء

و اولیاء و خلفا و سادات و علما و فضلا و مشایخ کبار و اماثل روزگار از اموات و احیاء از ابتدا تا انتها هرجا واقع شود از رای عزت و روی حرمت بعضی را به زرحل و بعضی را به لاجورد و برخی را به رنگهای دگر که مناسب باشد بنویسند و تعلیم ترکیب و تفهیم ترتیب هریك را از آن الوان مختلف اینست :

- زر حل بعد از آنکه استادان زرکوب، زر خوب از یك مثقال طلا تمام عیار، مقدار صد درم گرفته باشند از آن اوراق چند عدد بستاند و قدری سریشم سیاه را بگذارد واندکی از آن در کاسه افکند و دست را به آب گرم وصابون رقی پاك بشورد وکاسه را بدان سریشم بیالاید و به دو انگشت، یکی سبابه و یکی و سطی از دست راست بر گرداگرد کاسه بمالد تا چون داند که آمیخته شد آن صافی بسیار در کاسه کند و دست و اطراف کاسه را پاك بشوید و سر کاسه بپوشاند و از غبار وچربی و سیاهی محافظت کند و ساعتی بنهد تا تمام طلا تا بتك کاسه نشیند پس آنگاه آن آب زیادتی را بریزد و به قلم موی آن زر را بر کلك بیفزاید و کتابت کند وچون داند که خشك شد به سنگ یشم یا جزع یا عقیق جلا داده آهسته آهسته مهره زند و اگر تواند به سیاهی تحریر نیك باریك کند.

- نقره حل هم بدین طریق که زر را حل کنند و به آب صمغ غلیظ نیز حل توان کرد و به عسل مصفی هم حل می کنند. اما از خاك و گرد و غبار نیك محافظت باید کرد و هرگاه که کتابت تمام کند وچون زر و نقره حل کرده از کتابت زیادت آید هر آبی که در کاسه مانده تمام بریزد وکاسه را به آتش خشك کند که اگر زر و نقره حل بسیار در آب بماند تیره گردد وچون خواهد که بار دیگر کتابت کند زر و نقره به همان دو انگشت یا به آب صمغ یا سریشم قدری بمالد آنگاه بر آن منوال کتابت کند.

- برنج و مس حل قدری برنج مروی را یا صفحه مس صافی را بر سنگ آب بساید تا سوده آن اندك اندك جمع گردد پس آن سونش را در قدحی سنگین و آب گرم بشوید و چندان بگذارد تا به تك نشیند آنگاه آب زیادتی آنرا بریزد وبه سریشم سیاه یا آب صمغ عربی برهمان طرز و طور آرد زر و نقره بمالد تا حل شود و بدان کتابت بکند وچون خشك شود به سنگ جزع مهره زند خوب نماید.

- لاجورد از کوه بدخشان حاصل شود و آنرا صلایه کنند و بشویند و سر آب آنرا بگیرند و آنرا شمط خوانند وآنچه بماند، بغایت رنگین و شکفته باشد. پس چون خواهد که بکار برد باید که اول آنرا به آب صمغ خمیر کند و بسیار در تك کاسه بمالد بعد از آن آنرا به آب صمغ رقیق آن خمیر را به مرتبه رساند که لایق و موافق کتابت باشد بکار برد.

- [لاجورد عملی ترکیب آن از نیل خام سرابی و اسفیداج وآب صمغ باشد، که نیل بر وی سنگ ، به آب بساید و اسفیداج را بشوید، و نرم آنرا به نیل بیامیزد و تا آنگاه که به قوام آید به آب صمغ صلایه کند، و بکاربرد و کتابت بسیار پایدار باشد.](۱۲).

ـ شنجرف اصل آن از گوگرد و سیمات است. و از گل حکمت کوزه سازند و به آتش، نرم نرم آنرا بپزند. وبهترین آن در فرنگ سازند. پس کاتبانرا در بسیار محلها بکار آید. و در صلایه کردن آن احتیاط تمام بجای آوردن شرطست. اول بر سنگ بساید خشك، تا نیك نرم شود. بعد ازآن، اندك اندك به آب انار ترش صلایه کند، تا وقتی که هیچ جرم نماند پس به آب گرم سنگ را و دست را در کاسه بشوید، و ده ساعت بگذارد تا زردابی که دارد بر سر آید، آنرا بریزد. و باقی را بر خشت پخته نو آب نارسیده کند تا زود خشگ شود. پس قدری را به آب صمغ بسر شد و بدان کتابت کند.

ـ زنگار(۱۳) [دونوع باشد یکی آنك] توفال مس را مقداری بستاند و در ظرفی کند و همان مقدار از سرکه کهنه به آب بیامیزد ودر چاه آب آویزد و مدت چهل روز بگذارد. پس چون بیرون آرند زنگار شده باشد.(۱۳) [نوع دوم را از چقراست گیرند که گوسفندی باشد هم بدین منوال پس از زنگار اولین] قدری را به رکویی بپزند و در کاسه چینی به آب عنزورت صلایه کنند و به آب صمغ حل سازند و بدان هر چه خواهد بنویسد اما اگر مدتی برآید کاغذ را سوراخ سازد و بر دوام و قوام آن اعتماد و اعتضادی نباشد تدبیر آن است که اندکی از زعفران به آن ضم کنند تا فستقی شود ویایدار باشد.

ـ (۱٤)[طلق حل. سنگیست که از میان توده های خاك، که در کوههای بزرگ باشد، حاصل شود. وآن دو نوع باشد : یکی ورق ورق، برروی یکدیگر، مثال آبگینه ؛ و از آن تابهای حمام سازند. و دیگر، ورق او بغایت ریزه و روشن و تنك و پاك و درخشنده. پس ازین نوع ثانی، قدری را در خریطه کند، که از کرباس باشد، و پاره های یخ در خریطه اندازد، و بر سر کاسه دردست میمالد، و آب آن بتدریج در کاسه میریزد، تا چون یخ تمام آب شود ؛ بار دیگر یخ در خریطه کند، همچنین چند کرت صلایه کند. پس یك شب بگذارد. بعد از آن، آب زیادتی را بریزد، و به آب صمغ حل کند، و بدان کتابت کند بر کاغذ رنگین. و اگر اندکی زعفران با آن آب بیامیزد، مثل زر نماید. و اگر با شنجرف بیامیزد. همچون افشان نقره نماید، و اگر بر کاغذ آل نویسد، و به جزع مهره زند، همچون زر و نقره نماید. و این را طلق محلوب گویند. و اگر طلق را محلول تواند کرد، از وی بسیار عجایب و غرایب توان ساخت.

ـ زرنیخ حل. و این نیز دوگونه باشد ؛ زرنیخ ورق، و زرنیخ کلوخ. اما زرنیخ ورق، رنگین تر و درخشان ترست. قدری، از آن بستاند، و بر روی سنگ نرم کند، و بساید. پس بکرباس ببیزد، و به آب سرد صلایه کند، و بصمغ بسرشد، و بدان کتابت کند ؛ که بغایت رعنا نماید. اما نزدیك لاجورد، و برکاغذ کبود یا سیاه یا آل.

ـ گل هرموز. از قعر دریا حاصل شود. هرگاه آب با قعر افتد، مردم از آن بسیار

بردارند، و خشک کنند. قدری از آن بستاند، و در آب کند. بعد از آن، ازین طبق بدان قدح، و ازین قدح بدان کاسه، میکند. و هربار آنچه بر سر آب می آید، درقدحی میکند، تا آخر همه را دردوات کند. و قدری سوده بیخته با وی بیامیزد، عودی باشد.

ـ اسفیداج حل. از قلعی سازند. قدری از آن بستاند، و نرم بساید. و به آب صمغ خمیر کند. بعد از آن درمیان آب، بسیار نهد. تا اندك حل شود. آنرا نیز قدح بقدح پیماید. و اسراب آنرا که روح میخوانند. جمع میکند و آب زیادتی را میریزد، تا بقرار آید. به آب صمغ کند، ویدان هرچه بنویسد، پسندیده آید.

ـ [عروسك. از شاه آب معصفر سازند. چنانکه قدری شاه آب را در ظرفی کنند، و پاره یخ در آنجا افکنند، تا لخت لخت شود، چون جگر. پس اندك آبی که زیادت داشته باشد. پاره [یی] پشم را شانه کند، و بر لب آن قدح نهد و قدح را کژ کند، تا بمرور بچکد. بعد از آن، قدری صمغ سوده با آن بیامیزد، و بر نی انداید، تا در سایه خشك شود. بعد از آن، که احتیاج باشد، اندکی را در آب گرم حل کند، و بدان هُرچه خواهد بنویسد. و اگر شب در آب بماند، تیره شود.

وبدین مجموع الوان، که یادکرده شد، جدول توان کشید. و اگر جدول، حل طلا باشد، زیادتی تکلف و زینت گردد. و علی هذا القیاس، تا محل چه باشدو لایق که شناسد]. (١٤)

(١٥) **فایده** : منشی باید که چون فواید قواعد بعضی از خطوط متداوله مشهوره اطلاع یافت از منهیات که فرموده اند مجتنب و محترز باشد.

ـ اول آنك در وقت کتابت دست و جامه و بالای خانه خامه را سیاه نکند که با آنك در چشم و دل حاضران و ناظران مکروه می نماید بحسب خاصیت نیز سب تفرقه و ملالت خاطر کاتب می شود.

ـ دویم آنك دو کاتب در یکی حالت از یك دوات ننویسند که بی شك میان ایشان بضرورت کدورت افتد هرچند که محبت ومودت ومخالصت و موانست باشد به خصومت و عداوت مبدل شود این معنی سهل نباید شمرد.

ـ سیوم آنك چون از کتابت فارغ شود دوات و قلم بر جایهای بلند ننهد که مودب تنزل و نقصان مراتب و مناصب اهل قلم می شود و بسیاری از دبیران و مشیران و وزیران به سبب مداومت این عمل به معزولی افتاده اند و از روی تجربه اثری تمام دارد.

ـ چهارم آنك سیاهی غلیظ نگذارد و جائی کتابت نکند که محر باد و شعاع آفتاب باشد و سیاهی در دوات آهنین نکند که به اندك مدتی فاسد شود و زنگار آهن بسیاری مختلط شود از طراوت اصل بگردد و اگر ضرورت باشد چاره اصلاح آنست که قدری موم گداخته در دوات ریزد و اندرون آنرا بدان بیالاید بعد ازآن سیاهی در آن کند و بهترین

دواتها که می سازند از روی امتحان دوات چینی از همه بهتر است و اگر از آبگینه باشد در برودت هوا از شدت سرما سیاهی را محافظت باید کرد که هیچ آفتی سیاهی رااز سرمازدگی زیادت نباشد و از حاسدان و دشمنان و معارضان ایمن نباید بود که ناگاه آب تمبر هندی در دوات نکنند که از آن سیاهی یك حرف به قاعده نتوان نوشت و شرط کتابت آنست که در کتاب حك و اصلاح نکنند که بسیار عیب شمرده اند و اگر ضرورت افتد به انواع حك می توان کردن و ازهمه بهتر آنست که پاره موم گرم را بر بالای نوشته ریزد و باز بردارد و به انگشت موم را برخط بمالد چند نوبت خط تمام محو شود و باز مهره زند کاغذ به حال اول شود و به سرش عنجد حین عمل کند شاید و اگر به قلم تراش حك کند بر بالای سنگی یا تخته باید نهاد تا کاغذ سوراخ نشود و اگر خواهد اصلاح کند باید که به همان قلم و سیاهی اول باشد تا خط بیگانه ننماید.

فایده : منشی باید که سعی تمام نماید در اجتهاد مالا کلام تا خطوط خوانا واقع شود به تخصیص در محلی که مقصود و مطلوب آن باشد تا رنج و زحمت کتابت و تکلیف و مشقت رسالت ضایع نگردد و اگر چه متقدمان در دیباچه هرترسلی که تصنیف و تألیف کرده اند مبالغه نموده اند که کتابت نقط و علامت ننهند غالبا مراد ایشان آن بوده باشد که تا مستعدان و فاضلان تأمل و تخیل و تفکر و تدبر و شعایر ضمایر و دثار خواطر سازند اما به شرایط متأخران چنانست که در محلی که کلام در تجنیسات و تصحیفات واقع شود تعبیر و تفسیر متشابهات را امارات و نقاط ننهند تا لایح و واضح گردد و حسن الخط آنکه مفاتیح الرزق است بی ضابطه و رابطه و اصول معمول نگردد و همه کس آسان تواند خواند و در اظهار دثار مدات و تشمیرات و علامات و تشدیدات باید کوشید و بکسالت و بکلالت و عطالت و بطالت نباید و رزید.

فایده : منشی باید که چون کاتب در مراتب و مناصب از مکتوب الیه بزرگتر باشد بیاض بالای مکتوب را بسیار گذارد و پهنای کاغذ را زیادت از عادت گیرد و به قلم دلی سطور راز یکدیگر دورنویسد و سر مکتوب گشاده فرستد و محکم(١٦) [نپیچد و بر کاغذ مهر نکند مگر به ضرورت که این مجموعه خطبه بر ابهت و عظمت و جلالت دلالت کند چون مکتوب الیه و معروض علیه در مرتبت و منزلت از کاتب و خاطب به جاه و راه بزرکتر باشد] برعکس این مقدمه بیاض اول کمتر کند و عرض باریکتر گیرد و قلم از آن الوان تغییر دهد و خطوط را بهم نزدیك نویسد و محکم بپیچد و سر مکتوب مهر کند که این جمله به ادب نزدیکتر و نام خود را در زیر خط دوم نویسد اینجا که نوشته باشد که کمترین بساطبوس یا کمترین خاکبوس یا مخلص دولتخواه یا متخصص بی اشتباه یا محب جانی یا معتقد جاودانی یا بر ظهر رقعه نام خود به انگشتری مهر کند یا به خط ید خود

علامتی که معلوم شود که کیست و عرض از عرض آن همینست و اگر کاتب و مکتوب الیه در مرتبه برابر باشند طریقه اعتدال باید مرعی داشت و نام و تحیت خود بر یك طرف از آخر رقعه چنانچه لایق باشد بنویسد وپاره از کناره مکتوب قطع کند تا از شکل مربعی بیرون آید که حکما را در نحوست این صورت اتفاق است ومکتوب بدسن قاصد ندهد بلك برروی خاك افکند تا خود بردارد که ارباب تجربه را به کثرت ممارست در خواص اشیاء معلوم شده که چون رعایت این ترتیب کند مکتوب زود به مکتوب الیه برسد و در راه ضایع نشود و اگر این اسامی را منقطع بر ظهر مکتوب نویسد مکتوب زودتر واصل گردد و مأمول و مقصود زودتر به حصول موصول گردد و المقطع هذا یا ك ه ی ص یا ح م ع س ق(۱۷) یا ج ب ر ی ل(۱۸) یا م ی ك ا ء ی ل(۱۹) یا خ ض ر(۲۰) یا ا ل یا س.

البته در هرمکتوبی که یکی ازاین اسماء بی ترکیب بدین ترتیب بنویسند بی شك به مقصود رسد وچون از زبان بزرگی بنویسند و مهمی در ارسال آن مکتوب مطلوب باشد بعد از نوشتن نگاه کند و سطور را بشمارد که ناگاه سیزده سطر نشده باشد و اگرسیزده باشد چیزی در آن افزاید تا دفع آن نحوست شود و باید که از شش حروف احتراز کند که در آخر مکتوب واقع نشود و این شش حروف را امام زین العابدین رضوان اله علیه از امیر المؤمنین کرم اله وجهه روایت صحیح می کند که در فال قران مجید ازین شش حروف هیچ عاقل غافل نباشد که در هرنیت که ازین حروف سته یکی باشد مضرت آن کار از حضرت مبعث اکثر باشد و ازین جهت شاید که در فاتحه الکلام واقع نشده اینست ت ش غ لا ك م ترکیبها تشغلا کم باشد وخرده دانان ونکته بینان درین ترکیب و ترتیب تأمل بسیار کرده اند و به دقت طبع لطیف دریافته که حرفی ازین ترکیب بر هر حرفی دیگر مقدم است هیبت و صلابت آن بیشتر از آن حرفست که بروی مقدم است چنانك درین حرف میم اندك ملالتی مندرج است و در حرف ك کربتی که از ملالت زیادتست و در حرف لا لامتی که از کربت بیشتر است و در حرف غ غرامتی که از لامت افزون تر است و در حرف ش شامتی که از غرامت بیش و در حرف ت تفرقه که از شامت و غرامت و لامت و ملالت زیادتست و اگر به امتحان مکتوبی بنویسند که مجموع این حروف بر توالی این ترکیب در اوایل این سطور ترتیب یابد هیچ مطلوب از آن مکتوب حاصل نشود و اگر در حجتی واقع شود که دینی بر آن باشد هرگز آن دین مؤدی نشود عرض از تمهید این مقدمه بر آن

باشد[۲۱]، آن دین مؤدی نشود. دیگر آنکه م (میم) با که (ك) چون دانسته که حضرت از جناب و جناب از جانی و جانی از خدمه (. . .)

دیگر در فن انشا آنست که هرکس رقعه خواهد نوشت اول تأمل کند تا ناگاه عضوی از اعضاء و جزوی از اجزای مکتوب الیه معیوب و معلول نباشد مثلا سر یا چشم، یا دست یا پای، یا بینی یا گوش تا اگر این اسمای سند نوشته شود مکتوب الیه متغیر و متفکر گردد و اگر مثلا کسی اقرع باشد در مکتوب او بسیار نام سر وموی وکاکل [و فرق و گیسو و امثال این نویسد جمل بر تعرض خواهدکرد][۲۲].

و اگر کسی را چشم ناقص بود در رقعه او نام چشم و بینائی و نرگس و هرچه از لواحق قرانی آن عضو متهم باشد مذکور شود منحرف المرام گردد و مستمعان و حاضران به کنایت و رموز اشارت اظهار آن معنی کنند و در قامت طویل و قصیر و لون زرد و سیاه و محاسن کوسج و بلمه نیز احتیاط شرط است و در صفت کسی که ذات او بدان سبب بی حرمت می شود هیچ طعنه و توبیخ روا ندارد و نادانی را به علم و کمال و فضل صفت نکند و گربه منظر را به حسن و جمال تشبیه و تنبیه (. . .)

کشتی شکستگانیم ای بادشرطه برخیز باشدکه بازبینیم آن یار آشنارا

قضا را باد شرطه برجوابت تا کران بیستون لنگردار سبکرفتار چون شبدیز هامون گذار به رفتار درآمده در سطح آن بحر خونخوار و پست و بلند پشت امواج را به طریق برق دمان و بادوزان می نوردید «نظم».

قرارش چون قرار بیستون بود ولی دربیقراری اندو (ه) گین بود
نچندین ز خوش رفتاریش آب به ره می رفت اما بود در خواب
نبودش دست و پا در وقت رفتار بریدی راه چون با سینه مار
زمانی بحررا کردی توانگر فکندی هرکجا یك لحظه لنگر
به تیرش کهکشان پیچیده چون مار درآغوشش فلك چون (چرخ) دوار
چو دریا آسمان درزیرمایش کواکب چاکران ناخدایش
نمی زد باد چون موجش به هرسنگ که بودی جای غلطیدن برو تنگ
شدی گاو زمین را در کناره زجنگ لنگرش دل پاره پاره

تا رفته رفته به لطف سبحانی و فیض ربانی در اندك فرصتی طی مسافت شده کران از آن بیکران هوید (ان) و مرتبه مرتبه سواد کنار در نظر الوالد بصار کحل الجواهر می ساخت تا در لنگرگاه لنگر انداخت نظم :

آن سلامت رو گرانمایه مانده چون باد از پیش سایه
بر وش همچو روزگار خاموش چرخ اطلس چو بادبان بر دوش

دیده و روی چو مردم دریا داده درعین ختم جوشش جا

همچو یك نظر در آب روان بود رفتارش ازنظر پنهان

سنگ او همچو عمر در رفتار بی خبر من درو گرفته قرار

حاصل چون از خوف و خطر سالم حسب و اسم به مسمی پیوست و داعی هر نکات نمود چون اطفال خوشحال از معلم خلاصی یافته رخت حیات به زورق نجات افکنده ساحل امید برآید به مقضی کل شی یرجیع الی اصله خاك را در آغوش کشیده اطمینان قلب حاصل امید که حق سبحانه تعالی درماندگان محیط حرص و طمع را به ساحل آمن (و) قناعت برساند. تمام ۱۱۲۲

2. *Qânun al-sovar* by Sâdeqi Beyg Afshâr.

Text based on the edition of M.T. Dânesh-Pazhuh, with the variations of Kaziev's edition.

قانون الصور

سلاطین را درآغاز جوانی
به خدمت صرف کردم زندگانی

شمردم عار آیین دگر را
فرو نگذاشتم رسم پدر را

ولی گاهی ز طبع نکته زایم
بگوش دل رسیدی این ندایم

که از قرب سلاطین دوری اولی
ازین بزم هوس مهجوری اولی

مکن این نکته راازمن فراموش
که تا باشی پی کسب وهنرکوش

بدست آور هنر تا می توانی
که باشد بی هنر کم زندگانی

چو شد ذوق طلب با دل هم آغوش
به کلی کردم از خدمت فراموش

دلم را بخت و دولت رهنمون شد
پی کسب وهنر رغبت فزون شد

ولی شهباز طبع چرخ پرواز
بهرصیدی نمیشد چنگل انداز

بهرکاری که رغبت می فزودش
به پیش دیده آسان می نمودش

تمنای دلم این بود پیوست
که گیرد همت بهزادیم دست

کشم رخت هوس در کوی صبورت
شوم معنی طلب از روی صورت

دلم را کز فن صورت خبر بود
بخوددرراه معنی پی سپر بود

بود ظاهر به پیش مرد هشیار
که بی استاد گردد کار دشوار

بدینسان داد پیر عقلم ارشاد
که باید برد اول ره باستاد

بآیین هوس می شد زهرسو
دلم استاد بهزادی نسب جو

به رغبت هرکه را جویندگی هست
دهد جوینده را یابندگی دست

شد آخر هادیم روشن ضمیری
چراغ افروز را هم دستگیری

مروت پیشه ای نیکو نهادی
فرید عصر نادر اوستادی

یکی از وارثان کلك بهزاد
زشاگردی او بهزاد دلشاد

در ایوان قلم بالانشینی
بآیین بصارت دوربینی

به چشمی چشمه خورشید دیدی
به مویی هردو عالم را کشیدی

خردمندی که چون گشتی قلم زن
عطارد را زبان گشتی به احسن

شدی گر صورتی را چهره پرداز
توانستی شمردن سحر واعجاز

به تمثال کسی کردی چو رغبت
چنانش ساختی کز اصل صورت

نیارستی کسی فرقی نهادن
مگر از جنبش و از ایستادن

ز رعنایی چو گشتی صورت آرای　　هوس را پای لغزیدی بصدجای
به نقاشی چو سر دادی قلم را　　نمودی نوبت دیگر ارم را
دلیری را چو دادی صورت ازنقل　　تهور مومیایی جستی از عقل
برنگ و روغنش هرگه نظر بود　　صفاراازحیا خون در جگر بود
بآیین غلامی مدتی چند　　شدم درشیوه خدمت کمربند
ره صورت گری چندان سپردم　　که ازصورت به معنی راه بردم
چو نام نامی آن پیر پرور　　شدم برکشور این فن مظفر
زلطف حق چو گردد شادروحش　　منورباد روح پرفتوحش
تنقصیرت دنیای جدا باد　　غریق رحمت فیض بقا باد

سبب نظم این رساله

یکی از دوستان آدمی خوی　　که برراه وفایش داشتم خوی
دلش را ذوق نقاشی ز ره برد　　عنانش را بدست شوق بسپرد
شب و روز از خیال نقش صورت　　بیفزودی کدورت بر کدورت
نه شب آرام و نی روزش قراری　　نه جز نقش و صور مشغول کاری
شبی نیکوتر از روز جوانی　　درآمد از درم آن یار جانی
دلم را مرهم داغ نهان شد　　ز درج در چنین گوهر فشان شد
که ای مشهور علم ذوفنونی　　خردرا کرده رایت رهنمونی
مرا شمع طلب شد رغبت افروز　　که ذوقم می فزاید روزبروز
مرا زینگونه باشد کار دشوار　　ترا زینسان تغافل شیوه و کار
پی پاداش منت داری من　　مرتب ساز قانونی درین فن
اگر این کار بی قانون نباشد　　که باشد کز شما ممنون نباشد
کسی احوال فردا را نداند　　غرض نقشیست کز ما بازماند
چو برترتیب کارم ساخت مأمور　　به عذر اینکه «المأمور معظور»
درین قانون نوشتم صفحه ای چند　　به قانون الصور کردم نشانمند
الهی این عروس حجله ناز　　که کردازخلوت خود جلوه آغاز
دهی قرب قبول خاص وعامش　　کنی توقیع مقبولی بنامش

در نصیحت فرزند

مجو تعلیم ز استادان تصویر　　که از فرزند خود دارند تقصیر

اگر فهمت کند ستی درین فن   بشاگردی گرایی تا بمردن
وگر گردی بآسانیش تفهیم   حسد گردد حجاب راه تعلیم
بود مردی نه مرد ریش و دستار   که در قید حسد باشد گرفتار
نمیگویم که خود هرزه سپرباش   ولی جویای مرد راهبر باش
اگر زانگونه استادی نیابی   زقانون الصور رو برنتابی
که آوردم بهر آیین و دادی   ترا بی مزد و منت اوستادی
نباشد صادقی را غیر ازین کام   که گه گاهش بنیکویی بری نام
همین دارم زتو چشم دعائی   که هستی را نمی بینم بقائی

در صفت نقاشی و بستن قلم موی

شود چون [1]شوق نقاشیت غالب   قلم بستن بود اصل مطالب
مخوان حرف هوس از نامه کس   مکن عادت به طور خامه کس
ز کاتب این صفت نیکو نباشد   که کلکش را کسی دیگر تراشد
قلم را مو دم سنجاب باید   ولی آن مو که با نرمی گراید
به مقدار قلم ازوی جدا کن   ز یکدیگر بزور شانه واکن
بچین پهلوی هم زانگونه نیکو   که نبود زیر و بالا یکسر مو
[2]درست آندم شود آن خامه بسته   که نگذاری [3]در و سوی شکسته
چو داری از شکست مو امانش   سه جا باید که بر بندی میانش
[4](. . .)
مکن در عقد سیم سست کاری   که از پر غاز آسانش برآری
چو برکف خامه آید غنچه وارت   دهد گلهای امیدی ز خارت

در گرفتن قلم

گره کاه قلم گیری مکن مشت   قلم را جایگه ساز ازدوانگشت

---

۱ ـ ذوق
۲ ـ درست آنگه
۳ ـ که نگذاری در آن یکمو شکسته
٤ ـ مشو در عقد اول سخت تدبیر
مبادا خامه ات گردد گلوگیر

سه دیگر ستون آن دو باید / که تحریر قلم (۵)سنجیده آید
بگاه کار می باید دلیری / نمی باید قلم را سخت گیری
ز نقاشی چو خواهی کام یابی / گشایم بر تو ازهرسوی بابی
اگر امداد طبیعت کارسازست / تصرف را درو دست در ازست
ولی (۶)چون مفت نبود اصل این کار / چگویم زانکه دارد فرع بسیار
چنین کرد اوستادم رهنمایی / که هست (۷)اسلامی ودیگرختایی
زابرو (۸)داغ اگرآگاه باشی / چونبیلوفر فرنگی خواه باشی
مکن ازبند رومی هم فراموش / کنی چون اسم هریك جای در گوش
چو اصل کار دانستی درین کار / نگردد برتو فرع کار دشوار
رقم سازی چو ازهر اصل معلوم / مساوی بایدت هم برگ و هم بوم
بگلهای مدور باش سرراست / که (۹)پرکاریش سازی بی کم وکاست
(۱۰)بودبااوکه بی جان بسته آنها / زپیچك کن قیاس (۱۱)ریسمانها
بطرح کار مستعجل نباشی / ز جوش ریسمان غافل نباشی

در رنگ آمیزی

به رنگ آمیزی چون گردی هوسناك / ببایدرنگهای شسته پاك
بنه گربیش خواهی ساخت ورکم / دورنگ عاشق و معشوق باهم

در طریق شستمان

کنون پویم طریق شستمانرا / نمایم برتو این راز نهان را
دو طور شستمان نغزست و نیکو / یکی دم شوی دان دیگر میان شو

---

۵ ـ که تحریر قلم پیچیده آید
۶ ـ ولی جز هفته نبود اصل این کار
۷ ـ اسلیمی، خطایی
۸ ـ ابر و واق
۹ ـ که پرکاریست کار بی کم و کاست
۱۰ ـ بود با ارگ پیچان بسته آنها
۱۱ ـ ز پیچك کن قیاس از ریسمانها

کنی کز نقش بررنگ شکفته
مدار آیین دم شو را نهفته

بود برعکس آن کز بوم کارت
بباید از میان شو دست یارت

از آن پس قید روغن کن به احسن
چو آوردی برون از قید روغن

بگیر از خشت بغدادی جلایش
بده از شست و شو آنگه صفایش

به حل کاری بود [12]زان پس مدارت
که حل کاریست اصل [13]کاروبارت

ز حل کاری چو فارغ بال گردی
بباید کز جلا خوشحال گردی

در حل طلا و نقره

اگر از سیم و زرخواهددلت حل
بدین منوال کردم مشکلت حل

که بستان از سریشم پاك بی غش
بخیسان وپس آنگه نه برآتش

به صحنی کرده ازچربی تمیزش
[14]چوبگذ اردبدان گرمی بریزش

ولی از بیش وکم بودن بیندیش
مکن هرقطره را یك ورق بیش

ز ملح نیم سوده دانه ای چند
درو انداز و می مال ای خردمند

بخشکی دست مالیدن نشاید
چو از تری سوی خشکی گراید

سرانگشتان بآب گرم تر کن
بروافشان و ازسردی حذرکن

زمان مالشی او ساعتی بیش
[15]نبایدبودای مرد هنرکیش

(...)[16]زصحنش چونبشستن شد حواله
سر آبش را بگیر اندرپیاله

گرفتی چون سراب ای مژدآگه
ازو تا نیم ساعت دست کوته

[17]بیایدداشت تابرته نشیند
[18]کزو مردهنرورکام بیند

به کلی چون نشیندسیم با زر
نماند غیر آب صاف برسر

بریز آبش اگربسیارباشد
وگرنه آب هم درکارباشد

زیکسو اندك اندك کارگرشو
به ملك کامیابی راه برشو

---

۱۲ ـ بحال کاری بود آنگه مدارت
۱۳ ـ اصل جمله کارت
۱٤ ـ چون بگداز و بدان گرم بریزش
۱٥ ـ بباید
۱٦ ـ چو یك ساعت بمالیدش پیوست
بآب گرم از مالش بشو دست
۱۷ ـ ورا بگذار تا در ته نشیند
۱۸ ـ کزان مرد هنر در کام بیند

تعریف صورت گری

اگرصورت گری باشد مرادت بودپس آفرینش اوستادت
دراین وادی تتبع سست رایی است دررحمت بروی خودگشاییست
کی از قید غلط آزاد باشد اگر مانی و گر بهزاد باشد

درصفت جانورسازی

کنی گر جانورسازی اراده ز گلگون تصرف شو پیاده
بیك سو از طریق بیش و کم باش براه پیروی ثابت قدم باش
زراه و رسم استادان مکش پای بآیین تتبع راه پیمای
مدان صاحب روش از صد یکی را بجو آیین آقامیرکی را
مبادا ای در دریای حیرت ندانی جانورسازی صورت
بگویم جانورسازی کدامست چه سان وچندوهریك راچه نامست
یکی سیمرغ و دیگرهست اژدر هژبروگاوگنج است ای برادر
ولی معلوم این فن برسه قسم است گرفت وگیر حملش نام واسم است
شوی چون برگرفت و گیرراغب درین وادی سه چیزت هست واجب
(۱۹)زهستی جانور هادوربایـد ستون دست و پا (۲۰)پیروزبایـد
شوی گر از دوجنگی نقش پرداز (۲۱)نبایدبرتن هم پنجه انداز
مبادا پنجه ای (۲۲)پیکارباشد درین صورت مگر ناچار باشد
مکرر ساختن هم نیست مرغوب ولی غیر مکرر هست مطلوب
مکرر گرچه سحر آمیز باشد طبیعت را حلال انگیز باشد

دربیان رنگ و روغن

شوی گر رنگ و روغن را طلب کار ترا پاکیزگی باید بناچار
بود این هم دواصل ای یارجانی بگویم تا به فکرت درنمانی
یکی جسمی و دیگر نقره پوش است ولی این کار نیش پرزنوش است

---

۱۹ ـ ز ستی جانورها
۲۰ ـ دست و پا پر زور باید
۲۱ ـ بباید
۲۲ ـ پنجه بیکار

ازینها خواهی ار کامت برآید ... یکایك باتو گویم آنچه باید
ببایـد بوم کارت را رسانی ... بآیین بطانه تا بدانی
بطانه آسترکاریست درباب ... سریش است و سریشم گچ و دوشاب
ز بعد آسترکاری درین فن ... علاجت از سفیدابست و روغن
مکرر بایدت کردن سفیداب ... که تا گردد این کار نایاب
برو اکنون بهرراهی که خواهی ... بکن هرنگ دلخواهی که خواهی

در طریق رنگ جسمی

حرارت گر بود جسمی درین کار ... بدل از نقره کاری یاد مگذار
به غیر از لاجوردی رنگها را ... بروغن گیر و رونق ده صفارا
برای لاجوردی بر رخ کار ... کشی روغن ولی نه کم نه بسیار
زنی کف تا شود همواریکدست ... گذاری تا بلند او شود پست
برنگ آستر روغن هم آغوش ... شود چون ریزش با پای خرگوش
میان باب دگرروز دگرکن ... ولی از گرد واز باران حذرکن
بروز سیم از روکش صفا ده ... بچارم روز از روغن جلا ده
ز کاغذ لق مشو غافل که یاریست ... پی رفع کدورت سازگاریست
وگر روز تو بی گردوغبارست ... ترا با قید کاغذ لق چه کارست

در آداب نقره پوش

وگر از نقره پوشت کام جوییست ... مداربوم کارت برنکوییست
بکش روغن بنه بر آفتابش ... ولی خشکی [۲۳]صبر از حدبتابش
چوگردد نیم خشك آور بهنجار ... بچسبان نقره اش یکدست هموار
چوچسباندی و کردی خشك نیکو ... ز پیش دست وپا بگذار یکسو
کنون از رنگهای پاك بی عیب ... کشم بر صفحه تقریر لاریب

درقاعده رنگها

بود چون لاجوردی رنگ زنگار ... ولی اورا ببایـد ریخت یکبار

---

۲۳ ـ ولی خشکی مبر از حد بتابش

مکن زنگارریز بی تأمل — بکن از صبح تا پیشین تحمل
بریز آنگه بروی کار یکدست — بمالش پاچه خرگوش پیوست
چو گردد خشک از روغن جلاکن — صفای کار خودرا برملاکن

درروش رنگهای سریشمی

ز گلهایی که آید رنگ بیرون — بنفش و ارغوانی زرد و گلگون
بگیر آبش بهر طوری که دانی — شود ظاهرتر از راز نهانی
کنی گر بستمان ز اندازه بیرون — ولی شرینیش باید به قانون
چو در رنگ تو باشد چاشنی کم — جداگردد بگاه خشکی از هم
وگر بسیار شد جوشش نماید — برین تقدیر باید آزماید[٢٤]
رسد گر دست چربی بر رخ کار — بشو با انزروت آبش بهنجار
بکش برروی هم آن رنگ پیوست — که گردد رنگ تو همواریکدست
منه ز افزونی و قلت بدل بار — که گردد آخر کار تو هموار
چو گردد خشک روغن کاریش کن — ز کاغذ لق ولی غمخواریش کن
دراین وادی که نبود از خطر پاک — ترا بایاری طبع هوسناک

درساختن سفیدآب و سرنج

بود مشکل به منزل راه بردن — بخودسرراه هر منزل سپردن
کنم چون باتو دارم حق یاری — زتعلیمت رفیقی سازگاری
بگیر از سرب چندانی که باید — بدیکی از سفالینی که شاید
بنه بر دیکدان دیک مقرر — بکن آتش که گردد آب یکسر
بآهن کفجه اش یکسان بیاشور — چو خاکسترز سیالی شوددور
بسان سرمه گردد تیره خاکی — فتد آتش درو از تابناکی
بنه سرپوش و محکم دار پیوند — گشوده راه آتشگاه مپسند
چو گردد[٢٥] سرمه بایدپختن خوب — بآب ملح شستن پاک و مرغوب
سه بارش چون بشستی ای نکورای — بنه نوشادروباسرکه می سای

---

٢٤ ـ بدین تقدیر با اندازه باید
٢٥ ـ چو گردد سرد باید هم چنین خوب

به [٢٦]عضب ازوی نشادر پاك بستان   بكن خشك و دگرمی سای باآن
چو كردی شستن و سحقش مكرر   [٢٧]بپردازازخلاصش باردیگر
ز بعد آن خلاص اورا بشوپاك   كه گردی از صفای او فرحناك
بری گر باردیگر درخلاصش   بیفزایی خلاصی در خلاصش
چو فارغ بال گردی از دو آتش   برون آید سرنج پاك بی غش

در زنگار ساختن

بكن چاهی دو گز درجای نمناك   صفایح كن بتك لیك از مس پاك
بریز از سركه ناصاف چندان   كه گردد صفحها درسركه پنهان
در آن چاهش بنه یكمه كم و بیش   بپوشان از كم و بیشش میندیش
پس از یكماه بنگر كان تمامی   شود زنگار خاطرخواه نامی

درشنجرف ساختن

بدست آور گریزنده سه وچار   سه مثقال دگر كبریت كن یار
بسای اندر صلایه ساعتی بیش   شود خاكستر تیره میندیش
بنه در شیشه مطین و دلكش   بیفروز از پسین تا شام آتش
چو گردد سرد بیرون آر و بنگر   كه شنگرفی شود نیكو و احمر

در لعلی ساختن

زرنگ لاك بستان نغز و خوبش   بنیكویی جدا گردان ز چوبش
بگیراز آب آشنان پاك و بی غش   بكن در دیك و آنگه نه برآتش
درومیریز رنگ لاك كم كم   بزن با چوبكی هر لحظه برهم
چوخالی گشت لاك از رنگ بی شك   ز لتر سوده در وی ریز اندك
پس از ده جوش دیگر صاف كن پاك   كه دل از دیدنش گردد فرحناك
ز صاف او شود لعلی پدیدار   زمر باشد ز درد او نگهدار
بگیر از سندروس پاك یكمن   بضرب تیشه فندق وار بشكن

---

٢٦ ـ بغصب
٢٧ ـ ببر اندر

بدیکی نو که در وی گنجد آن بار
بکن بر دیکدان آن دیك را بار

بکیر از چارجانب در گل آن دیك
که تا گردن بگل گرددنهان دیك

کناردیك رااز خشت واز سنگ
برآور کزهمه جانب شود تنگ

ز بعد آن بیفروز آتش تیز
ز تند و تیزی آتش مپرهیز

بتفسان دیك را زانسان که حداد
درون کوره آهن را و فولاد

درون دیك گردد پرستاره
بیفگن سندروس و کن کناره

دگرباکفچهٔ آهن بیاشور
مرو نزدیك و خودرا دار ازودور

چو گردد سندروست آب یکسر
بریز از روغن بزر ای برادر

درو زن سندروس اما بهنجار
که در روغن فتد آتش بیکبار

وگر طغیان کند روغن ز آتش
دمی از دیکدان آتش برون کش

چو جوش چنددادی قطره ای زان
چکان در آب اگر شد منعقد آن

بود پخته وگرنه همچنانش
بجوشان تا شود ظاهرنشانش

ولی این کار در منزل نشاید
مقامی دورتر از شهر باید

تمت قانون الصور بتوفیق الملك الأکبر[۲۸]

۲۸ ـ دانشگاه : قدتم قانون الصور

GLOSSARY

âb-e khun, (?) or *khun-âb,* binding for paint : 28, 81, 91, 102
âbgine, polisher made of glass : 27, 98
âbi, light blue; also, colours for marbling, "diluted" : 42-43, 48
abr, "cloud", one of the "seven principles of painting" : 109, 112, 115
abri (kâghaz), marbled paper : 45-49, 112, 118, 122, 161
afshân, (see *zar-afshân*) flecking : 45, 49-51, 143, 161
âftâb-gardesh, sunflower : 40, 42-43
aftimun, epythimum : 64
âhak, lime : 124
âhâr(i), starch(ed) : 27, 48, 50, 119
'aks, painting with stencilled designs : 51-52, 161
âl, bright pink, safflower : 39, 43
'alak, chewing gum : 124
alsi,* linseed : 94
'amal, the "bulk" of the work in the mentions made in the margins of the manuscript paintings : 57, 65, 157
anâr, pomegranate : 41, 45, 80
angâre, sketch : 65-66
angur, grapes : 29
'anzarut, sarcocolla : 81, 92, 124
arghavâni, purple : 40, 43
'arusak, ruby red : 43, 80
arwali,* kind of paper : 23, 25
arziz, tin : 75-76
âshnân, saponaria : 80, 92
asrâsh, glue : 91
âstar, lining; the colour base; lining for the binding : 94-95, 122

ashkhvâr (or *shakhâr*), soda : 25, 86, 124

bâdanjâni, colour of brinjal : 40, 43
banafshe, violet : 39, 42-43, 80, 90
band-e neyshekar, a kind of headband : 121
band-e rumi, geometrical traceries, one of the "seven principles" : 109, 111, 115
baqam, logwood or sapanwood : 40, 43, 80
batâne, mastic, lacquer base : 29-30, 76, 86, 92-93, 122
bazr-e qatunâ, psyllium : 27
berenj, brass : 82
beyze, egg : 91-92
bostân-afruz, amaranth : 40
bostemân, binding for paint; flotation additive for marbling : 48, 91
*bul**, myrrh glue : 48
bum, the background of the painting : 29, 96, 123
burâq, borax : 80
bure-ye kâghaz, paper pulp : 30

carbe, fine paper for pounced drawing : 65
cehre-goshâ'i (or *-pardâzi),* portrait : 57, 65, 106, 143-144, 156
cini, light green : 38, 42-43

dam-shu, a kind of *shostemân* : 96
davâle, a kind of *jadval* (frame) : 60-61
*dhelki**, mortar (for paper) : 23
dibâce, preface, frontispiece : pl. 9, 62, 112-113
do-rang, dye in two colours : 43
dude, lamp black : 48, 63-64

esbaghul, psyllium : 27
eslimi or *eslâmi*, decorative foliage, one of the "seven principles" : 109-110, 115, 123
esparag, yellow weed : 64
ezhdar, dragon, animal design in illumination : 108

farangi, "European", acanthus foliage, one of the "seven principles" : 109, 111, 115
farise or *farishe,* bluish green : 42-43, 82
fassâli, one of the "seven principles"; also, the assembling of

jalâ dâdan, polishing : 97-98
jânevar-sâzi, animal design : 108
jasmi, "consistent" colours in flat tints : 93, 95
jowzi, brown : 41, 44
joz-bandi, stitching of the quires : 117, 119-120

kabud, blue : 42-44
kâghaz, paper : 15-28, 45, 112, 152, 161, pl.4
kâghazliq, oiled paper : 25
kâhi, straw yellow : 38, 44
kâjere, safflower : 38-39
kalbod, mould, matrix (see also *qâleb*) : 30
karbâs, rag, for numerous kinds of use : 22, 28
kasambhi,* safflower : 52
katirâ, tragacanth : 27
katreme (or *batreme ?),* a design in illumination : 111
kebrit, sulphur, see *gugerd.*
kharboze, melon : 27
khatâ'i, 1) colour, mixture of henna, ink and indigo : 32, 38, 41, 44
2) type of paper : 17, 28, 32
3) "Chinese type" illumination design, one of the "seven principles" : 109-111, 115, 145
khesht-e baghdâdi, (brick from Bagdad), polishing device : 98, 103
khodrang, skin colour : 40, 44
khun-e siyâvush, Dracaena cinnabaris : 39, 77
konj, corner design, associated with the *toronj* : 113, 122
korsi-neshâni, drawing of reference marks.
kuh-pardâzi, drawing of mountains, landscape : 108, 144

lâjvard, lapis-lazuli (or other blue stones) : 48, 51, 64, 75, 80, 82-87, 129, 143, 161, 178
lâjvard-e soleymâni, cobalt : 86
lâjvardi, lapis colour : 42, 84, 90
lâk, lac : 38-40, 48, 80, 92, 178
lâle, tulip red : 39, 44
la'li, ruby red : 44, 80
langar, stone press : 123
late, a kind of *zarafshân* : 50
limu, lemon : 38, 45, 119
limu'i, lemon yellow : 44

noqre, silver : 43, 64, 82
noqre-push, silver background for lacquer : 93, 95
nokhodi, brown, chick pea colour : 39, 44
nushâdor, ammonia : 64, 82

ogar-gun, skin pink : 90
'onnâbi, jujube red : 38, 39, 44
'onvân, title, initial illumination : 62, 112-113
ostokhvân-bandi, composition : 65-66
owre, the "stuff" of the colour, as against the *âstar,* the lining : 91, 94, 102

*peori**, Indian yellow (see *goguli**).
*phatkari**, alum : 48
pirâze, stitching of the back of the quires : 117, 120-121
piyâzi, reddish brown, onion peel : 39, 44
*poti**, red dye

qal', tin : 75
qal'i, colour (pale green or violet) : 42, 44
qalam, reed pen : 27, 67, 80, 123, 141, 171
qalam-e jadval, pen for making borders : 59, 61, 120, pl.10
qalam-mu, brush : 67, 122
qalam-e siyâhi (or *mosavvede),* drawing in black ink : 65
qâleb, frame, mould or matrix : 22, 28, 91
qat'(e), the format of the sheets; also the cut paper : 26-27, 52-53, 58-59, 66, 161, 171
qeliyâ, soda : 124
qermez-dâne, kermes : 39
qunnâb, flax : 21

*râl**, resin of *Shorea robusta* : 94
rang kâri rikhtan, to get down to work.
rang-o-rowghan, oil colours, lacquer : 29, 91, 93, 122, 157
rasm, drawing : 94
*ritha**, soap tree : 48
rowghan-e kamân, varnish for lacquer ; 30, 93, 122
rukesh, cover board : 95, 117, 122
runâs, madder : 40, 63

soranj, minium : 75, 77-78, 178
sorb, lead : 75-78
sorkh, red : 39-40, 44, 52, 77-78
sorme, antimony : 84
suratgari, portrait : 104-107, 109, 143, 157
susani, iris colour, violet : 37, 39, 42, 44

tahrir, the contours of the letters and illuminations : 50, 52, 60-61, 68
*takankhâr**, borax : 48
takht-e sang or *sang-e zir-e dast,* stone press, stone slab : 119, 122
talâ kardan, to knead.
tqlq (sefid), talc : 75-76
tamr-e hendi, tamarind tree : 45
tarh-(e mosavvede), drawing (in black) : 57, 65-66, 69, 143, 157
tarkib bastan, to make the composition : 66
*târpin**, turpentine : 94
*tât-pati**, rags (for paper) : 22-23
tâvusi, peacock blue : 42, 44, 64
toghrâ, style of calligraphy, particularly for royal signatures : 156, 165
tokhm-e morg, egg : 92
toronj, oval medallion : 113, 122
tuti or *tutaki,* parrot green : 38, 42-44
tutiyâ, tutie (zinc sulphide) : 76, 89

'ud, aloe : 64
'udi, colour of aloe, brownish violet : 38, 40, 42-44

vâq (or *dâgh*), one of the "seven principles" : 109, 112
vâshe, ammonia gum : 124
vasme, woad : 43, 64
vassâli, assembling of sheets for binding : 118-119, 143, 161

za'farân, saffron : 37-38, 63-64, 76-77, 81
za'farâni, saffron yellow : 38, 44
zâg or zâj, alum : 45, 63-64, 80
zanjire, "chain", margin : 122
zâj-e kabud, blue vitriol, copper sulfate : 38, 40, 43
zarafshân, gold flecked paper : pl.5, 38, 49-51
zar, gold : 50-51, 64, 88-89

BIBLIOGRAPHY

ABBREVIATIONS

Abst. Ir.: *Abstracta Iranica.*
B.L.: British Library, London
B.N.: Bibliothèque nationale, Paris.
BWG: BINYON, WILKINSON & GRAY, *Persian Miniature Painting.*
E.I.: *Encyclopédie de l'Islam.*
J.A.: *Journal Asiatique.*
KASHANI: ABU al-QASEM KASHANI
Maj.: *Majmu'at al-sanaye'.*
Khosh.: *Resâle-ye Khoshnevisi.*

1. Manuscripts:

'ABD-ALLAH SEYRAFI, *Osul-e khotut-e sette yâ resâle-ye khatt.* See *Resâle-ye khoshnevisi.*

'ABD-ALLAH KUHDEZI, *Adât al-kâteb.* Ms. Asiatic Society of Bengal, Calcutta (Cat. IVANOW, Curzon coll. no. 635) dated 1247/1831, 15 fol.

ANAND RAM MOKHLES, *Camanestân.* Khuda Bakhsh Lib., Patna, Ms. no. 865 (Cat. ABDUL MUQTADIR, IX no. 882, iv), n.d., fol. 68b-134b.

----*Mer'at al-estelâh.* Khuda Bakhsh Lib., Patna, Ms no. 796 (Cat. ABDUL MUQTADIR, IX no. 810). dated 1820, 283 fol. See also RIEU III, p. 997.

----*Perikhâne.* Khuda Bakhsh Lib., Patna, Ms no. 865 (Cat. ABDUL MUQTADIR, IX no. 882,ii), n.d., fol. 37b-55a.

(*Album of the Crafts of Kashmir*). Kashmir, 1850-60. India Office, Add. Or. no. 1666-1745. 79 fol.

Bayâz-e khoshbu'i (anonymous). India Office, (Cat. ETHE I, no. 2784) 182 fol., dated 1109/1698.

Kholâsat al-mojarrabât. Ms. India Office (Cat. ETHE no. 2346) Acc. no. 2814, dated 1180/1766, 181 fol.

Majmu'at al-sanâye'. B.L. (Cat. RIEU II, p. 489-90) Add. no. 17 960, n.d., 51 fol., and Asiatic Society of Bengal, Calcutta (Cat. IVANOW I, p. 749 no. 1621) 56 fol, n.d.

NASR-ALLAH KHAN KHURJAVI, *Nomov al-sabbâghin*. Ms. Andhra Pradesh Oriental Lib., Hyderabad (Cat. Asafiyah II no. 262) no date (ca. 1280/1863) 10 fol.

QAZI AHMAD QOMI, *Golestân-e honar* or *Tazkere-ye khoshnevisân va naqqâshân*. Salar Jang Library, Hyderabad (Cat. ASHRAF, II nos 598 et 599) Acc. no. T-K.1, dated 1004/1596, (autograph) text 48 fol.; Acc. no. T-K.2, n.d., 76 fol.

RAFI' al-DIN Ebrâhim Shirâzi, *Tazkerat al-moluk*. Ms. Salar Jang Lib. Hyderabad (Cat. M. ASHRAF vol. I no. 362) acc. no. Hist. 142, dated 1148/1735, 184 + 24 fol.

Resâle-ye 'atr va rang. Ms. India Office (Cat. ETHE no. 2785). 30 fol., dated 1211/1797.

Resâle-ye buqalamun (in fact, a Persian translation of the *'Umdat al-kuttâb* attributed to Ebn Bâdis). India Office (Cat. ETHE vol.I no. 2977) Acc. no. 1348, dated 1010/1601-2, fol. 108b-139a

Resâle-ye Jeld-sâzi or *Resâle-ye manzum dar sahhâfi*. Government Oriental Manuscripts Library, Madras, no. M.437, dated 1228/1812, 11 fol.; Asiatic Society of Bengal (Cat. IVANOW, II p.114 no. 919) Acc. no. A.J. 56, dated 1275/1859. 96 fol. (see ed. I. Afshâr, *Sahhâfi-ye sonnati*).

Resâle-ye Khoshnevisi, anonymous, attributed to 'Abd-allâh Seyrafi. Ms. Patna (Cat. ABDUL MUQTADIR, XI, p. 86-89 no. 1076) acc. no. H.L. No. 1066, 36 fol., dated 1120/1708.

SIMI NEYSHAPURI, *Jowhar-e Simi*. B.L., Ms.Or. 7465 (Meredith Owens, p. 92) n.d., fol. 38a-49b; Bodleian Lib., Oxford (Cat. SACHAU-ETHE, I p. 762) dated 1122/1710, fol. 344a-356b.

Tarkib-e tayyâri-ye kâghaz-e Dehli. Ms. B.L. (Cat. RIEU, III p. 1012) Acc. no. Or. 1733. n.d., fol. 48a-50a.

(*Traité dans lequel il est parlé du papier et de sa fabrication*). Ms. B.N. (Cat. BLOCHET, IV no. 2206, I) Acc. no. Decourdemanche S.P. 1942. n.d., fol. 1-13.

VAJED 'ALI KHAN, *Matla' al-'olum va majma' al-fonun*. Ms. Asiatic Society of Bengal, Calcutta (Cat. IVANOW, Curzon coll. no. 486) Acc. no. P. 635, dated 1274/1858, 343 fol.

2. Printed works:

'ABD-ALLAH KUHDEZI, see manuscripts.

'ABD al-BAQI NAHAVANDI, *Ma'âser-e Rahimi*. ed. M. Hidayat Husain, Calcutta: Bibliotheca Indica, 1910-1931, 3 vols.

'ẠBDI BEYG SHIRAZI, *A'in-e Eskandari*. ed. Abu al-Fazl Rahimof, Moscow: Dânesh, 1977, 142 p.

----*Dowhat al-azhâr*. ed. 'Ali Minâ'i Tabrizi and Abu al-Fazl Rahimof, Moscow: Dânesh, 1974, 177 p.

----*Rowzat al-safât*. ed. Abu al-Fazl Rahimof. Moscow: Dânesh, 1974, 70p.

ABDUL AZIZ, Sh., *The imperial Library of the Mughals*. Delhi: Idarah-i Adạbiyat, 1974. vii + 62 p.

ABDUL MUQTADIR, *Catalogue of the Arabic and Persian Manuscripts in the Oriental Public Library at Bankipur*. (Khuda Bakhsh Lib., Patna). 34 vols. since 1908.

ABU al-FAZL 'ALLAMI, *A'in-e Akbari*. transl. H. Blochmann, 2nd ed., Calcutta, Asiatic Society, 1927. vol. I, lix + 741 p., xvii pl.; vol. II-III.

----*Akbar-nâme*. transl. H. Beveridge, Calcutta, Bibliotheca Indica, 1902-1939 - reprint Delhi, Ess Ess, 1979. 3 vols.(vol. I, 667 + xxxii p. + index; vol. III, 1274 p. + index 68 p.

ABU al-MA'ALI, *Bayân al-adyân*. ed. H.Râzi. Tehran, Farâhâni, 1342/1964. 574 p.

ABU al-QASEM KASHANI, *'Arâyes al-javâher va nafâyes al-atâyeb* ed. I. Afshâr, Tehran, Anjoman-e âsâr-e melli, 1348/1969. 405 p.

ADLE, Chahryar, ed., *Art et société dans le monde iranien*. Paris, ADPF, 1982. 380 p., ill. b.w.

ADLE, Chahryar, "Recherche sur le module et le tracé correcteur dans la miniature orientale, I", *Le Monde Iranien et l'Islam*, vol.III (Paris, 1975) pp.81-105, figs.

----"Recherche sur le module et le tracé correcteur, II", *Art et société dans le monde iranien*, ed. C. Adle, Paris, A.D.P.F., 1982, p. 199-218, pl.; figs.

'AFIF, Shams-e Seraj, *Târikh-e Firuz-shâhi*. ed. M.V. Husain, Calcutta, Bibliotheca Indica, 1891. ii + 516 + index 81p.

AFSHAR, Iraj, *Fehrest-e maqâlât-e fârsi*. Tehran, 1348/1969 to 2535/

1976. 3 vols.
----*Sahhâfi-ye sonnati*. Tehran, Ketâbkhâne-ye markazi-ye Dâneshgâh, 1357/1978. 164 p.; coul. pl. and b.w.
----"Sahhâfi az negâh-e farhang va târikh", *Sahhâfi-ye sonnati*, ed. I. Afshâr, pp. 77-94.
----*Seyr-e ketâb dar Irân*. Tehran, Markaz-e asnâd, 1344/1965. 72 p., ill.
AKIMUSHKIN, O.F., "Persidskaja rukopisnaja kniga", in *Rukopisnaja kniga v kul'ture Narodov Vostoka*. Moscow, Nauk, 1987, pp. 330-406.
'ALI b. 'AZIZ-ALLAH TABATABA, *Borhân-e ma'âser*. ed. Seyyed Hâshemi. Delhi/ Hyderabad, Jâme'e, 1355h.q./1936. 632 p. + 22 p. index.
'ALI MOHAMMAD KHAN, *Mer'at-e Ahmadi*. transl. M.F. Lokhandwala, Baroda, Oriental Inst., 1965. xxiii + 945 p., index.
ALLAN, J.W., "Abû'l-Qâsim's Treatise on Ceramics", *Iran* vol. XI (London, 1973), pp. 111-120.
ALLCHIN, F.R. & N. HAMMOND, ed., *The Archaeology of Afghanistan from Earliest Times to the Timurid Period*. London, 1978. 451 p., ill.
AMES, Frank, *The Kashmir Shawl*. Woodbridge, Antique Collector's Club, 1986. 347 p., index, 66 col. pl., 222 b.w.
AMIR KHOSROW DEHLAVI, *Qerân al-sa'deyn*. ed. fac-sim., intr. A.H. Dani. Islamabad, Iran Pakistan Inst. of Persian Studies, 1976. 39 p. + 363 p. fac-sim., ill. b.w.
AMMIANUS MARCELLINUS, *Rerum gestarum*. ed. & transl. J.C. Rolfe. 3 vols. Cambridge, Mass., Harvard U.P., 1937. vol. 2, 693 p.
ANAND RAM MOKHLES, see manuscripts.
ANDREWS, Fred H., *Catalogue of Wall-Paintings from Ancient Shrines in Central Asia and Sistan*. Delhi, Central Asian Antiquities Museum, 1933. xiii + 201 p., pl.
AQAJANI, H., "Ta'mirât-e naqqâshi", *Asar* vol. I, pp. 79-90 & vol. II-IV, pp. 160-175. ill. (Tehran, 1359/1980).
Archéologie du livre médiéval. C.N.R.S. (Institut de Recherche et d'Histoire des Textes) & Bibliothèque Nationale. Paris, CNRS, 1987. 72 p., ill.
ARCHER, Mildred, *Company Drawings in the India Office Library*. London, British Library, 1972. xiv + 298p., ill.
ARNOLD, Thomas W., *Painting in Islam*. Oxford, 1928; reprint New York, Dover, 1965. xviii + 159 p., lxiv ill.
ASHRAF, K.M., *Life and Conditions of the People of Hindustan*. Delhi,

. 1970. 312 p.

ASHRAF, Muhammad, *Catalogue of the Persian Manuscripts in the Salar Jung Museum and Library*. Vol. I, History. Hyderabad, Salar Jung, 1965. 611 p.; vol. II. Biographies, 1966. 287 p. + indices.

ASLAH, Mirzâ Moh., *Tazkere-ye sho'arâ-ye Kashmir*. Karachi, Iqbal Academy, 1346/1967. 3 vols., 1577 p.

'ATTAR, Farid al-din, *Elâhi-nâme . Le livre divin*. transl. F. Rouhani. Paris, Albin Michel, 1961. 480 p.

----*Tazkerat al-owliyâ'*. ed. Nicholson, vol. II. London/ Leyden, Brill, 1907. 361 p.

AYNI, K., *Salâmân va Absâl. Jâmi*. ed. fac-sim. with intro. Doshanbe, 'Erfân, 1976. 48 p. + fac-sim. n.p.

AZARPAY, Guitty, "The Development of the Arts in Transoxiana", *Cambridge History of Iran*, III,2, pp. 1130-1148.

----*Sogdian painting*. Berkeley, Univ. of California, 1981. 212 p.+ 30 pl., ill.

BABUR SHAH, Zahir al-din, *Bâbur-nâme*. transl. A.S. Beveridge, 1922; reprint Delhi, Oriental Books Reprint, 1979. 2 vols. lxi + 716 p. + lxxxi + index.

BADA'UNI, 'Abd al-Qâder, *Montakhab al-tavârikh*. ed. A.'A. Kabir & W.Nassau Lees, Calcutta, Bibliotheca Indica: 1864-9 3. vol.; transl. T.W. Haig, Calcutta, Bibliotheca Indica, 1899-1925. reprint Delhi, 1973. 3 vols.

BARNI, Ziâ' al-din, *Tarikh-e Firuz-shâhi*. ed. S. Ahmad Khan, Calcutta, Bibliotheca Indica, 1862, 602 p.

BARBIER DE MEYNARD, C., *Dictionnaire géographique de la Perse*. Paris, Imprimerie Impériale, 1861. 640 p.

BAYANI, Mehdi, *Ahvâl va âsâr-e khoshnevisân*, vol.I, *Nasta'liq nevisân*. Tehran, Enteshârât-e Dâneshgâh, 1345/1966. 304 p.

----*Ketâb shenâsi-ye ketâbhâ-ye khatti*. Tehran, E.A.A.M., 1353/1974. 64 p. + pl.

Bayâz-e khoshbu'i, see manuscripts.

BECKER, C.H., *Das Wiener Qusair-'Amra-Werk*. Strasbourg, Zeitschrift für Assyriologie, Bd. XX, 1906.

BEHZAD, Tâherzâde, "The Preparation of the Miniaturist's Materials", *Survey of Persian Art*, ed. A. Pope, vol.V, pp. 1921-1927.

BEYHAQI, Abu al-Fazl, *Tarikh-e Mas'udi*. ed. Ghâni & Fayyâz. Tehran, 1324/1945. 764 p.

BINYON, L., WILKINSON, J. & GRAY, B., *Persian Miniature Painting*. London, 1931; reprint, New York, Dover, 1971. 212p., ill.

BIRUNI, Abu Reyhân, *al-Jamâher fi ma'refat al-javâher*. ed. F. Krenkov, Hyderabad, Da'irat al-Ma'arif, 1355/1936. 273-11-51 p.

----*Kitâb al-Hind*. transl. Edward C. Sachau. 2 vol. London, 1910; reprint Delhi, Oriental Reprint: 1983. 408 + 431 p.

BJÖRKMAN, W., *Beiträge zur Geschichte der Staatskanzlei im islamischen Ägypten*. Hamburg, de Gruyter, 1928. vi-217 p.

BLOCHET, E., *Catalogue des manuscrits persans de la Bibliothèque Nationale*. Paris, 1905 to 1934. 4 vols.

BLOOM, J., "The Blue Koran, an Early Fatimid Manuscript from the Maghrib", in F. DEROCHE, ed., *Manuscrits du Moyen-Orient*, pp. 95-99.

BOSCH, G., CARSWELL, J. & PETHERBRIDGE, G., *Islamic Bindings and Bookmaking*. Chicago, Oriental Institute: 1981. 235 p., ill.

BOTHMER, Hans-Caspar Graf von, "Architekturbilder im Koran. Eine Prachthandschrift der Umayyadenzeit aus dem Yemen", *Pantheon* (1987), XLV, pp. 4-20.

BOURNE & al., *Lacquer, an International History and Collector's Guide*. Malborough, The Crowood Press, 1984. 256 p., ill., index.

BRAND, Michael, "The City as an Artistic Center", *Fatehpur-Sikri*, ed. M. Brand & G. Lowry, pp. 93-120, 25 ill.

BRAND, Michael & G. LOWRY, ed., *Fatehpur-Sikri*. Selected papers from the International Symposium on ... Bombay, Marg Publications, 1987. xii + 204 p., col. & b.w. ill., plans.

BRIQUET, C., "Recherches sur les premiers papiers employés en Occident & en Orient, Xe - XVIe siècles", *Mémoires de la Société Nationale des Antiquaires de France*, Paris, 1886.

BUSSAGLI, Mario, *La peinture d'Asie Centrale*. Genève, Skyra: 1978. 137 p., ill.

The Calligrapher's Craft, Ahuan Gallery of Islamic Art, Summer Exhibition 1-27 June 1987. London, Ahuan: 1987. 24 p.

The Cambridge History of Iran. vol. III, 1-2. ed. E. Yarshater. Cambridge, Univ. Press, 1983.

CENNINO CENNINI, *Il libro dell'Arte*. transl. D.V. Thompson, *The Craftman's Handbook*. New York, Dover, 1960. 142 p., ill. French transl., Victor Mottez, Paris, F. de Nobele: 1911 (reprint 1982). xxxix + 189 p.

CHANDRA, Moti, *The technique of Mughal Painting*. Lucknow, U.P. Historical Soc., 1949. 108 p. + x pl.

CHARDIN, *Voyages du Chevalier Chardin en Perse*. éd. L. Langlés, Paris, Le Normant, 1811. vol. IV & V. 464 + 500 p.

Le Coran. transl. R. Blachère. Paris, Maisonneuve & Larose: 1980. 748 p.

CORBIN, Henry, "*Mundus imaginalis* ou l'imaginaire & l'imaginal", *Cahiers internationaux du symbolisme* no. 6, Bruxelles, 1964, pp. 3-26.

DANESH-PAZHUH, Mohammad Taqi, "Moraqqa' sâzi va jong nevisi", *Farkhonde payyâm*, essais à la mémoire de Q.H. Yusefi. Mashhad, Enteshârât-e Dâneshgâh no. 74, 1360/1981, pp. 148-229.

----"Rang-sâzi dar kâghaz va rang zedâ'i az ân", *Honar va mardom*, no. 181 (Tehran, 2536/1977), pp. 16-36.

----"Sar-gozasht-e nâmehâ-ye khoshnevisân va honarmandân", *Honar va mardom* no. 86-87 (Tehran 1348/1969) pp. 31-43.

DARIDAN, J., & STELLING-MICHAUD, S., *La peinture séfévide d'Ispahan*. Paris, Les Beaux-Arts, 1930. 24 p.+ 21 pl.

DEHKHODA, 'Ali Akbar, *Loghat-nâme*. Tehran, Majles, 1325/1956-..., 37 vols.

DE LAET, Joannes, *The Empire of the Great Mogol*. transl. J.S.H. Hoyland, Bombay, 1928

DELLA VALLE, Pietro, *Voyages de Pietro della Valle.*, Rouen, 1745. vol.III. 452 p.

DENNY, Walter B., "Turkish Ceramics and Turkish Painting: the Role of the Paper Cartoon in Turkish Ceramic Production", *Essays in Islamic Art and Architecture in honor of K. Otto-Dorn*, ed. A. Daneshvari, Malibu, 1981, pp. 29-36.

DEROCHE, François, ed., *Les Manuscrits du Moyen-Orient*. Essais de codicologie & de paléographie. Actes du Colloque d'Istanbul, 1986. Istanbul/Paris, I.F.E.A./C.N.R.S., 1989. 143 p. + xxxii pl. b.w.

DESMAISONS, J.J.P., *Dictionnaire persan-français*. Rome, Imprimerie Vaticane, 1908-1914. 4 vols.

DIGBY, Simon, "The Literary Evidence for Painting in the Delhi Sultanate", *Bul. of the American Academy of Benares*, vol.I (Varanasi, 1967).

DOERNER, Max, *The Materials of the Artist*. London, Granada. 1984. xvi + 435 p., 8 pl.

DOIZY, M.A. & IPERT, S., *Le papier marbré*. Paris, Technorama: 1985. 251 p., ill.

DOWLATSHAH SAMARQANDI, *Tazkerat al-sho'arâ'*. ed. E.G. Browne, London/Leyde, Gibb Mem., 1901. 621 + 16 p.

DREGE, Jean-Pierre, "Le livre manuscrit & les débuts de la xylographie", *Le livre & l'imprimerie en Extrême Orient & en Asie du Sud,*

Revue Francaise d'Histoire du Livre, n.s. no. 42 (Bordeaux, 1984), pp. 19-39.

DU MANS, Raphaël, *L'état de la Perse en 1660*. ed. C. Scheffer, Paris, Leroux, 1890. 465 p.

DUST MOHAMMAD, Preface to the Album of Bahrâm Mirzâ (*Hâlât-e honarvarân*). ed. M. Bayâni, *Ahvâl va âsâr-e khoshnevisân*. vol. I, Tehran, 1345/1966, pp. 188-203.

EBN BADIS, Mu'izz (attributed to), *'Umdat al-kuttâb*. transl. M. Levey, "Chemical Technology in Mediaeval Arabic Book-Making", *Transactions of the American Phil. Soc.*, vol. 52, no. 4 (1962), pp. 5-66.

EBN-e ESFANDIYAR, *Târikh-e Tabarestân*. ed. 'A. Eqbâl. Tehran, 1320/1941. vol. I, 331 + 175 p.

EBN al-FAQIH al-HAMADANI, *Kitâb al-buldân*. ed. De Goeje, Bibli. Geograph. Arabicorum, V, 365 p.

EBN al-NADIM, *The Fihrist of al-Nadim*. transl. B. Dodge, New-York, Columbia U.P., 1970. 2 vols., 1149 p., index.

ECHRAGHI, Ehsan, "Description contemporaine des peintures murales disparues des palais de Sâh Tahmâsp à Qazvin", *Art & société*, ed. C. Adle, pp. 117-126, phot.

Encyclopédie de l'Islam. 1st ed., Leyde/Paris, 1913-1934 . 4 vols.; 2nd ed., Leyde, Brill, 1960 -> . 5 vols. published.

'ESAMI, *Fotuh al-salâtin*. ed. M. Husain, Agra, 1938; ed. A.S. Usha, Madras, University of, 1948. 786 p.

ESKANDAR BEYG MONSHI, *Târikh-e 'âlam-ârâ-ye 'abbâsi*. ed. I. Afshâr, Tehran, Amir Kabir, 1335/1956. 2 vols.

ETHE, H., *Catalogue of the Persian Manuscripts in the Library of the India Office*. Oxford, 1903-1937. 2 vols.

ETTINGHAUSEN, Richard, "*Abri* Paintings", *Studies in Memory of Gaston Wiet*, ed. Myriam Rosen-Ayalon, Jerusalem, 1977, pp. 345-356, ill.

----(ed.), *Highlights of Persian art*. Boulder, Westview, 1979. 391 p., ill.

FALK, T. & FERRAR-ROCHAT, U., ed., *Trésors de l'Islam*. Catalogue of the Exhibition at the Musée Rath, Geneva. Geneva, 1985. 400 p., 567 ill. coul.

FANSHAVE, H.C., *Shah Jahan's Delhi, Past and Present*. reprint from ed. 1902, Delhi, Sumit, 1979. xxiii + 337 p.

FARROKHI, *Divân*. ed. M. Dabir Siyâqi. Tehran, Zavvâr: 1349/1970. 519p.

FATTAHI NEYSHAPURI, *Dastur al-'oshshâq*. ed. R.S. Greenshields. London, Luzac, 1926. 412 p.

FEKRI SALJUQI, *Zekr-e barkhi az khoshnevisân va honarmandân bar dibâce-ye Dust Mohammad.* Kabul, Anjoman-e târikh: 1349/1970. 136 p.

FERDOWSI, *Shâh-nâme.* ed. Bertels & al. Moscow, Nauka, 1965-1971. 9 vols.

Flora Iranica. ed. K.H. Rechinger. no. 157, Papilionaceae II. Graz, 1984.

FORBES, R.J., *Studies in Ancient Technology.* vol. III, Leyde, Brill, 1955. 268 p., index.

FOUCHECOUR, Charles-Henri de, *La description de la nature dans la poésie lyrique persane du XIe siècle.* Paris, Klincksieck, 1969. 263 p.

FRUMKIN, Grégoire, *Archaeology in Soviet Central Asia.* Leiden/Köln, Brill, 1970. 217 p., 47 pl.

FRYKENBERG, R.E., ed., *Delhi through the Ages. Studies in urban culture, history and society.* Delhi, Oxford U.P.: 1986. 566 p., 8 ill., 12 figs., plans.

GABAIN, A.M. von, "Irano-Turkish Relations", *Cambridge History of Iran,* II, 1, pp. 613-624.

GASPARINI, E., *Le pitture murali della Muradiye d'Edirne.* Padova, Quaderni dell'Università di Venezia no. 18, 1985. 55 p., 75 pl., 4 figs.

GHARNÂTI, Abu Hamid al-Andalusi, *Tuhfat al-albâb.* ed. G. Ferrand, in J.A. (Paris, Jul.-Sept. 1925).

GHAZZÂLI TUSI, *Ehyâ' 'olum al-din.* Cairo, 1962. vol. III.

GHIRSHMAN, Roman, *Iran, Parthes & Sassanides.* Paris, Gallimard, 1962. 407 p., ill.

GHOLAM MOHAMMAD DEHLAVI, *Tazkere-ye khoshnevisân.* ed. M.Hidayet Husain, Calcutta, Bib. Indica, 1910. index, 39 p. + 131 p.

GIGNOUX, Philippe, "Middle Persian Inscriptions", *Cambridge History of Iran,* III, 2, pp. 1205-1215.

GODARD, Y.A., "Pièces datées de céramique de Kashân à décor lustré", *Athar-e Iran,* II, 2 (Paris, 1937) pp. 309-337, ill.

GOL BADAN BEYGAM, *Homâyun-nâme.* ed. & transl. A.S. Beveridge, London, 1902; reprint Delhi, Munshiram, 1983. 331 p., index, persian text 96 p.

GOLOMBEK, Lisa, "The Chronology of Turbat-i Shaikh Jam", *Iran,* IX (London, 1971) pp. 30-31, pl. ii-iii.

----"The Timurid Shrine of Gazur Gah", *Art and Archaeology Occasional Papers,* 15. Toronto, Royal Ontario Museum: 1969. 227 p., 160 p.

GRABAR, O. & BLAIR, S., *Epic Images and Contemporary History. The Illustrations of the Great Mongol Shâhnâma.* Chicago/London,

Univ. Chicago Press, 1980. 210 p., ill.

GRAY, Basil, ed., *The Arts of the Book in Central Asia*. London/Paris, Unesco, 1979. xiv + 314 p., ill.

----"The Tradition of Wall-Painting in Iran", *Highlights of Persian Art*, ed. R. Ettinghausen, pp. 312-329, ill.

GUNASINGHE, Siri, *La technique de la peinture indienne d'après les textes du Silpa*. Paris, Annales du Musée Guimet, 1957. 96 p.

HABIB, Irfan, *An Atlas of the Mughal Empire. Political and Economic Maps with Detailed Notes, Bibliography and Index*. Delhi, Oxford U.P., reprint cor. 1986. xvii + 106 p.

----"Capacity of Technological Change in Mughal India", in *Technology in Ancient and Medieval India*, ed. A.Roy & S.K. Bagchi, pp. 1-13.

HABIBI, Abd al-Hayy, "Literary Sources for the History of the Arts of the Book in Central Asia", *The Arts of the Book in Central Asia*, ed. B. Gray, pp. 273-280.

HÂFEZ-e ABRU, *Majma' al-tavârikh*. transl. extr., *A Persian Embassy to China*. ed. K.M. Maitra, Lahore, 1934.

HAIG, WOLSELEY, The Cambridge History of India, vol. III. Cambridge, 1928. 752 p., pl.

HAMID QALANDAR, *Kheyr al-majâles*. ed. K.A. Nizami. Aligarh, 1959.

HAMZE ESFAHANI, *Sani moluk al-arz va al-anbiyâ'*. transl. J. Sho'â'i. Tehran, B.F.I., 1346/1967. 261 p.

HERZFELD, Ernst, *Iran in the Ancient East*. Oxford U.P.: 1941 363 p. 131 pl.

----*Der Wandschmuck der Bauten von Samarra*. (Samarra, Bd. 3) Berlin, 1923.

HILLIARD, Nicholas, *A Treatise Concerning the Art of Limning*. ed. R. Thornton. Ashington, Mid Northemberland Press, 1981. 139 p., ill.

Hodud al-'âlam. ed. M. Sotude. Tehran, E.D.T., 1340/1961. 255p.

HOERNLE, R., "Who was the Inventor of Rag Paper ?" in *Journal of the Royal Asiatic Society*, (London, 1903) pp. 663-684.

HOEY, William, *A Monograph on Trade and Manufactures in Northern India*. Lucknow, 1880. 215 p., glossary.

HOJVIRI, *Kashf al-mahjub*. ed. V. Zukovski (reprint M. 'Abbâsi). Tehran, Amir Kabir, 1336/1957. 607 p.

HOMAYUNFARROKH, Rokn al-din, *Ketâb va ketâb-khânehâ-ye saltanati-ye Iran*. Tehran, Vezârat-e farhang va honar: 1345/1966. 157 p., ill.

HOPKIRK, Peter, *Foreign Devils in the Silk Road*. Oxford U.P.: 1984. xi

+ 252 p., 13 phot.

HUART, Clément, *Les calligraphes et les miniaturistes de l'Orient musulman*. Paris, E. Leroux, 1908. 388 p., 10 pl.

IPSIROGLU, M. S., *Saray-alben*. Wiesbaden, Steiner, 1964. 135 p., ill. + 47 pl.

IVANOV, A.A. & AKIMUSHKIN O.F., "The Art of Illumination", in *The Arts of the Book in Central Asia*, ed. B. Gray, pp. 35-57.

IVANOW, W., *Concise Descriptive Catalogue of Persian Manuscripts in the Asiatic Society of Bengal*. 2 vols., Calcutta, Asiatic Soc., 1924 (I) & 1926 (II, Curzon collection).

JAGGI, O.P., *History of Science and Technology in India*, vol. 7, Science and Technology in Medieval India. Delhi, Atma Ram, 1977. 258 p., ill.

JAHÂNGIR PADSHAH, Nur al-din, *Tozuk-e Jahângiri yâ Jahângir-nâme*. transl. A. Rogers & H. Beveridge, London, 1909-1914; reprint, Delhi, Munshiram, 1978. 2 vols. in one, xiii + 478, index & vii + 315 p., index.

JAMÂLI YAZDI, *Farrokh-nâme*. ed. I. Afshâr, Tehran, Amir Kabir: 1346/1967.

JAMES, David, *The Chester Beatty Shah-Namah of Shah Abbas*. Dublin, P.D.I.

KARABACEK, M., "Neue Quellen zur Papiergeschischte", *Mitteilungen Sammlung Erzh. Rainer*. VI, 79 (1888).

KERMÂNI, 'Ali b. Mahmud, *Ma'âser-e Mahmudshâhi*. ed. Nur al-Hasan Ansâri, Delhi, Jamâl Printing Press, 1968. 148 p., index.

KEVORKIAN, A.M., & SICRE, J.P., *Les jardins du désir. Sept siècles de peinture persane*. Paris, Phébus, 1983. 267 p., ill., 94 pl.

KHADIVJAM, Hoseyn, *Vâzhe-nâme-ye ghazalhâ-ye Hâfez*. Tehran, 1362/1983. 136 p.

KHANDALAVALA, K. & RAHMAT ALI KHAN, *Gulshan-e-musawwari*. Seven Illustrated Manuscripts. Hyderabad, Salar Jang Mus. 1986. 59 p., 13 pl. col., 56 figs. b.w.

KHVANDAMIR, *Habib al-siyyar*. ed. J. Homâ'i, Tehran, Khayyâm, 1333/1954. 4 vols.

----*Kholâsat al-akhbâr*. ed. part. G. E'temâdi, *Fasli az Kholâsat al-akhbâr mo'alefe-ye Khvândmir*, Kabul, Modiriyat-e 'omumi-ye târikh, 1324/1945. 80 p.

----*Nâme-ye nâmi*. ed. & transl. of excerpts, L. Bouvat & M.M. Qazvini, "Deux documents relatifs à Behzâd", *Revue du Monde Musulman*, XXVI (Paris, 1914) pp. 146-161.

----*Qânun-e homâyuni*. ed. M. Hidayat Hosain. Calcutta, Bib. Indica, 1940. xxxvi + 141 p., index.

KIEFER, C. & ALLIBERT, A., "Les céramiques bleues pharaoniques & leur procédé révolutionnaire d'émaillage", in *Industrie céramique*, no. 607 (Paris, 1968), pp. 395-402.

KLEIN, Robert, *La forme & l'intelligible*. Paris, Gallimard, 1970. 496 p.

KOSTROV, P.I., "Tekhnika zhivopisi i konservatsija rospisei drevnego Piendzhikenta", *Zhivopis drevnego Pendzhikenta*, Moscow, 1954, pp. 162 ss.

LABROUSSE, A. & R. BOUCHARLAT, "La fouille du palais de Chaour à Suse en 1970-71", *Cahiers de la D.A.F.I.*, II (Paris, 1972), pp. 61-168.

LAFFITTE, M.P. & al., *Les tranchefiles brodées*. Etude historique & technique. Paris, Bibliothèque Nationale, 1989. 92 p., ill.

LAHORI, 'Abd al-Hamid, *Pâdshâh-nâme*. ed. Kabiru'd-Din Ahmad & Abd'ur-Rahim. Calcutta, Bibliotheca Indica, 1866-72. 2 vols.

LAUFER, Berthold, *Sino-Iranica. Chinese Contributions to the History of Civilisation in Ancient Iran*. Chicago, 1919. 630 p.

LAURIE, A.P., "The Pigments and Medium", *Survey of Persian Art*, ed. A. Pope, vol. V, pp. 1918-1920.

LE COQ, Albert von, *Auf Hellas Spuren in Öst-Turkistan*. Berlin, 1926. 166 p., ill.

----*Chotscho*. Königlich-Preussische Turfan-Expedition. Berlin, 1913.

----*Die manichäische Miniaturen, Die buddistische Spätantike in Mittelasien*.II. Berlin, 1923. reprint Graz, Akadesmische Druck, 1973. 63 p., 9 pl.

LEVEY, Martin, "Chemical Technology in Mediaeval Arabic Bookmaking", *Transactions of the American Philologic Society* vol. 52, part 4 (1962) pp. 5-65.

LEVI STRAUSS, Claude, *Le regard éloigné*. Paris, 1983.

LOWRY, G. D. & T.W. LENTZ, *Timur and the Princely Vision*. Washington, 1989.

LUSCHEY SCHMEISSER, Ingeborg, *The Pictorial Tile Cycle of Hasht Behesht in Isfahân*. Rome, IsMEO, 1978. 240 p., ill.

----"Ein safavidischer Drachen-bogen in der Ermitage", *A.M.I.*, 17 (1984), pp. 315-321, pl. 41-45.

----"Der Wand-und Deckenschmuck eines safavidischen Palästes in Nayin", *A.M.I.*, N.F. no. 2 (1969) pp. 183-192, ill.

MACKENZIE, D.N., "Khwarazmian Language and Literature", *Cambridge History of Iran*, III, 2, pp. 1244-1249.

MAHFUZ ul-HAQ, "The Khan Khanan and his Painters", *Islamic Culture*, vol. V no. 4 (Hyderabad, 1931).

Majmu'at al-sanâye', see Manuscripts.

MAJNUN RAFIQI HERAVI, *Resâlehâ-ye khatt-e Majnun Rafiqi Heravi.* ed. Mâyel-e Heravi. Kabul, Anjoman-e Târikh, 1355/1976. xviii + 44 - x p.

MAQBUL AHMAD, "A Persian Translation of the Eleventh Century Arabic Alchemical Treatise *'Ain as-san'ah wa 'aun as-sana'a*". *Memoirs of the Asiatic Society of Bengal*, vol. VIII no. 7 (Calcutta, 1929), pp. 419-460.

MAQDISI, *Ahsân al-taqâsim*. ed. De Goeje, Leiden, Brill, 1906. 498 p.

MAS'UDI, *Muruj al-zahâb*. transl. Barbier de Meynard, *Les prairies d'or*. Paris, Imprimerie Impériale, 1861-77. 9 vols.

----*Kitâb al-tanbih wa al-ashrâf*. ed. M.J. de Goeje. Bib. Geogr. Arabicorum VIII. Leyde, Brill, 1894. 588 + 43 p., index.

MAYEL HERAVI, *Loghêt va estetêhêt-e fann-e Ketêbsêzi.* Tehran, 1353/1974.

MELIKIAN CHIRVANI, A.S., "Khwâje Mirak Naqqâsh", *J.A.*, (Paris, 1988), pp. 97-145, 12 figs.

----"Le Livre des Rois, Miroir du Destin", *Studia Iranica*, 17-1 (Paris, 1988), pp. 7-46.

----"Trois manuscrits de l'Iran seldjoukide. Matériaux pour servir à l'histoire de la peinture persane, I", *Arts Asiatiques* no. 16 (Paris, 1967), pp. 3-51, figs. 1-24.

----"Varqe va Golshâh, essai sur les rapports de l'esthétique littéraire & l'esthétique plastique dans l'Iran pré-mongol", *Arts Asiatiques* vol. XII (Paris, 1970).

MEREDITH-OWENS, G.M. *Handlist of Persian Manuscripts* 1895-1966. London, 1968. 127 p.

MINORSKI, V., See QÂZI AHMAD

MIR 'ALI HERAVI, *Medâd al-khotut*. ed. Fekri Saljuqi, *Zekr-e barkhi az khoshnevisân va honarmandân*, pp. 110-122.

MIRKHVOND, *Rowzat al-safâ'*. ed. 'A. Parviz, Tehran, Markazi, 1338/1959, 7 vols.; *Histoires des Sassanides*. ed. Paris, F. Didot, 1843. pp. 173-282.

MIRZA HAYDAR DUGHLAT, *Târikh-e Rashidi*. transl. E. Denison Ross, London, 1898; reprint Delhi, 1972 (not complete); excerpts transl. by Th. Arnold in *BWG*, pp. 189-191.

MIRZA RAFI'A, *Dastur al-moluk*. ed. M.T. Dânesh-Pazhuh, *Majalle-ye dâneshkade-ye adabiyât va 'olum-e ensâni*, 16e an., no.1-2, pp.62-93 and no. 4 , pp. 416-440.

MO'ALLEM, Mortezâ, *Nouveau dictionnaire persan-français*. Tehran, Amir Kabir, 1344-48. 2 vols.

MOHAMMAD AMIN b. Mirzâ Mohammad Zamân Bokhâri, *Mohit al-tavârikh*. transl. chap. X, Akimushkin & Ivanov, *Art & Société*, ed. C. Adle, pp. 127-138.

MOHAMMAD TAHER NASRABADI, *Tazkere-ye Mohammad Tâher Nasrâbâdi*. ed. Vahid-e Dastgerdi, Tehran, Armaghân, 1317/1938. 576 p.

MONSHI TEK CHAND, *Bahâr-e 'ajam*. ed. Lucknow, 1916 (litho) 2 vols.

MONZAVI, Ahmad, *Fehrest-e noskhehâ-ye khatti-ye fârsi*. vol.III, Tehran, 1350. (5 vols.).

MOORCROFT, William, & G. TREBECK, *Travels in the Himalayan Provinces of Hindustan and the Panjab*. London, 1837; reprint, Delhi, Anubhav, 1986. xlvii + 565 p.

MOWLAVI BALKHI, *Masnavi-ye ma'navi*. ed. R. Nicholson, vol. I. London, Gibb Mem., 1925. 462 p.

Museum für Indische Kunst, Berlin. Katalog 1986, Ausgestellte Werke. Berlin, Museum, 1986. 240 p., col & b.w. ill.

NAHATTA, Agar Chand, "Chitra aur rang banane ki prachin vidhiyan", *Akriti* (Hindi Quaterly), vol. 12, no. 1 (July 1977), pp. 5-9.

NAIK, C.R., *'Abdur'-Rahim Khan-i Khanan and his Literary Circle*. Ahmedabad, Gujerat Univ., 1966. xxii + 583 p.

NAQVI, Hamida Khaton, *Agricultural, Industrial and Urban Dynamism under the Sultans of Delhi*, 1206-1555. Delhi, Munshiram, 1986. 205 p., tabl.

NASER-e KHOSROW, *Safar-nâme*. transl. C. Schefer, Paris, Leroux, 1881. 348 p.

NASIRI AMINI, Fakhr al-din, "Rukesh-e jeld va anvâ'-e ân", *Sahhâfi-ye sonnati*, ed. I. Afshâr, pp. 1-35.

NASR-ALLAH KHAN KHURJAVI, *Nomov al-sabbâghin*, see Manuscripts.

NAVA'I, 'Ali Shir, *Majâles al-nafâyes*. transl., Fakhri Amiri Heravi, *Latâ'ef-nâme*. ed. 'A. A. Hekmat, Tehran, 1323/1945. 471 p.

NEUMANN, R., "Eine safawidische Seide aus den Beständen der staatlichen Kunstsammlungen zu Dresden", *Persica*, XI (1984), pp. 115-127, 6 pl.

----*Persische Seiden*. 1986. 200 p., 15 col. pl.

NEZAMI 'ARUZI, *Cahâr maqâle*. ed. M. Qazvini, Tehran, Zavvâr,

1333/1952. 136 p.
NEZAMI GANJAVI, *Haft Peykar*. ed. Vahid Dastgerdi, Tehran, Yâdegâr, 1315/1936. 368 p.
----*Sharaf-nâme*. ed. Vahid Dastgerdi, Tehran, 1335/1956. 528p.
----*Khosrow va Shirin*. ed. Vahid Dastgerdi,Tehran, 1334/1955.
ÖNEY, G., "The Interpretation of the Frescoes in the Kharraqan Mausoleum near Qazvin", *Akten VII Int. Cong.iran. Kunst Archäologie* (1976), 1979, pp. 400-408.
ORSATTI, Paola, "Epigraphes poétiques dans des Manuscrits persans du XVe & XVIe siècle & exergue du Sâhnâma de Firdawsi", in F. DEROCHE, ed. *Manuscrits du Moyen-Orient*, pp. 69-75.
PANOFSKI, E., *Idea*. Contribution à l'histoire du concept de l'ancienne théorie de l'art. Paris, Gallimard, 1983. 284 p.
----*L'oeuvre d'art et ses significations.Essais sur les arts visuels*. transl. Paris, Gallimard, 1969. 119 p., ill.
PEDERSEN, Johannes, *The Arabic Book*. transl. G. French, Princeton U.P., 1984. 220 p. 45 ill.
PICKETT, Douglas, "Inscriptions by Mohammad Ridâ al-Imâmî", *Iran* XXII (London, 1984), pp. 91-102, 4 pl.
PLATTS, John T., *A Dictionary of Urdu, Classical Hindi and English*. reprint, Delhi, Oriental Repr., 1977. 1259 p.
PLINY, *Histoire naturelle*. ed. & transl. Littré, Paris, Didot, 1860. 2 vols.
POPE, John A., *Chinese Porcelain from Ardabil*. Washington, Freer, 1956. 194 p.+ pl.
POPE, Arthur U., ed., *A Survey of Persian Art*. Oxford U.P.: 1939, 6 vols. (reprint Tokyo/Tehran, 1977, 16 vols.)
PORTER, Yves, "*Kâghaz-e abri*, notes sur la technique de la marbrure", *Studia Iranica*, 17, 1 (Paris, 1988), pp. 47-55.
----"Notes sur le *Golestân-e honar* de Qâzi Ahmad Qomi", *Studia Iranica*, 17, 2 (Paris, 1988), pp. 207-223.
----"Une traduction persane du traité d'Ibn Bâdis 'Umdat al-kuttâb", in F. DEROCHE, ed. *Manuscrits du Moyen-Orient*, pp. 61-67.
----"Un traité de Simi Neyshâpuri, artiste et polygraphe", *Studia Iranica*, 14, 2 (Paris, 1985), pp. 179-198.
QALQASHANDI Abi al-'Abbâs, *Subh al-a'shâ*. Le Caire, al-Mu'asasat al-misriya al-'âma, (1963), 14 vols.
QAZI AHMAD QOMI, *Golestân-e honar* or *Tazkere-ye khoshnevisân va naqqâshân*. ed. A. Soheyli Khvânsâri, Tehran, B.F.I., 1352/1973. x-lxii + 216 p., index, ill.
----transl. V.Minorsky, *Calligraphers and Painters*. Washington, Smith-

sonian, 1959. x- 223 p., 4 pl.; see also Manuscripts.

QOTB al-DIN QESSE KHVAN, (*Resâle'i dar târikh-e khatt va naqqâshi*); Preface to the album of Shâh Tahmâsp. ed. Khadivjam, *Sokhan*, 17, no. 6-7 (Tehran, 1346/1967) pp. 666-676.

RAHMAT ALI KHAN, "The Grand Court of the Khan Khanan", *Lalit Kala*, no. 21 (Delhi, 1986), pp. 27-35.

RASHID al-DIN FAZL-ALLAH, *Vaqf-nâme-ye rob'-e Rashidi*. ed. I. Afshâr & M. Minovi, Tehran, A.A.M., 2536/1977. 344 p.

RAVANDI, *Râhat al-sodur*. ed. M. Iqbâl, London, Gibb Mem.: 1921. 575 p.

RAZI, Amin b. Ahmad, *Haft eqlim*. ed. E. Denison Ross & Abdul Muqtadir, Calcutta, Bib. Indica, 1918 (vol.I).

Resâle-ye Jeld-sâzi or *Resâle-ye manzum dar sahhâfi*. Ed. I. Afshâr, *Sahhâfi-ye sonnati*, ed. I. Afshâr, pp. 108-149

RICHARD, Francis, "Un lectionnaire persan des Evangiles copié en Crimée en 776H./1374", *Studia Iranica*, 10-2 (Paris, 1981), pp. 225-245.

----"Les manuscrits persans d'origine indienne à la Bibliothèque Nationale", *Revue de la Bibl. Nat.*, no. 19 (Paris, 1986) pp. 30-46, ill.

RIEU, CHARLES. *Catalogue of the Persian Manuscripts in the British Museum*. London, 1879-1895. 4 vol.

RIZVI, S.A., *Fathpur-Sikri*. Bombay, Taraporevala, 1975. xxiii + 175 p., xlviii pl.

ROBINSON, B.W., "Ismâ'il II's copy of the Shâhnâma", *Iran*, 14 (1976), pp. 1-8.

----"A Survey of Persian Painting (1350-1896)", in *Art & société*, ed. C. Adle, pp. 13-82, ill.

ROY, Aniruddha & BAGCHI, S.K., eds., *Technology in Ancient and Medieval India*. Delhi, 1986. 167 p., 38 pl.

SA'ALEBI, *Latâ'ef al-ma'âref*. ed. P. de Jong; transl. part. C.E. Bosworth, Edinburgh U.P., 1968. 164 p.

SACHAU-ETHE, Catalogue of the Persian ... Mss in the Bodleian Library. Oxford, 1889. 3 vol.

SADEQ BEYG AFSHAR 'SÂDEQI', *Qânun al-sovar*. ed. A.Y. Kaziev (Baku, 1963) & M.T. Dânesh-Pazhuh in *Honar o mardom*, no. 90 (Tehran 1349/1970), p. 13-20; critical ed. Y. Porter, based on the former, see text in annexe 2. Transl., see S.C. Welch, *The Houghton Shahnamah*.

SA'DI, *Golestân. Kolliyât*, ed. 'A. Eqbâl, Tehran: 1340/1961. 424 p.

SAKISIAN, Arménag, "Esthétique & terminologie persanes", *Journal*

Asiatique (Paris, 1935) pp. 144-150.

SALEH, Mohammad Kanbuh Lâhori, *'Amal-e Sâleh*. ed. Gh. Yazdani, Calcutta, Bib. Indica, 1912-38 (3 vols. + index).

SAM MIRZA, *Tohfe-ye Sâmi*. ed. Vahid Dastgerdi, *Armaghân* sup. 16th year. (Tehran, 1314/1939); transl. excerpts. Mahfuz ul-Haq, *J.A.S.B.*, n.s. XXVII no. 1 (Calcutta, 1932) pp. 239-249.

SCHIMMEL, Annemarie, *Calligraphy and Islamic Culture*. New York U.P.I., 1984. xi + 264 p., 4 pl. coul., 8 pl. b.w.

----"Poetry and Calligraphy", *Highlights of Persian Art*, ed. R. Ettinghausen, pp. 177-210, ill.

SCHLUMBERGER, Daniel, *Lashkari Bazar. Une résidence royale ghaznévide et ghoride*. In collaboration with M. Le Berre. vol. 1A, L'architecture. Paris, Mémoires de la D.A.F.A. XVIII, 1978. 2 vols. texte 110 p.; planches 152 pl.

SCHÖFFLER, H.H., *Die Akademie von Gondischapur*. Stuttgart, Freies Geistesleben, 1980. 158 p.

SEYLLER, John, "Scribal notes on Mughal manuscript - illustration." *Artibus Asiae* 48 (1987) pp.247-277, 24 fig.

SEYRAFI SHA'ER, *Golzâr-e safâ*. ed. M.T. Dânesh-Pazhuh, *Honar va mardom* no. 93 (Tehran, 1349/1970) pp. 30-43.

SHARAF-e YAZDI, *Zafar-nâme*. ed. Calcutta, Bib. Indica, 1887. 813 p.

SHO'A'I, Hamid, *Amsâl-e she'r-e fârsi*. Tehran, 1351/1972. vol.I.

(SIMI) editions of the anonymous version, ed. Golcin-e Ma'âni, "Yek resâle-ye nafis-e kohansâl-e honari", *Nashriye-ye dâneshkade-ye adabiyât-e Tabriz* (Tabriz, 1341/1962), XIVe year no. 3, pp. 287-303; ed. P. Azkâ'i, "Resâle-ye khatt", *Honar va mardom*, no. 85 (Tehran, 1348/1969) pp. 51-57; ed. Dânesh-Pazhuh, (without title, in annexe to his article "Rang-sâzi", pp. 34-35, based on a ms. from Hamadan); see also Manuscripts. Essay of critical edition see text in annexe 2.

SOJÂN RAY BHANDARI, *Kholâsat al-tavârikh*. ed. Zafar Hasan, Delhi (litho) 1918. 540 p.+ index 32 p.-vii

SOLTÂN 'ALI-MASHHADI, *Serât al-sotur*. ed. A. Soheyli Khvânsâri in Qâzi Ahmad, *Golestân-e honar*, pp. 64-78; transl. in Minorski.

SOUCEK, Priscilla, "Nizâmî on painters and painting", *Islamic art in the Metropolitan Museum of Art*, ed. R.Ettinghausen, pp. 9-21, 5 ill.

SOUSTIEL, J. & DAVID M.C., *Art Musulman*, Galerie J.Soustiel, Paris, 1988. n.p., 12 pl.

SRIVASTAVA, R.P., *Punjab Painting*. Delhi, Abhinav Pub., 1983. col. pl. & b.w.

STAPLETON, H.E., & al., "Chemistry in Iraq and Persia in the tenth

Century A.D.", *Memoirs of the Asiatic Society of Bengal*, vol. VIII no. 6 (Calcutta, 1927) pp. 317-418.

STAUDE, W, "Les artistes de la cour d'Akbar", *Arts Asiatiques* II, 1 (Paris, 1955) pp. 47-65, ill.

STCHOUKINE, Ivan, *Les peintures des manuscrits Timûrides*. Paris, Imprimerie Nationale, 1954. vi + 177 p., 44 pl.

STEIN, Aurel, *Ancient Khotan*. (reprint) Delhi, 1981. 3 vols., 621p. + pl.

----*Innermost Asia*. Oxford, 1928; reprint, Delhi, 1981. 4 vols.

----*Serindia*. Oxford U.P.: 1921; reprint, Delhi, 1980. 5 vols. 1581 p. + pl. + plans.

STEINGASS, F., *A Comprehensive Persian-English Dictionary*. reprint Delhi, Oriental Repr., 1981. 1539 p.

STOREY, A., *Persian Literature, a Bio-bibliographical Survey*. London, Luzac, 1927-77. 3 vols.

STRONACH, D. & T. Cuyler Young, "Three Octogonal Tomb Towers from Iran", *Iran*, IV (London, 1966) pp. 1-20, ill.

Sublime indigo. Musées de Marseille. Marseille/Paris, Vilo, 1987. 256 p., ill. coul. & b.w.

TAFAZZOLI, A., "A List of Trades and Crafts in the Sassanian Period", *A.M.I.*, N.F. Bd.7 (Berlin, 1974), pp. 191-196.

TALBOT RICE, Tamara, *Ancient Arts of Central Asia*. London, Thames & Hudson, 1963. 288 p., ill.

Tarkib-e tayyâri-ye kâghaz-e Dehli, see Manuscrits.

TAVERNIER, J.B., *Tavernier's Travels in India*. London, 1889. *Les six voyages de...en Turquie, en Perse & aux Indes*. Paris, 1692. 2 vols.+ 1 (1712).

Tazkerat al-moluk. ed. & transl. V. Minorsky, London, 1943. 218 + 130 p.

TEFLISI, Habish b. Ebrâhim, *Bayân al-sanâ'at*. ed. I. Afshâr, *F.I.Z.* V,4 (Tehran, 1336/1957) pp. 298-457.

THEOPHILUS, *De artibus*. transl. J.G. Hawthorne & C.S. Smith. New-York, Dover, 1979. 216 p., 45 ill.

THOMPSON, Daniel V., *The Materials and Techniques of Medieval Painting*. New-York, Dover, 1956 (reprint s.d.), 239 p.

TITLEY, Norah, *Persian Miniature Painting*. London, British Museum, 1983 . 272 p., ill.

TOSI, M., "The Lapis-lazuli Trade across the Iranian Plateau in 3rd millennium B.C.", *Gururâjanjarikâ* in onore G. Tucci. Naples, 1974. vol. I pp. 3-22, pl.

TUSI, Khvâje Nâser al-din, *Tansukh-nâme-ye ilkhâni*. ed. Modarres

Razavi, Tehran, EBFI, 1348/1969. liii + 359 p., index.
VAJED 'ALI KHAN, *Matla' al-'olum*, see Manuscripts.
VALLAT, F., "Deux nouvelles chartes de fondation d'un palais de Darius I à Suse", in *Syria* 48 (Paris, 1971) fasc.1-2, pp. 53-59.
VESEL, Zhiva, *Les encyclopédies persanes*. Paris, A.D.P.F., 1986. 65 p.
VITRUVIUS, *Les dix livres d'architecture*. transl. C. Perrault (Paris, 1684), reprint Paris, Mardaga, 1979. 354 p., pl.
WATSON, William, "Iran China", *Cambridge History of Iran*,III, 1, pp. 537-558.
WELCH, A, *Artists for the Shah*. New Haven/London, Yale U.P.: 1976. 234 p., ill.
WELCH, S.C., ed., *India, Art and Culture, 1300-1900*. New-York, Metropolitan Museum, 1985. 478 p., ill. col. & b.w.
----*Persian Paintings*. New-York, Braziller, 1976. 127 p., ill.
----*Wonders of the Age*. Harvard, Fogg Museum, 1979. 223 p., ill.
WELCH, S.C., & DICKSON, M.B., *The Houghton Shahnamah*. Cambridge, Mass., 1981. 2 vols.
WIDENGREN, Geo, *Mani and Manicheism*. London, Weidenfeld, 1965. 168 p., ill.
WILKINSON, Charles K., "Life in Early Nishapur", *Bul. of the Metropolitan Museum of Art*, n.s. IX (New York, 1950) pp. 60-72, ill.
----*Nishapur, Pottery of the Early Islamic Period*. New-York, Metropolitan Mus., 1974. 374 p., ill.
----*Nishapur. Some Early Islamic Buildings and their Decoration*. New-York, Metropolitan Museum, 1986. 328 p., 33 ill.
WULFF, Hans, *The Traditional Crafts of Persia*. Cambridge, Mass., M.I.T. Press, 1966. xxiv + 405 p., index, 423 figs.
YAGHMÂ'I, H., *Ferdowsi va shâhnâme-ye u*. Tehran, E.A.A.M., 1349/ 1970. 359 p.
YÂQUT, *Mo'jam al-boldân*. ed. D.Sadr & D. Beyrouth, Beyrouth, 1956. 5 vols.
ZÂBEH, A., "Honar e qalamdân sâzi", *Muzehâ* no. 6 (Tehran, 1364/ 1985) pp. 22-31.
ZANDER, G., *Travaux de restauration de monuments historiques en Iran*. Rome, IsMEO, 1968. 491 p., pl.
ZÂVESH, Mohammad, *Kâni shenâsi dar Irân-e qadim*. Tehran, EBFI: 1348/1969. 339 p., index.
ZELNINSKAYA, Z.M. & al., "Analizy krasok nastennykh rospisej Dil'berdzhina", *Drevnjaja Baktrija*, ed. I.T. Kruglikova, Moscow, Nauka, 1979, pp. 166-172.

ZERDOUN BAT-YEHOUDA, Monique, *Les encres noires au Moyen-Age*. Paris, C.N.R.S., 1983. 437 p.

ZOKÂ', Yahyâ, *"Dust Mohammad Mosavver, Dust Mohammad Kâteb, Dust Mosavver"*, *Ayande*, 8e an. no. 5 (Tehran, 1361/1982) pp. 244-253.

INDEX